THE WORLD ECONOMY BETWEEN THE WORLD WARS

THE WORLD ECONOMY BETWEEN THE WORLD WARS

Charles H. Feinstein
Peter Temin
Gianni Toniolo

OXFORD

UNIVERSITY PRESS

2008

OXFORD

UNIVERSITY PRESS

Oxford University Press, Inc., publishes works that further
Oxford University's objective of excellence
in research, scholarship, and education.

Oxford   New York
Auckland   Cape Town   Dar es Salaam   Hong Kong   Karachi
Kuala Lumpur   Madrid   Melbourne   Mexico City   Nairobi
New Delhi   Shanghai   Taipei   Toronto

With offices in
Argentina   Austria   Brazil   Chile   Czech Republic   France   Greece
Guatemala   Hungary   Italy   Japan   Poland   Portugal   Singapore
South Korea   Switzerland   Thailand   Turkey   Ukraine   Vietnam

Copyright © 2008 by Oxford University Press, Inc.

Published by Oxford University Press, Inc.
198 Madison Avenue, New York, New York 10016

www.oup.com

Oxford is a registered trademark of Oxford University Press

Library of Congress Cataloging-in-Publication Data
Feinstein, C. H.
The world economy between the world wars / Charles H. Feinstein,
Peter Temin, and Gianni Toniolo.
p. cm.
Includes bibliographical references and index.
ISBN 978-0-19-530755-9
1. Economic history—1918–1945. I. Temin, Peter. II. Toniolo,
Gianni, 1942–   III. Title.
HC57.F45 2007
330.9′041—dc22   2007018792

1   3   5   7   9   8   6   4   2
Printed in the United States of America
on acid-free paper

Preface

Given that the lead author of this volume died in 2004, we think that readers are owed a brief history of this book. The three of us wrote *The European Economy between the World Wars*, which appeared in 1997. It was received well, and all three of us enjoyed both writing the book and using it in classrooms. We believe others enjoyed the latter activity as well. Some time ago, Charles approached his coauthors and Oxford University Press about a revised edition. The suggestion was received warmly by all.

Charles then outlined the revision, emphasizing the need to expand our focus from Europe to the world. He laid out a plan of action, indicating where we had to add material and where recent scholarship needed to be included. Alas, his death prevented him from completing the plans he had made. The present authors decided to continue with the revision, acknowledging Charles's part in stimulating and planning it.

We therefore want to take the unusual step of thanking Charles, even though we have kept him as first author to highlight his role. We want to thank him for the intellectual vitality that led him to continue his professional work up to the time he died. This is shown not only in this volume, but also in the fine economic history of South Africa that he completed shortly before his death and which is cited in references here (Feinstein, 2005). He was a good friend to us both, and we wish he had been able to share more of the joys of revisiting, revising, and expanding our joint work.

Peter Temin
Gianni Toniolo
March 2007

Contents

Tables

Figures

THE WORLD ECONOMY BETWEEN THE WORLD WARS

Introduction

When this crisis is looked back upon by the economic historian of the future it will be seen to mark one of the major turning-points [of history].
     — John Maynard Keynes, "An Economic Analysis of Unemployment"

Chaos, crisis, and catastrophe are terms that feature prominently in the economic history of the interwar world economy. They are applied to price and money supplies, foreign-exchange rates, gold and capital movements, banking systems, external trade, and, worst of all, mass unemployment. Early in the period there were several spectacular episodes of hyperinflation in central and eastern Europe, and many other countries suffered severe though less drastic inflation and corresponding depreciation of the external value of their currencies.

There was a short-lived postwar boom followed by a slump, and a number of countries experienced serious banking crises in 1920–1921. These inflationary and financial problems were a direct consequence of the First World War. So too was the colossal burden of inter-allied debts, as were the attempts of the allies, particularly France, to extract huge sums in reparations from Germany. The struggle to cope with these enormous obligations was one of the critical factors in the financial instability of the 1920s.

A further aspect of great significance was the widespread belief in financial and political circles that it was essential to return to the prewar gold standard if the growth and prosperity of the pre-1914 era was to be reestablished, regardless of the sacrifices their countries would have to make in order to force down wages and prices so that the prewar value of the currency could be restored. The attempt to achieve this reconstruction of the gold standard dominated the financial policies of many nations.

An apparent measure of progress was achieved by the mid-1920s, and confidence and production revived. Improved economic understanding among the major European powers was reflected in the acceptance in 1924 of the Dawes Plan for the future payment of reparations. A new measure of political agreement was achieved with the ending of the French occupation of the Ruhr and the signing of the Locarno Pact. A brief interlude of relative stability and economic growth followed but could not be sustained. In the mid-1920s, agricultural producers around the world were hit by falling prices, especially for wheat and sugar, and signs of impending recession were evident in Germany from 1928 onward. The following year saw the beginning of a series of damaging banking panics and failures in America and Europe, culminating in serious currency and bank crises in Germany and the United States in 1931.

The collapse in output and employment in both industrial and primary producing countries combined to create the "Great Depression," a worldwide slump of unprecedented intensity and duration. In September 1931, Britain was no longer able to meet its obligations to supply gold to its international creditors and was forced to abandon the gold standard. Numerous other countries followed her example, and the international economic system established at such high cost in the 1920s was completely shattered at the beginning of the 1930s.

With the disintegration of the gold standard and the breakdown of international monetary cooperation, the world economy fragmented into hostile blocs, with mounting economic and political competition among the sterling area, the gold bloc, and the group of countries dominated by authoritarian regimes such as Nazi Germany and Japan. The period was marked by successive currency devaluations, the introduction of exchange controls, and the imposition of a wide variety of barriers to trade, all taking the major countries further away from the orthodox ideals of laissez faire, free trade, and stable currencies.

For many nations, it was a time of deep distress and slow recovery. This was true for the United States, even after the suspension of gold payments in 1933 and the devaluation of the dollar in early 1934. It applied particularly to those gold-bloc countries that were determined to maintain their commitment to gold. As their competitive position deteriorated, the attempt to cling to their pre-1931 gold parities became increasingly untenable, and they were finally compelled to devalue. In eastern Europe and other continents, growth was severely restricted by the collapse of farm prices and the contraction of multilateral trade.

Unemployment was widespread in industrial areas, while underemployment was the norm in the agricultural settings of Latin America, Africa, and Asia. All countries tried to alleviate the suffering, even if only to preserve political stability. Discontent flared up into political chaos or revolution in some countries, but not in others. It is hard to see a pattern when the results were the rise of fascists in the center of industrial Europe and the Iberian Peninsula and of militarists in Japan, while populist regimes emerged in Latin America.

The decline of the French franc and a growing sense of the need for political solidarity among the democracies eventually pushed a reluctant France, Britain, and the United States to take limited and tentative steps back toward a more cooperative international framework. This effort was given formal expression in the Tripartite Agreement, under which the three countries undertook to relax quotas and exchange controls and to avoid competitive devaluations. Germany and Italy stood outside this framework, with Hitler and Mussolini forcing their economies progressively further in the direction of state control, militarism, and autarky, dragging with them many neighboring countries in a web of exchange controls, tariffs, and special bilateral trading arrangements.

These successive developments had profound economic, social, and political effects on those who lived through these disturbed decades, and their recollection continued to reverberate during the reconstruction and evolution of the postwar economic system. The aim of this book is to provide a brief description of these events and to analyze the primary causes of the successive financial and economic developments of the interwar period and of their interrelationship. The Great Depression of 1929–1933 and the financial crisis of 1931 are placed at the center of the narrative and are presented both as the culmination of the policies and practices of the 1920s and as a powerful influence on the subsequent economic history of the 1930s. The unifying theme of the narrative is the impact of various forms and aspects of international economic organization on world economic stability.

In order to place the events of the interwar period in their historical context, we begin our account by looking briefly at the pattern of economic growth before and after this period. We also outline two key propositions or hypotheses relating to the organization of international economic relations that have been advanced by various writers who address this period: the decline and demise of empires, and the role of political actions in economic prosperity and depression. These propositions recur throughout our account of the interwar period, with differing emphases in different phases.

Chapter 1

The Interwar Economy in
a Secular Perspective

1.1 Modern Economic Growth in a
Twentieth-Century Perspective

The years between the two world wars were turbulent, both politically and economically. This book chronicles the economic events of those years. To understand them fully, the events noted here must be seen in the context of preceding and succeeding events. We start therefore by placing the interwar years in the context of modern economic growth. This sustained growth in per capita incomes started a century before the period described here, but it had affected only part of the world economy by the time our story begins.

During the first part of the nineteenth century, and in some regions for long after that, the standard of living—diet, clothing, housing, life expectancy, and literacy—of the average peasant family in the most advanced areas of western Europe and North America had far more in common with the standard of living of their medieval ancestors serving on feudal manors than with their post–Second World War great-grandchildren. Most industrial workers did not fare much better, packed as they were in filthy cities and burdened from childhood with long working weeks in unhealthy working conditions.

An Italian working-class family of four had an average monthly consumption in the early 1990s of about $1,600. In the 1890s, that family had to survive on less than $180 (inflation-adjusted), out of which they also had to cover expenses for health care and education, now provided free by the state. Such a low level of consumption allowed for bare subsistence on a diet that included meat only on rare occasions and left little for tobacco and a glass of cheap wine in the local *osteria*—and that only for the head of the household (Rossi and Toniolo, 1993).

The large majority of people living outside of western Europe and the so-called European overseas offshoots survived on an amount of resources possibly 30 to 50 percent lower than those available to the masses in the areas of the world where an "industrial revolution" of some kind had sparked the transformation of the daily life of ordinary people for which Simon Kuznets coined the term "modern economic growth." At the heart of this process, the most far-reaching revolution in the history of mankind, Kuznets saw an "epochal innovation" consisting of the "spreading application of science to processes of production and social organization" (Kuznets, 1966, p. 487).

Kuznets showed that those countries in which modern economic growth occurs experience a number of similar quantitative developments related to the long-run rates of growth of aggregate and sectoral production, consumption and saving patterns, and structural changes in the economy. Modern economic growth is typically characterized—and, some would say, defined by—"high rates of increase in per capita product, ranging from less than 15 to about 30 per cent per decade" (Kuznets, 1966, p. 490). Its main features include an acceleration in the growth of population and consumption, a rise in savings and investment ratios, and a shift in the composition of GDP away from agriculture. Aggregate product derives increasingly from the manufacturing and service sectors, with a similar change in the pattern of consumption.

Kuznets also saw a tremendous increase in the international movement of goods, services, and factors of production as a prominent feature of modern economic growth. A rapid increase in cross-border trade and factor mobility was, however, neither constant nor irreversible. Historians talk about a "first globalization" taking place roughly between 1860 and 1913, a "globalization backlash" during the years covered by this book, and a resumption of international economic integration after 1945, taking place slowly at first and then gaining strength. It was probably only in the 1990s that trade and capital mobility again reached the weight in the world economy that they had attained at the beginning of the century, allowing scholars to identify a "second globalization." Labor mobility, however, has never again been as pronounced as it was before the First World War.

Before introducing the overall quantitative dimensions of the 1914–1945 "globalization backlash," the topic of this book, let's take a brief look at some of the secular trends in the world economy, in order to better understand the peculiarities of the interwar years.

In the early part of the nineteenth century, modern economic growth had spread from its cradle in England to Belgium, France, Switzerland, the Rhineland, and the United States. Some decades later, it reached Prussia and the Scandinavian countries, and eventually it spread to some parts of Russia and central Europe, to the Italian and Iberian peninsulas in the Mediterranean, to Canada and Argentina in the Americas, and to parts of Oceania. Japan was the only country outside the areas of European settlement where a robust process of modern economic growth took place in the nineteenth century. It was only after the Second World War that industrialization and GDP-growth acceleration became an increasingly common feature of other countries,

Table 1.1 Average annual rates of growth, 1870–1998, world and main regions

	1870–1998	1870–1913	1913–1950	1950–1973	1973–1998
World	1.48	1.30	0.91	2.93	1.33
Western Europe[a]	1.74	1.32	0.76	4.08	1.78
Western offshoots[b]	1.87	1.81	1.55	2.44	1.94
Japan	2.63	1.48	0.89	8.05	2.34
Asia (excluding Japan)	1.33	0.38	−0.02	2.92	3.54
Latin America	1.41	1.81	1.42	2.52	0.99
Eastern Europe[c]	1.22	1.15	1.50	3.49	−1.10
Africa	0.88	0.64	1.02	2.07	0.01

Note: Estimates are weighted averages.
[a] Twenty-nine western European countries.
[b] Australia, New Zealand, Canada, and the United States.
[c] Seven eastern European countries and Russia/the Soviet Union.

Source: Maddison (2001), 126 and passim.

particularly in Asia. The progress of Latin America was less buoyant, patchier, and more prone to reversals of fortune. Sub-Saharan Africa, with the exception of the Cape region, remained almost entirely cut off from the spread of modern economic growth. Even in many industrial countries, workers still had not derived much benefit from this process before World War I.

Table 1.1 puts the years between the two World Wars in the context of long-term modern economic growth. For a period of almost 130 years, from 1870 to the end of the twentieth century, the world's annual rate of increase in the real GDP per capita—a rough proxy for the standard of living—averaged about 1.5 percent per annum.

Even a quick glance at table 1.1 will reveal two features of the long-term growth of the world economy: the uneven path of growth both across regions and over time. Economists do indeed expect productivity (proxied by GDP per capita) growth to differ across countries and regions, but their assumption is that backward areas will catch up with the more advanced ones. The history of modern economic growth tends to show that, if anything, the opposite has been the case for a long period of time. In 1870, western Europe and the western offshoots were already more "advanced" in terms of GDP per capita than the world's average (about 2,200 international dollars vs. 867),[1] yet their secular growth rates have been higher than those of the initially poorer countries.

---

[1] At 1990 purchasing power.

Divergence, rather than convergence towards the productivity leaders, has tended to characterize the long-run growth process of the world economy, at least until the 1980s. The big exception, the rapid catcher-up, has been Japan.

Rates of growth also differed over time, beyond the normal cyclical fluctuations, suggesting that in each given period in table 1.1, factors such as technology, institutions, and economic policies affected the world economy in different ways.

As shown in table 1.1, during the first (1870–1913) and the last (1973–1998) periods, real per capita GDP in western Europe and the western offshoots grew at about the average secular rate. In contrast, the two other subperiods deviate sharply from this trend. In the 1950s and 1960s, the economies of western Europe grew at a rate twice as high as the secular trend. This tremendous increase in production and the full employment that accompanied it turned out to be compatible with low inflation and overall external stability, at least until the mid-1960s. The western offshoots also outperformed secular average growth, if in a less spectacular fashion.

While the rapid growth from 1950 to 1973 looks like a golden age of economic growth, the preceding period, from 1913 to 1950, appears to be a pause in the onward progress of rising per capita income. Almost every area distinguished in table 1.1 grew more slowly in 1913–1950 than in the preceding period and far more slowly than in the golden age. The slowdown was particularly sharp in western Europe, which will occupy a prominent place in this narrative.

This brief survey of the aggregate changes in the world economy since 1870 was intended to put the interwar years, the subject of this volume, in a longer-term perspective that should help us to better understand the specific features of those momentous, defining years. We now turn to a brief exposition of the main macroeconomic aspects of the interwar period, by way of introduction to the specific issues dealt with in the following chapters.

1.2 Some Quantitative Features of the Interwar Years

The marked slowdown in the world's real per capita growth between 1913 and 1950 provides the background to the present history. Against this general background and before proceeding to analyze the various aspects of the international economy during the interwar years, it is useful to discuss briefly a few "stylized facts" that are prominent features of the aggregate quantitative changes between 1913 and 1950 (or between 1921 and 1938, as may be the case). They may be summarized as follows: (1) while the slowdown in economic activity was a worldwide phenomenon, it affected individual areas in quite different ways; (2) the overall slowdown was the result of quite satisfactory rates in the 1920s and of dismal economic performance in the 1930s; (3) far from keeping pace with output trends, international trade declined in real terms; (4) high and structural unemployment was the shocking new phenomenon of those years; and (5) labor productivity increased more rapidly than in 1890–1913; the pace achieved in the 1920s was particularly good.

Slower Growth

Table 1.2 shows that the reduction in the growth of real per capita GDP between 1870 and 1913 and between 1913 and 1950 characterized all the regions in the table, except for the Soviet Union, which was the most notable exception to the general gloom of the 1930s (see table 1.2).

There is one dominant explanation for the severity of the European slow-down between 1913 and 1950 (and, paradoxically, also for the golden age of the 1950s and 1960s): war. The catastrophic impact of two global military conflicts, both fought with unprecedented destructive strength on European soil, explains the poor performance of western Europe relative to North America, its main competitor and trading partner. During 1913–1921, western Europe's output declined on average by 1.2 percent per annum, while GDP per capita in the United States remained roughly constant. During 1938–1950, the United States enjoyed its fastest growth on record for a period of comparable length, 3.8 percent per annum, while Western Europe only grew by 0.3 percent per annum. This is why, in what follows, special emphasis will be placed on the immediate and long-term effects of the Great War (including, among the latter, the second global conflagration of 1939–1945). On the other hand, in 1921–1938, Europe's growth considerably exceeded that of the United States. Japan's record (1913–1950) was also deeply affected by the Second World War.

Growth deceleration in Latin America was roughly in line with that of the western offshoots in North America and Oceania. Most of Asia (excluding Japan), which had remained quite untouched by the growth acceleration process of the "first globalization" (1870–1913), experienced a long-term decline in output and welfare during the period covered by this book.

Table 1.2 Growth of real GDP per capita in Europe, the United States, Latin America, Japan, China, India, and the Soviet Union, 1913–1950 (average annual rates of growth)

	Western Europe	United States	Latin America	Japan	China	India	Soviet Union
1913–50	0.8	1.8	1.4	0.9	−0.8	−0.3	1.1
1921–38	2.0	0.8	1.4	1.8	n.a.	−0.1	n.a.
1921–29	3.5	3.3	2.6	2.0	n.a.	0.9	n.a.
1929–38	0.7	−1.3	0.4	1.7	0	−1.0	4.9

Source: Maddison (2001), 104–11, 180–87.

As already mentioned, the Soviet Union in the 1930s provided a striking contrast to the dismal performance of most of the market economies. Even allowing for recent revisions of earlier Soviet and western estimates, total GDP growth in the Soviet Union averaged 5.30 percent per annum between 1928 and 1940 (Allen, 2003, 217), in striking contrast to the dim performance of the world's other main areas. Given the record of the Soviet Union's planned economy, it is no wonder that the Third International could tout the Soviet Union's performance as the "proof" of the superiority of the socialist system; nor is it surprising that many in the West prophesied the end of capitalism, including Mussolini and Hitler, who preached and practiced their own supposed "third way" between the two systems. Needless to say, the subsequent development of the world economy proved the resilience of well-run market economies.

The whole period stands out as one of major divisions and lack of cooperation, with devastating results for the pace of economic progress. This is shown, among other things, by the above-average performance in 1913–1950 of countries, that remained consistently neutral, such as Sweden and Switzerland.

The "Globalization Backlash"

It has become common for scholars to refer to the second of the quantitative "stylized facts" outlined above—namely, the disruption of international trade and the sharp reduction in the cross-border movements of factors of production (capital and labor)—as "globalization backlash."

International movements of goods, services, capital, and labor typically depend on two sets of factors: technology, which reduces transport and communication costs, and institutions, both domestic and international, that may either favor or hinder international economic integration. Transport and communication technology continued to improve in the period under consideration, not least due to military research and developments stimulated by the First World War. Larger and more energy-efficient ships reduced the unit cost of sea transport. Developments in the internal combustion engine provided a competitive alternative to railways in land transport for both people and goods. A passenger airline industry took off, providing ever-safer and progressively cheaper services. Telephone and radio revolutionized international communication, having a particularly strong impact on financial market integration. All other things being equal, therefore, technology created increasingly favorable conditions for cross-border economic integration. Therefore, we must seek other reasons to explain why August 1914 put an end to a long era of progressive, if slow, integration of the world economy, an era that then came to be known as the "belle époque" and that we now call "first globalization." As mentioned above, continuous tension, misunderstandings, and lack of cooperation characterized international relations in 1919–1938, resulting in the creation of an institutional environment inimical to trade and to the cross-border movement of people—and, in the 1930s, of capital as well. On the domestic front, countries were busy erecting tariff and nontariff walls, limiting immigration, and minutely regulating international financial transactions. The international monetary system, painfully re-created in the 1920s, collapsed early in the next decade. International economic organizations, such as the economic commission of the League of Nations and the Bank for International Settlements, were almost powerless in a context of extremely strained international relations. On balance, man-made obstacles outweighed the favorable impact of technology on international economic transactions. Pre-1913 globalization was put in reverse.

In 1870–1913, the income elasticity of world exports was certainly greater than 1 and probably close to 2. In the subsequent sixteen years, international trade growth slowed down everywhere; in 1929–1950, it almost stagnated (see table 1.3). Europe's trade performance stands out as particularly disappointing. Japan's exports grew rapidly in the 1920s, while they decreased in the 1930s, in spite of a fairly good output growth, marking the shift to autarky imposed by the military regime. The export performance of the United States was twice as good as the world's average in the 1920s. While U.S. export performance sharply decreased in the subsequent decade, it still remained well above average.

Europe was largely responsible for the dramatic fall in international trade growth during the Great War and the interwar years. In the 1930s, the volume of western European exports actually declined. Europe's sluggish trade impact on the Atlantic routes, both North and South, depressed trade from and to the Americas as well.

Table 1.3 Growth of value of merchandise exports at constant prices for twenty-four countries (annual average rates)

	1870–1913	1913–1929	1929–1950	1950–1973	1973–1998
Western Europe[a]	3.23	0.21	−0.32	8.03	4.55
United States	4.86	3.33	1.68	6.27	5.98
Russia/Soviet Union	n.a.	−4.66	3.08	9.98	2.95
Latin America[b]	3.40	3.89	1.46	4.10	5.70
China	2.59	2.90	0.06	2.74	11.81
India	2.37	−1.02	−1.90	2.46	5.94
Japan	8.47	7.00	−0.97	15.54	5.30
World	3.35		0.89	7.88	5.07

[a] Twelve countries.
[b] Seven countries.

Source: Maddison (2001), 361–62.

As the result of the interwar trade trends, western Europe's share of world exports declined from 60.1 percent in 1913 to 41.1 percent in 1950, highlighting one of the structural changes in the world economy brought about by two world wars and the Great Depression: the shift of the center of the world economy away from western Europe.

As a feature of the interwar globalization backlash, migration flows stand out even more strikingly than trade. In the century after 1820, about 55 million Europeans left the continent. In the twentieth century, war and the United States Immigration Acts, which introduced immigrant quotas by national origin, put an end to the "age of mass migration," which was a salient aspect of the first globalization. The depression of the 1930s, with the attendant mass unemployment in the New World, further depressed the flow of people crossing the Atlantic. Intra-European migrations were also somewhat reduced.

If voluntary migration sharply decreased, forced migration increased, highlighting the most tragic features of the European interwar history. Persecution made Jews leave central Europe in the 1930s. Spaniards left for Mexico during the Spanish Civil War. Poles and Baltic people were forcibly deported to Siberia.

Cross-border capital flows reached an all-time peak in 1913. They became a casualty of the Great War and remained depressed in the following two decades, characterized as they were by administrative controls on cross-border monetary transactions (the so-called "exchange controls") and by uncertainty regarding future exchange rates.

The Rise in Unemployment between the Wars

High unemployment rates, particularly but not exclusively in the 1930s, stand out in collective memories as the most deeply felt economic feature of the interwar period. Visual artists and writers, as well as a largely diffused oral tradition, have passed on stories of homeless people, long queues for a free meal, \workers sitting idle outside their humble dwellings, helpless families, discouraged long-term unemployed people. Photographs, paintings, and novels describe the Great Depression in North America and Europe in quite similar fashions, meaning that, as far as unemployment is concerned, in the 1930s the contrast between the two sides of the Atlantic was not perceived to be very pronounced. On the contrary, a contrast existed in the 1920s when, in many European countries, a fairly large number of people were out of work, while the United States experienced almost full employment.

Comparing unemployment over time and across countries is a daunting task. The term "unemployment" appeared for the first time only in 1888 (Royal Institute of International Affairs, 1935, 26); the compilation of official statistics began much later. Moreover, because such statistics often derived from

Table 1.4 Average European unemployment rates, 1921–1993 (percent)

1921–1929	1930–1938	1950–1959	1960–1973	1974–1981	1982–1989	1990–1993
8.3	15.8	4.2	2.5	5.2	8.8	9.2

Note: Arithmetic average of average annual unemployment rates. 1921–1938 covers France, Germany, and the United Kingdom; for 1950–1993, Italy is also included.

Sources: For 1921–1938, Galenson and Zellner (1957), 455. For 1950–1993, Maddison (1991), 262, and OECD data from Crafts and Toniolo (1996), 7.

the records either of those receiving some sort of benefit or of those register-ing with labor-exchange offices, they depend heavily on specific institutional arrangements in individual countries. It is thus impossible to make an accurate comparison of the levels of interwar unemployment with those prevailing in the quarter of a century before 1914. However, there seems to be some con-sensus among scholars that unemployment before the First World War was of shorter average duration than that experienced after 1918.

More can be said about the relative magnitude of the phenomenon in the interwar period and the years after the Second World War. Table 1.4 covers only a few western European countries and may not be very precise as far as the absolute levels of unemployment rates are concerned, but it probably provides a broadly correct indication of relative variations across time (Eichengreen and Hatton, 1988, 7). Exceptionally high unemployment rates stand out as a fea-ture of the 1930s, while unemployment in the 1960s was exceptionally low. At the same time, the relative number of those out of work in the troubled decade of the 1920s looks, on average, to be broadly comparable with that of the 1980s and early 1990s, an aspect we shall return to in the concluding chapter.

Productivity Continues to Improve

While the number of unemployed rose, available evidence shows that product per hour worked by those who retained their jobs continued to increase. From 1913 to 1950, the pace of productivity growth in western Europe was roughly the same as in the previous half century. In the United States, productivity growth was more rapid than in the pre-1914 decades. Productivity growth in Japan, on the other hand, slowed down (see table 1.5).

There are three plausible reasons why productivity continued to grow in the period under review, in spite of the disruption of human and physical capital brought about by two world wars and of the interwar globalization backlash. The first is that the 1920s and 1930s were rich in technological innovations. A number of inventions produced by the pre-1913 "second industrial revolu-tion" had a measurable impact on aggregate output only during or after the war. This was the case, for instance, with regard to the internal combustion engine, the assembly line pioneered by Henry Ford, and the electrical network

Table 1.5 Growth of productivity, 1870–1998, selected areas (average annual rate of growth)

	1870–1913	1913–1950	1950–1973	1973–1990	1990–1998
Western Europe[a]	1.55	1.56	4.77	2.29	2.16
United States	1.92	2.48	2.77	1.41	1.74
Japan	1.99	1.80	7.74	2.97	2.13

Note: Productivity is defined as real GDP per hour worked.
[a] Twelve countries.

Source: Maddison (2001), 352.

and motor. The latter was a typical "general purpose innovation" capable of application in a large number of production processes. The second reason for continued productivity growth in the interwar years is probably traceable to the continuation of the prewar trend of extending elementary and secondary education to an ever-larger number of people and of investing in higher education. Investment in education typically has a lagged impact on the stock of human capital and thus on productivity growth, but if sustained is a major source of long-term growth in output per hour worked. Finally, productivity growth in the 1930s might also have been the unintended consequence of unemployment itself, as layoffs tend to affect the least productive members of the workforce.

Whatever caused it, the observed trend in productivity growth is interesting and important for at least two reasons. First, it reinforces one of the main contentions of this book: that slow growth and depression were man-made rather than "natural" phenomena. Second, it explains, at least in part, the extraordinary growth rates of the years after the Second World War. Once man-made obstacles were removed, the European economies could exploit a vast backlog of accumulated technical knowledge and human capital.

Output Growth: Belligerents and Neutrals

In this brief quantitative survey, we have so far considered Europe as an aggregate. But, over the interwar period, nation-states actually reinforced their protagonist role. The dissolution of four large empires (the Russian, Prussian, Austro-Hungarian, and Ottoman empires) between 1917 and 1919 resulted in the addition of a number of new independent states to the prewar lot. Nation-states received ideological support from the Wilsonian ideology and a full international endorsement at the Versailles Peace Conference. Moreover, in retaining or gaining full economic sovereignty, it was the nation-state that was responsible for policies affecting economic growth. Tense relations between nation-states were also responsible for the autarkic trends that disrupted the international economy.

Table 1.6 shows the growth rates of nine European countries, the United States, Canada, and Japan during 1913–1950 and two relevant subperiods. The first column in the table covers the full period 1913–1950. Countries are ranked by growth order, starting from the slowest. No simple organizing principle is possible here; given the length and complexity of the period, growth rates were the result of participation or neutrality in one or both world wars, the speed of respective recoveries, monetary and exchange-rate policies, semiplanned fascist economies, and other factors. However, one obvious prima facie observation is possible: two of the fastest-growing countries, Sweden and Switzerland, remained neutral during both the First and the Second World Wars, and two others, Finland and Norway, were neutral in the first conflict.

The second column covers the years from 1913 to 1929. Here, countries are classified according to their participation in the Great War, the most important single factor to affect individual performances, at least during the first half of the decade. The results are quite indicative: neutrals outperform all winners, while the winners (with the possible exception of the United Kingdom) do better than the cores of the two pre-1918 central empires that were defeated in the war and lost significant parts of their territories. The third column takes into account the most important item in the economic policies of the 1930, namely the adherence to the gold standard until 1935–1936, or its early demise in 1931. Here, too, the results are quite suggestive. Those who left gold definitely outperform the members of the gold bloc and Switzerland. Germany is listed under "other" because its currency remained only formally anchored to gold, while in practice policy makers were quite successful at insulating the country from the deflationary effects of the gold-standard rules.

It goes without saying that the associations in table 1.6 cannot be taken as proofs of causal links. At best, they may be suggestive of research hypotheses. If so, they indicate again that in order to understand the slowdown in modern economic growth experienced in the period of our study, it is appropriate to explore first and foremost the effects of the war and of ill-advised economic policies. In this vein, we have selected four relevant propositions from among the large number of explanations scholars have provided for the poor performance of the European economy during the interwar years.

1.3 Two Propositions about International Economic Organization

Structural Imbalances and the End of Empires

The traditional explanation for the depth and persistence of widespread postwar difficulties is the problem of "structural imbalance" within and

Table 1.6 Growth in real GDP, selected European countries, the United States, Canada, and Japan, 1913–1950 (average annual rate of growth)

1913–1950		1913–1929		1929–1938	
		WWI neutrals		*Off gold in 1931*	
Austria	0.2	Sweden	1.9	UK	1.9
Belgium	1.0	Finland	2.4	Denmark	2.2
Germany	1.1	Denmark	2.7	Sweden	2.6
France	1.2	Switzerland	2.8	Norway	3.1
UK	1.3	Norway	2.9	Finland	3.9
Italy	1.5	Netherlands	3.6		
Netherlands	2.4			*Gold bloc*	
Denmark	2.5	*WWI winners*		France	−0.4
Switzerland	2.6	UK	0.7	Belgium	0.0
Finland	2.7	Belgium	1.4	Netherlands	0.3
Sweden	2.7	Italy	1.7	Switzerland	0.6
Norway	2.9	France	1.9	Italy	1.6
		WWI losers		*Other*	
		Austria	0.3	Austria	−0.3
		Germany	1.2	Germany	2.5
Extra-Europe					
Japan	2.2	Canada	2.5	United States	−0.6
United States	2.8	Japan	3.7	Canada	0.0
Canada	2.9	United States	3.1	Japan	3.6

Source: Maddison (1995), 180–83.

between countries. The origins of this dislocation are found in the changes in the composition of production and demand resulting from the wartime disruption of international trade, from the geopolitical effects of the Treaty of Versailles, and from postwar changes in technology and patterns of demand.

Although the effects of these changes are not always clearly spelled out, they may be taken to relate particularly to a misallocation of resources that was responsible for the high rate of unemployment in Europe in the 1920s and that also made the adjustment process longer and more costly. The effects of these structural changes were felt in both labor markets and product markets, in each of which, it is argued, there was appreciably less flexibility after 1918 (Svennilson, 1954).

In eastern Europe and beyond, the collapse of the Austro-Hungarian, Ottoman, and Russian empires created entirely new conditions for a whole region. This part of the world is geologically unstable, as it sits on top of the fault that created the Great Rift Valley in Africa and oil deposits farther north. The region turned out to be unstable politically as well in the early twentieth century, as the rulers of these empires tried to compete with the more indus- trial countries in the First World War. Mobilization in these largely agrarian economies stripped the country of productive resources, leading to food short-ages in major cities. The results were civil disturbances and the collapse of traditional governing structures (Broadberry and Harrison, 2005).

As a result of these far-reaching changes, there were many new countries led by inexperienced leaders in the interwar years. The results were inauspi-cious in most cases, leading to economic chaos in the form of hyperinflations in some cases and less severe problems in others. The Soviet successors to the old Russian Empire separated themselves from much of the economic activity we will describe here, although we will also discuss developments in the Soviet sphere. Other successor countries struggled for independence and stability, leading to the interaction of economics and politics that is the subject of our second proposition.

Conflict in Asia both within China and between China and Japan impeded economic growth and prosperity there, too. The collapse of the Chinese Empire was not as closely tied to the war as was the collapse of the empires nearer to the actual conflict. The coincidence in timing, however, suggests that some of the same forces were at work. China was doubly disadvantaged by having inexperienced leaders at home and an aggressive Japan on its doorstep. As we will describe later, Japan's recovery from the Great Depression led to its inva-sion of China, which impeded economic progress there.

Politics and Economics

The lack of leadership by governments, central banks, and international institu-tions in the operation of the restored gold standard—and, more generally, in international economic policy making—has been noted by Brown (1940) and Kindleberger (1973). The proposition is summed up in the phrase "no longer London, not yet Washington." The diminished political, military, and financial status of the United Kingdom meant that London was unable to act as sole conductor of the international orchestra (or, in more modern terminology, to operate as the "hegemon"), while the United States was not yet willing to take over this role, despite the enormous improvement in its international standing.

The ability of London to perform its traditional role as the dominant eco-nomic power was further undermined by the strength of France's relative financial position after the stabilization of the franc in 1926 and the large accumulation of gold by the Bank of France. Lack of leadership manifested itself in a number of crucial political and economic areas where consensus could not be reached. The failure of the numerous economic conferences, the fruitless disarmament efforts, and the unresolved issue of German repara-tions are all cases in point. The specific financial manifestation of this lack of leadership was that there was no country able and willing to stabilize the global monetary environment, for instance by acting as an international lender-of-last resort.

The lack of leadership was compounded by the absence of international cooperation between the United States, Britain, France, and Germany, and the failure of the major nations to coordinate their domestic economic policies. Clarke (1967) argued this specifically in relation to the period from mid-1928 to the collapse of the gold standard in 1931, claiming that after the 1928 death of Benjamin Strong, governor of the Federal Reserve Bank of New York, the central bankers failed to achieve the necessary coordination of policy. Friedman and Schwartz (1963), writing about the United States, gave even more weight to Strong's unfortunate death.

More generally, Eichengreen (1985, 1992a) suggested lack of cooperation as a central feature of the entire period, manifested particularly in the attempt of each of the main powers to secure for itself a disproportionate share of the world's limited stocks of monetary gold. Prior to the collapse of the gold standard in 1931, their uncooperative behavior involved the imposition of tight monetary policies not only by countries in deficit, but also by those that were in surplus, notably the United States and France. This added to the deflationary pressures on the world economy and increased the vulnerability of the weak currencies, such as the pound sterling and the mark, to speculative attack.

In other variants on this theme, the shortcomings of the interwar adjustment mechanism are explained by the unwillingness of central banks to operate the gold standard according to the "rules of the game," under which all movements in gold should have been fully reflected in compensating changes in domestic money supplies. The main reason for this tendency to neutralize changes in gold and foreign-exchange reserves, rather than allowing them to influence internal monetary conditions, was that postwar governments were no longer willing to give unconditional support to external equilibrium and the defense of the reserves, due to the increased political cost of the necessary measures.

Democratic electorates increasingly required that governments should attach greater weight to internal stability of prices and incomes. "When the precepts of the gold standard ran counter to the requirements of domestic monetary stability, it was the latter that usually prevailed," wrote Nurske (1944, 105). But the new position was not entirely symmetrical: there was always greater pressure to neutralize an outflow of gold than an inflow, and this imparted a deflationary bias to the whole system.

The inability of the powers to cooperate was dramatically symbolized at the World Monetary Conference in the summer of 1933, which met in London shortly after the United States had abandoned the gold standard and allowed the dollar to depreciate. The gathering had been specifically convened to promote the coordinated stabilization of exchange rates, but in the middle of the proceedings, Roosevelt announced that he was not yet willing to stabilize the dollar. He brusquely dismissed "the specious fallacy of achieving a temporary and probably an artificial stability in foreign exchanges on the part of a few large countries only" (Hodson, 1938, 194). This disastrous meeting starkly exposed the total lack of any common ground between countries and hastened the further disintegration of the international monetary system. With global political relations also deteriorating rapidly, the decade witnessed an epidemic of competitive currency depreciation; extended resort to exchange controls; the rise of protectionism, bilateralism, import quotas, and other barriers to trade; and the development of hostile, noncooperating trade and currency blocs.

Finally, even when leaders acted responsibly and cooperation was tried, problems arose from the hold that old-fashioned political and financial ideologies exerted on policy-makers. The former is seen as responsible for the insistence on substantial reparations. This produced a new pattern of international settlements that made the smooth functioning of international payments dependent upon the capability and willingness of the United States to continue lending to Europe indefinitely. The destabilizing potential of this "arrangement" is self-evident. Still more important was the financial ideology reflected in the priority attached to the reintroduction of the gold standard, even where this could only be achieved by subjecting the economy to a severe program of deflation and obstructing future trade by the imposition of an overvalued currency.

Under the discipline that this doctrine enjoined—or the values it implied—country after country surrendered its "monetary sovereignty" and restricted its ability to accommodate balance-of-payments disturbances by any means other than retrenchment. The consequences of this situation became apparent in the early 1930s, when the constraints of the gold standard prevented countries from initiating policies to alleviate economic distress and even induced some countries to pursue policies that intensified the economic decline (Temin, 1989).

We shall return to these two propositions and discuss their validity and applicability at appropriate points in the subsequent narrative.

Chapter 2

The Legacy of the First World War

2.1 The Economics of "Total War"

It is impossible to understand interwar economic history—and, more specifically, interwar international economic organization—without considering the long-lasting effects of a war that was first bitterly fought both on the battlefield and on what came to be known as the economic front, and that then continued, more subtly, in later postwar political and economic policies.

The First World War marked the true watershed between the nineteenth and twentieth centuries. This fact is particularly relevant when we consider our central theme of international economic organization. The late nineteenth century was characterized by a relatively well-functioning international payment system based on the gold standard. London played a pivotal and stabilizing role, and the leading central banks cooperated as necessary. In addition, there was almost perfect mobility of factors of production, reflected in large-scale movements of labor and capital from Europe to the New World. Commercial treaties mitigated the impact of tariffs on international commodity trade, stimulated by rapidly falling transportation costs. This was the nineteenth-century international economic order.

The war itself was a major economic revolution. In pre-1914 peacetime economies, the role of the state was extremely limited. Governments provided for defense, foreign policy, domestic security, and free universal elementary education in some cases; they subsidised railways and built national roads. Total revenue seldom exceeded 15 percent of GDP in the final years of peace; the same was true of total expenses (Lindert, 1994). This pattern was so firmly established in everybody's expectations that a "short-war theorem" had developed among governments and chiefs of staff. This theorem held that any 'modern' war was bound to be brief, given the limited resources available and the disruption in economic and social life that a war would create.

As it turned out, the short-war theorem was based on very shaky foundations. It disregarded both the flexibility of a modern economy and the adaptability of mankind to almost any situation. The revolutionary aspect of the war economy consisted mainly in the rapid shift of resources from consumption to arms production and the attendant reorganization of the entire economic life of the belligerent nations. In a relatively short period of time, thrifty nineteenth-century governments were turned into twentieth-century big spenders. In the United Kingdom, military expenditure rose from about 4 percent of GDP in 1913 to 38 percent in 1916–1917, bringing total government expenditure close to half of national income. In Germany, military spending alone rose to 53 percent of GDP by 1917 (see table 2.1, in which these

Table 2.1 Military expenditure as a percentage of net national product at factor cost, selected countries, 1913–1920 and 1937–1951

	UK	USA	USSR	Germany	Japan
First World War					
1913	4	1	—	—	—
1914	9	1		14	—
1915	34	1	—	41	—
1916	38	1	—	35	—
1917	38	6	—	53	—
1918	32	13	—	32	—
1919	13	9	—	—	—
1920	4	3	—	—	—
Second World War					
1937	—	—	9	—	13
1938	7	—	—	17	—
1939	16	2	—	25	—
1940	49	2	21	44	17
1941	55	12	—	56	25
1942	54	34	75	69	36
1943	57	44	76	76	47
1944	56	45	69	—	64
1945	47	38	—	—	—
1946	19	10	—	—	—
1947	11	5	—	—	—
1948	8	5	18	—	—
1949	8	6	17	—	—
1950	8	5	16	—	—

Sources: UK, USA, USSR, Germany, 1938–1945: Harrison (1988), 184.

UK: Feinstein (1972), tables 1, 3, 12, and 33, and supporting worksheets.
USA: U.S. Department of Commerce (1975), series F1, F6, Y458–59.
USSR: Bergson (1961), 128, 303.
Germany: Stolper, Hauser, and Borchardt (1967), 57; Sommariva and Tullio (1987), 226–27.
Japan: Milward (1977), 85; Ohkawa and Shinohara (1979), 269, 375.

proportions are compared with those of World War II). A colossal amount of labor had to be swiftly diverted from peacetime production to military service and to rapidly expanding armament factories, chemical industries, shipyards, and the like. Female labor was widely used in the countryside. The capital needs for this colossal resource reallocation were met chiefly by borrowing or simply by printing large quantities of bank notes.

As soon as the illusion of a short war had vanished, all the contenders organized for a "total war." In Germany, Walther Rathenau, the brilliant head of the AEG electrical combine, was put in charge of an agency set up to exercise control over military supplies. In Italy, capable industrialists and top generals were given similar jobs. Germany's central planning of the supply of raw materials and their distribution to companies working for the government turned out to be particularly effective. It was accompanied by an industrial reorganization that more often than not entailed compulsory cartelization. Small industry was sacrificed to the needs of industrial giants.

In Britain, the Ministry of Munitions was created in 1915 under Lloyd George. The new ministry slowly acquired most of the features of Germany's War Raw Material Office, supervising private business and supplementing their efforts with direct investment when necessary. At the end of the war, Britain had some 200 government-owned plants.

In many areas, this colossal productive effort was coupled with an acceleration of technical progress both in products and production processes. Internal-combustion-engine vehicles, surface ships, submarines, airplanes, and several other products were drastically improved during the war, most of them subsequently enjoying peacetime development. At the same time, plants became larger and more efficient; the workforce—subject to military discipline—was "scientifically" organized.

With hindsight, one may say that perhaps the most revolutionary aspect of "total war" was general conscription. Society, particularly in the countryside, was deeply changed by the departure of almost all acceptable men and their replacement by women, children, and older workers. While serving in the trenches, men were exposed to mass propaganda of various kinds as never before, and some of them learned ways of organizing large numbers of people for political purposes. After the war, it was almost impossible for the ruling classes to ignore the reality of mass movements or to revert to the old, cozy ways of elite politics.

The extreme form of this political change came when the mass movements overwhelmed the government, leading to fundamental political changes. In Germany, the Kaiser abdicated and was replaced by a republic. The Austro-Hungarian Empire collapsed into a set of small countries. The Russian and Ottoman Empires collapsed in opposite ways. The Russian Empire was taken over by the Bolsheviks, who established a new Soviet empire with new economic policies to be described later. The Ottoman Empire also collapsed, but only Turkey and Egypt emerged as independent countries. The rest of the empire became mandates of England and France and only later became independent political entities.

The British and the French empires, while enlarged by the acquisition of German possessions in Africa, were also weakened by the war as local movements for autonomy or even independence began to gather strength at a time when the home countries found it more difficult to mobilize resources for overseas expenditure. The Japanese Empire, on the other hand, emerged stronger from the war: Tokyo's almost costless alliance with the Entente allowed it to make some territorial gains and to consolidate its colonial holdings (particularly Taiwan and Korea) and its commercial influence in Asia.

A somewhat similar mechanism led to the demise of these various empires. In the advanced, industrialized countries, mobilization generated a large demand for food and led to agricultural prosperity. In the more agricultural regions of these empires, mobilization took workers—and often horses as well—from the countryside. The reduction of trade and of domestic production of consumer goods during the war meant that farmers had little to buy if they sold their output. The result was that the farmers felt hard-pressed and reluctant to sell food. This led to acute food scarcity in the cities and abundant food in the countryside with no market. Lack of food is a classic source of civil unrest, and the inevitable result was revolution. If the empires had been either industrial or sufficiently isolated from the conflict so that they did not mobilize, they could have survived. But being at the periphery of Europe and determined to participate in all things European spelled their downfall (Broadberry and Harrison, 2005).

In the international economy—the matter that interests us here—the war brought about two major developments. First, the displacement of the agricultural sector in the belligerent countries led to the lifting of import duties in order to gain access to the cheapest overseas supplies. The production of grains and meat in the fertile regions of the United States, Canada, Argentina, and Australia expanded to exploit those nations' comparative advantage in supplying European markets.

Second, financial cooperation was undertaken by the Entente powers in the form of inter-Allied loans. At first, Britain lent to its financially weaker allies, France, Italy and Belgium. Later on, the United States provided war loans to all the European countries fighting against the central empires. As a result of this cooperation, the allies' exchange rates could be pegged at politically acceptable levels, and hard currency was made available to buy overseas supplies, mostly in the home markets of the creditor countries themselves.

2.2 The Economic Consequences of the War

The most enduring legacy of the war was social and political instability, both domestic and international. It is not our aim here to discuss this issue. Suffice it to say that, on the various domestic fronts, the war's ultimate results took the names of Mussolini in Italy and Hitler in Germany. And, of course, it was the war that opened the way to the October Revolution in Russia. More stable democracies, such as France and Britain, also suffered from immediate postwar instability, and for a brief time even they feared revolution.

In the international arena, the period between the Armistice of November 11, 1918, and the crisis of 1923–1924 that led to some kind of "stabilization" was one of great upheaval. The war left a permanent scar on international relations that made cooperation much more difficult for many years to come. In the Balkans and in parts of the former Russian Empire, active fighting remained endemic for a long time after the official end of the war, often dragging European powers into costly and useless interventions. Even more damaging in the long run was the way in which the peace treaties, particularly the one with Germany, were drawn. The unnecessarily punitive nature of reparations, the military occupation of the Rhineland, and eventually the direct intervention in the Ruhr all carried momentous consequences, some of which are related in the coming chapters.

Though we are convinced that unsettled domestic and international conditions played a major role in generating an unstable international economic environment, we confine our attention to those consequences of the First World War that directly affected the postwar organization and activity of the international economy. Some of these consequences were an immediate effect of the war; others followed from the way in which the great powers dealt with the issues that had still to be resolved when the armies finally called a halt to the slaughter and destruction. We look first at four direct effects of the war.

The Two Exogenous Shocks

As we have seen, the war caused a major disruption of the real economy, both on the demand side and on the supply side. In every belligerent country, there were swift changes of great magnitude in production and consumption patterns, such as those briefly outlined above. In particular, heroic efforts were made to increase productive capacity in war-related industries such as engineering, iron and steel, and shipbuilding.

The second exogenous shock occurred when much of this capacity became superfluous once the war was over. It proved exceptionally difficult to adjust to the required patterns of peacetime production as swiftly as required by sudden changes in demand created by unfulfilled wartime needs. This difficulty was to a certain extent the consequence of the devastation of transport networks and of fields, houses, factories, and mines during the fighting. The destruction was worst in France, Belgium, Italy, and Poland, but many other countries had also endured considerable loss of fixed assets. Much more important were the difficulties connected with the relocation of physical assets and labor to peacetime production. For instance, huge investments were made in shipbuilding, a particularly asset-specific industry that found itself perennially saddled with excess capacity.

Another difficulty in returning to prewar patterns was created by the changes that had occurred in world markets. Competitors whose economic circumstances were affected relatively little by the war, notably the United States and Japan, had seized the opportunity created by the inability of European manufacturers to maintain their normal trading activity and had successfully invaded their markets. Japan, in particular, rapidly increased her sales to many Asian countries that had previously looked mainly to Britain for their imports. Moreover, as we have seen, huge export capacity had been built by cheap primary producers. The war also stimulated domestic production in non-European countries in order to substitute for imports from Europe. This is what happened, for example, to cotton textiles and other light manufactures in India and Latin America, thereby reducing the markets upon which the prewar output of the exporting nations had depended.

The end of empires in eastern Europe and the Middle East further disrupted international relations. Large markets were replaced by tariff barriers that restricted the flow of goods. Banks that previously had been able to draw funds and make loans widely were restricted to the new political boundaries by the attempts of new countries to establish and protect their own banks. And the new Soviet government found itself in a war to preserve itself and no revenues with which to do so. Hyperinflation—a tax on real balances—was tried and found wanting as real balances disappeared when inflation outran the rate of money creation. Requisition—communism from the barrel of a gun—was tried, but this method generated too much hostility and opposition. Finally, the Bolsheviks relented slightly in their communist zeal and instituted a New Economic Policy in which parts of the economy, notably agriculture, were allowed to function as if they were privately owned.

A More Rigid Economic Environment

Once the war was over, the greatest possible degree of flexibility in prices and practices would be required in order to adjust to these devastating domestic and external shocks, but in fact the prevailing trend was toward greater rigidity. A long-run tendency for the flexibility of price and wage structures to decrease is likely to be a feature of all advanced democratic economies that give high priority to the stability of incomes, prices, and employment, but the war considerably hastened this process. In the postwar labor market, wage flexibility was diminished as many more decisions were centrally negotiated in a greatly extended process of collective bargaining. Behind this change lay the growth of working-class militancy and the dramatic rise in the membership and strength of the trade union movement.

In the goods market, there was a similar tendency toward reduced flexibility of property incomes and prices. The war contributed to this tendency by causing an increase in government intervention in economic life, the formation or strengthening of trade associations and cartels, and the imposition of numerous controls. Each of these features survived in varying degrees into the postwar period.

More fundamentally, the war accelerated the trend toward larger business units. In the extremely difficult circumstances of the 1920s, many firms looked to collusion, cartels, and the exercise of monopoly powers to escape the consequences of increasing competition for shrinking markets. In Germany, cartels and other forms of industrial combination were already well established before the war, and the increase in their scope and strength during the 1920s enabled them to resist falling prices by restricting production. In Britain, a similar trend was strongly encouraged by the government, which deliberately promoted legislation and other measures to reduce competition in industries such as cotton, shipbuilding, and coal mining.

A Weaker Financial Structure

The financial sector was also greatly affected by the war and the extensive interference in the peacetime patterns of domestic and international markets that it stimulated. Most obviously, the war and its aftermath gave rise to unprecedented needs for revenue. It is estimated that the direct cost of the war in constant prewar prices was the equivalent of five times the worldwide national debt in 1914 (Woytinski and Woytinski, 1955, quoted in Aldcroft, 1977, 30).

In all countries, note issues and bank credits were expanded by immense amounts, with little or no attempt either to raise taxes or to borrow from the public on the scale needed to offset the additional demand on resources generated by the enormous military expenditures. The United Kingdom did more than any other nation to impose additional taxes, but even this was sufficient to cover only one-third of its expenditure (Morgan, 1952, 104). In France and Germany, the proportion financed in this way was very much lower, although the precise figure for the latter is complicated by the role of local taxes.

After the war, finance ministers faced the need to service these swollen internal public debts. Many of them were short-term debts and thus threatened monetary stability. There were also external demands for payment of war debts and reparations, while at the same time, international financial cooperation had entirely vanished. The reduction of budget deficits was made more difficult by the need to provide for reconstruction and by new demands for higher expenditure on social security and unemployment benefits advanced by active trade unions.

A large body of literature exists on some aspects of international financial dislocation, especially on reparations, inter-Allied debts (more generally on

Continental Europe becoming a net debtor), and the new pattern of international lending. Less is known about changes in the web of international banking that provided the grassroots connection for the international transfer of short- and long-term capital, as well as for the actual day-by-day functioning of an international payment system.

A Fragile International Monetary System

The classic gold standard was an early casualty of the conflict. Within a few months of the declaration of war, almost all European central banks, including those in countries that were to remain neutral, had unilaterally suspended gold payments. During the war, the powers of the Entente developed their own payment system backed by the inter-Allied loans, as noted above. This cooperation was designed to allow the belligerent countries to sustain the level of imports required to achieve the maximum military contribution to the common cause.

Once the war was over, cooperation ceased almost overnight. Inter-Allied financial assistance was suspended, and creditor countries immediately made clear that they expected reimbursement of their war loans. At the same time, the victorious powers insisted on extracting an unrealistic amount of reparations from those they had defeated. French retaliation for the terms that Germany had imposed on her after victory in 1870 was the dominant factor in preventing a more realistic settlement. A typical interwar British view of the overall financial outcome is given in the following scathing comment by Lionel Robbins (1934, 6): "The inordinate claims of the victors, the crass financial incapacity of the vanquished, the utter budgetary disorder which everywhere in the belligerent countries was the legacy of the policies pursued during the war, led to a further period of monetary chaos."

We turn next to the developments that followed from the end of the war, including the shock to the domestic economies of the former belligerents, the signing of the peace treaties that settled the relations between the former enemies, and the changes in the relations between the allies. All these factors had further profound consequences for the financial and economic developments of the 1920s and beyond.

2.3 The Economic Consequences of the Postwar Settlements

The Shock of Economic Restructuring and Social Unrest

During the war, as much as 30–40 percent of the belligerents' GDP was directly or indirectly controlled by the state. While supplies to the army came to be the direct responsibility of governments, the rest of the economy was to a great extent subject to various forms of state supervision. Thus, forms of administrative controls on prices, wages, capital, and foreign-exchange markets were introduced more often than not. The return to peacetime economic organization and production entailed a huge process of resource reallocation that, contrary to what is assumed in economics textbooks, not only required a long period of time but also met with the resistance of the vested interests that had been created by the war.

Businessmen and industrialists were almost everywhere divided between those who favored an immediate return to a laissez faire economy and those—usually the suppliers to the army—who argued in favor of a slow "return to normality," with strong state help in the process. While most proponents of the latter view only wanted the state to provide forms of financial support to ailing industries and to guarantee the social peace, a militant minority in France, Germany, and Italy came to herald the birth of a "technocratic" and "corporatist" state that would actively support economic growth, particularly in the technologically more advanced sectors.

Whatever the pace was to be, industrial restructuring implied the closing of a number of plants (the case of shipyards is of particular relevance because of the magnitude of the supply cuts that were needed). Capital for the creation of factories that would meet consumers' demand was scarce at home and unlikely to come from foreign sources. The result was unemployment. At the same time, householders were frustrated by the fall in the real value of the wartime savings they wanted to use to satisfy their pent-up demand for consumer goods. In several countries, the combination of these two conditions produced a short but deep recession between 1920 and 1921.

Social unrest was, however, the main postwar problem. Its discussion would lead us away from the particular economic focus of the present text, but the economic implications of the political must not be underrated. The almost universal explosion of working-class struggles and protests after the war can be primarily attributed to two factors.

The first was the powerful growth of the organization, strength, and solidarity of the working class. Workers had already formed increasingly successful unions in the years before the war, not only in Britain, where they dated back several decades, but on the Continent as well. The war provided a tremendous boost to these organizations. Maintaining the discipline and morale of huge armies raised through compulsory conscription entailed both pressures and concessions, and the latter included promises of a better life for the masses as soon as hostilities were over. Life in the trenches also proved to be a tremendous catalyst for the emerging "mass society": workers from various areas and occupations got to know each other's needs and local strengths, and at the same time, socialist propaganda could be much more effective in such huge concentrations of working-class people.

In addition, at home, the urgent need to increase production of military supplies and overcome traditional restrictive practices required recognition of, and concessions to, the trade unions. From 1916 onward, trade-union membership increased steeply in the United Kingdom, Germany, and France.

Second, the Russian revolution exercised considerable influence on working-class movements, even though this influence was ambiguous: a model for a militant minority, but at the same time a highly divisive factor for those who did not share this ideology.

The economic impact of social developments differed according to the relative weakness of the economies and of the governments that emerged from the war. Thus, in Germany, the social democratic government undertook a number of social reforms, certainly out of its own political conviction but also to undermine working-class support for the revolutionary movement. Mines and metal-making were "socialized," trade unions were fully recognized, and the eight-hour week was introduced. Deficit spending by the state followed, partly feeding into the price spiral. As a result, however, social unrest diminished considerably; by early 1920, hours lost in strikes were already half the number counted one year earlier.

Other defeated countries saw more dramatic developments that undoubtedly contributed to economic destabilization in central and eastern Europe. Thus, Bulgaria was swept by quasi-revolutionary winds, while in 1919 Hungary was actually briefly governed by the communists in the so-called "Councils' Republic."

In Italy—socially and economically the weakest amongst the large countries on the winning side—workers took over the management of a number of companies during the "red biennium" (1920–1921). The working-class movement was eventually weakened by the division resulting from the creation of a Communist Party in 1921, while reactionary forces gained sufficient strength to enable them to seize power violently by the March on Rome (1922) that inaugurated twenty years of fascist dictatorship. The latter event, however, was mostly the result of the failure of the old liberal politicians to provide viable solutions to postwar problems, particularly for social issues.

In France and Britain, the enormous number of strikes during 1919 affected both industrial output and investors' expectations. In both countries, governments regained control of the situation during 1920, often by the adoption of rather harsh repressive measures. However, while in France the trade-union movement suffered a serious setback, in Britain the circumstances and the results of the social conflict were different, because the trade unions had already developed strong roots and because the victory of Lloyd George in the 1918 elections brought in a relatively sympathetic government.

The Economic Consequences of the Peace Treaties

The war finally ended, and after much wrangling, peace treaties were signed in 1919 with Germany (at Versailles), Austria (at St. Germaine-en-Laye), and

Bulgaria (at Neuilly), and in 1920 with Hungary (at Trianon) and Turkey (at Sévres). Various aspects of these treaties were to be a cause of severe disturbance to postwar trade and production. First, the way in which the political map of central and eastern Europe was redrawn disrupted long-standing economic relations and created new barriers to trade. Second, the attempt to hold Germany responsible for the war by imposing huge demands for reparations for the losses suffered by the victorious powers became a major cause of political antagonism and economic discord.

Pre-1914 trading patterns, communications, and financial relations had long been adjusted to the existing political boundaries. In the large central empires, these arrangements had evolved to coincide with customs and monetary unions. This well-established state of affairs was disrupted when the formation of new nation-states led to the creation of numerous smaller political units in the territories of the former Russian, German, Austro-Hungarian, and Ottoman empires.

The most extensive territorial changes came from the breaking up of the Habsburg Empire, leading to the loss of territory to Italy and the creation of six small nation-states (Czechoslovakia, Poland, Romania, Yugoslavia, and the much-diminished Austria and Hungary) in place of a single large multiethnic geopolitical entity. Germany lost all her overseas colonies and some of her best industrial and agricultural land, including Alsace-Lorraine and the Saar coal mines, to France; Upper Silesia and other territory to Poland; and smaller areas or towns to Denmark, Belgium, Lithuania, and Czechoslovakia. The Russian Empire also suffered major territorial losses, including four areas that became independent states (Finland, Estonia, Latvia, and Lithuania). Bulgaria was forced to cede territory to Greece, and there were substantial changes in the former Ottoman Empire, though the areas that Turkey lost were outside Europe. The final outcome was that there were 38 independent nations in Europe in 1919, 12 more than in 1914 (see figure 2.1).

In deciding on these changes to the map of central and eastern Europe, the victorious powers were primarily guided by the principle of national self-determination, not by economic considerations. This led to the creation of nation-states: political entities encompassing people of the same language, culture, and tradition. This principle was perhaps consistent with the political needs and ideology of the time, but it did not necessarily respond to economic needs. Foreign trade, in particular, was affected by the new frontiers, with significant consequences both for the development of the region and for the overall performance of the international economy.

Furthermore, this huge process of border adjustments and state formation inevitably failed to reconcile and satisfy all the conflicting interests and aspirations involved, leaving behind a permanent residue of social and national resentments. In the view of one historian, the territorial realignments may have created more problems than they removed (Thomson, 1966, 633). The

Figure 2.1. Europe before and after the First World War. Source: Martin Gilbert (1970), *First World War Atlas* (London: Weidenfeld and Nicolson). Reprinted by permission.

potential for further conflicts translated into the expectations of economic agents, particularly investors. In some cases, endemic fighting continued well into the 1920s, increasing the overall sense of instability.

Poland, Czechoslovakia, Yugoslavia, Latvia, Lithuania, Estonia, and Finland were each established as separate states. Romania was enlarged. Austria and Hungary were reduced in size and entirely separated from each other. Each new state created its own currency, erected trade barriers to protect domestic industry, and inaugurated independent fiscal and monetary policies. In particular, the imposition of tariffs (whether as a source of urgently needed revenue or as a means of protection), the loss of gold and exchange reserves, and the diminished possibilities for foreign borrowing by countries already overburdened by debts or claims for reparations all helped further to restrict the scope for foreign trade. Even from a narrowly defined economic point of view—that is, without taking into account the adverse impact of political uncertainty on the expectations of economic agents—these developments had a deep effect on the international economy by distorting trade and capital flows relative to the pre-1914 situation.

By the last decade of the nineteenth century, the Habsburg Empire had become a well-functioning customs union; it was also a rather efficient, if not optimal, currency area. Each region within the empire tended to specialize in those industrial and agricultural products for which it enjoyed a comparative advantage. Vienna, and to a lesser extent Budapest, had developed into well-functioning money and capital markets providing for the financial capital needs of the whole Dual Monarchy.

In the Danubian region, where industrialization had hardly begun by 1914, the establishment of independent policy-maker regimes implied the encouragement of industrial development. Thus Romania, Yugoslavia, and Bulgaria tended to favor high-cost native firms by erecting tall tariff walls around them at a considerable cost to the consumer and to the large agricultural sector. In Hungary, a more industrially advanced country, this policy was less extreme but had a negative impact on trade and growth nonetheless.

The case of Czechoslovakia was different in that the new state included the most highly industrialized parts of the former empire. Here the problem was that Czech industry was highly dependent on export markets that were severely affected by the new wave of protectionism. At the same time, the moderately protective agricultural policy of the Prague government had serious effects on the export outlets of other former members of the empire, given the high income of Czech consumers.

Although less industrialized than Czechoslovakia, Poland had a similar problem. While it was not heavily dependent on the Danubian markets for its agricultural exports, its natural outlets for industrial trade were disturbed by the new frontiers. In the previous four decades, the manufacturers of central Poland had developed "as part of the wider Russian market in which, in certain branches, they had taken the technical lead . . . . In the interwar years this market vanished, and Polish trade was virtually nil" (Radice, 1985, 34).

The international economy was also affected by the Bolshevik revolution and by the Russian civil war that continued until the early 1920s. In the last part of the nineteenth century, the Russian Empire had been increasingly integrated into European trade and capital flows. After signing a separate peace treaty with Germany, the Bolsheviks effectively severed most of the country's prewar links with the rest of the world. Trade was reduced to a fraction of its pre-1914 level, and western European capital was scared off by the repudiation of the tsarist regime's foreign debt. True, new countries—Finland, Latvia, Estonia, and Lithuania—emerged at the edge of the former empire, but these were economically too small to compensate for the loss of trade with Russia.

To sum up: the dismemberment of the Dual Monarchy, the splitting off of parts of the German and Russian empires, and the latter's autarkic evolution all represented a major shock to the international economy. These developments caused widespread resource misallocation, resulting in lower output and higher prices, particularly in central and eastern Europe. In the decades immediately preceding the war, this large area had made significant progress along the road of modern economic growth and was thus becoming ever more important to Europe's overall trade and production. In due time, of course, markets adjusted trade and capital flows to the new situation, but this structure was less conducive to economic efficiency than the one that prevailed before the war. Moreover, such adjustments were slow to come about, with the market process always taking far longer than economists are ready to admit.

In the aftermath of the war, the adjustment was made even slower by uncertainty regarding the stability of the new regimes, fear of revolution, the persistence of endemic conflicts, lack of information in western capitals about the new leaders, and the incompetence of some among the latter. For instance, it took long years of diplomatic effort and a number of international conferences to reestablish more appropriate levels of trade with the Soviet Union. And it was not until the mid-1920s that German exports resumed their prewar importance in the Reich's traditional central European markets.

The End of Financial Solidarity among the Allies

The abrupt end to the system of inter-Allied loans that had been put in place during the war delivered yet another shock to the international economy. The system had implied a flow of financial capital from the United Kingdom to the European members of the Entente, and from the United States to the Entente as well as to Britain. At the same time, part of this flow of capital was used to stabilize the belligerents' exchange rates, for both political and economic reasons. If the downward trend in the currencies were too steep, that might have been interpreted as the expression of a pessimistic market assessment of the outcome of the war. If the fluctuations around the trend were too wide and erratic, this would have increased the cost of supplies in neutral markets.

Inevitably, however, the support for the European exchange rates served to weaken the dollar on the Japanese and neutral markets. While maintaining the domestic convertibility of the dollar, Washington had to impose an embargo on the export of gold. All this was politically acceptable as long as it could be presented to the American public as part of an overall set of measures—military, economic, and diplomatic—aimed at maximizing a coordinated effort that would produce swift victory. Once the latter was achieved in November 1918, few saw the necessity for—or even the possibility of—a continuation of the wartime financial policy.

The war had been tremendously demanding of Europe's resources, both human and economic. In various parts of the continent, particularly in the defeated countries, food emergencies developed that could be addressed only with considerable difficulty, given the lack of foreign exchange to pay for agricultural imports. In other areas, particularly in France, Belgium, and to a lesser extent Italy, reconstruction required considerable amounts of capital. Finance was needed all over Europe to carry on the reallocation of resources from war-related production to peacetime production. In these circumstances, the European countries, most notably Britain and France, argued in favor of a "soft landing." This would have meant a continuation of financial assistance from the United States and a slow relaxation of wartime controls on exchange rates and on the international economy more generally.

At the same time, however, France demanded the imposition of very harsh conditions on the defeated powers, particularly on Germany. These required the payment of huge reparations to fund not only France's reconstruction and war pensions, but also its foreign debt. Indeed, the French insisted that the reimbursement of their debts to the United States and Great Britain must be linked to the actual receipt of reparations from Germany. The two sets of requests were not mutually consistent. If the aim was international solidarity to rebuild the European economy, then everyone should have been required to pay a price for the success of the cooperative effort, especially those European countries that stood to benefit most from the continent's swift recovery. If, on the other hand, the aim was equitable justice—with everyone paying for the obligations incurred during the war—then there was no reason to establish a link between debts and reparations.

While individual European countries, particularly those on the Continent, proved to be short-sighted in their narrow focus on their own immediate interests, it was the attitude of the United States that had by far the largest impact on subsequent developments. The political weight of the United States was considerable, because it had to be reckoned that U.S. intervention in the war had been decisive in tipping the scale in favour of the Entente; and, most important, America was now the world's dominant financial power.

However, the United States did not respond adequately to its newly acquired responsibility as world leader. There were good political reasons—both domestic and international—for this attitude, but in retrospect it is evident that there was a cultural gap as well. The leaders of the United States lacked the necessary insight to understand where the long-term interests of the country actually lay. The Victory Loan Act passed by Congress in March 1919 authorized the government to open credit to foreign countries only for the purchase of goods directly or indirectly belonging to the government, and of grains the price of which was guaranteed by the United States. Europe was thereby provided with a safety net against a fall in food consumption below subsistence levels, but it was denied U.S. credit for reconstruction and for postwar industrial conversion to peacetime production. The pace of both shifts was thus slower, and the economic and political impacts of the postwar shock to the world economy more substantial, than they would otherwise have been.

One of the features—both cause and effect—of the postwar shock was immense turmoil in the world markets for foreign exchange. Before 1914, the most severe financial crises resulted in currency devaluations of only a few percentage points, even for those European countries that were forced out of gold. Nevertheless, they were considered a national disaster. With the end of U.S. wartime financial support of Europe and of the attendant pegging of Entente currencies to the dollar, exchange rates were left to their own fate. The United States resumed gold payments in 1919. In 1920, the pound had lost about 25 percent of its value relative to its prewar parity. The exchange rates of the other members of the Entente soon lost more than fifty percent of their 1914 value, and they continued to fall. As an average for 1920, the French franc stood at 36 percent of its prewar gold parity; the Italian lira stood at 25 percent. In the defeated countries of central Europe, colossal exchange-rate devaluations ended up feeding into hyperinflation. By 1920, the German mark was worth only 7 percent of its 1914 value, and in the following two years it disappeared as an international currency.

Of course, the blame for this situation cannot all be laid at the door of the United States. Wartime currency pegging was obviously untenable after the end of hostilities, and it was necessary for the exchange rate of each individual currency to adjust to changes in purchasing-power parity driven by their respective rates of inflation. Insofar as markets reacted to uncertainty, it must also be recognized that domestic circumstances were of paramount importance.

Nevertheless, errors of judgment and policy by international leaders were an important additional factor. The retreat from wartime financial solidarity was too abrupt. The lack of international credit for reconstruction and industrial restructuring magnified the markets' unfavorable expectations for the pace of recovery in France, Belgium, and Britain. Uncertainty about the amount of reparations and the settlement of inter-Allied debt was also a major source of volatility in international markets. Finally, the idea of re-creating an international monetary system based on gold was not only highly ill-advised (as we shall see) but was also left to the initiative of central bankers rather than being part of a larger political design issuing from the world's leaders.

Reparations

In discussing the economic consequences of the war and the peace treaties, we have several times mentioned reparations without actually discussing them. In fact, they deserve specific treatment: they were by far the most controversial issue in the peace treaty with Germany and are widely regarded as one of the critical elements underlying the political and economic failures of the interwar period.

Article 231 of the Versailles Treaty held Germany responsible for the war, therefore establishing the legal ground for reparations. These were supposed to cover war-related material damages. To start with, the definition of "war-related material damages" was ambiguous. While the cost of reconstruction was undoubtedly included, a controversy soon developed over the inclusion of compensation for personal losses (mainly pensions to widows and disabled men).

Keynes was the first to condemn reparations as economically irrational and politically unwise. In a famous polemic (Keynes 1919), he argued that it was not sensible—indeed that it was ultimately against the best interests of the victorious powers—to cripple Germany economically, because much of Europe's pre-1914 welfare had depended on German economic growth. Moreover, Keynes envisaged difficulties in transferring real resources across borders, given the uncertainty about how the postwar international capital market would work. His overall view was thus that reparations were "vindictive," "insane," and ultimately "unworkable."

Many modern historians regard Keynes' castigation of European leaders on this issue as excessively harsh. Negotiators at Versailles were aware that "if the Weimar Republic was unduly hampered in employing its skilled population and material resources productively, the continent as a whole would not easily recover its prosperity" (Schuker, 1988, 14). However, they faced enormous budgetary problems themselves as a result of the war, and public opinion could not possibly be convinced to bear all the burden after the huge sacrifices made during the conflict itself. "La Boche payera" (Germans will pay) was a powerful political slogan in early postwar France. Whatever awareness European leaders had of the intricate web of problems created by the war, the fact remains that the reparation issue injected a considerable additional amount of uncertainty and acrimony into the volatile postwar economy.

An official of the British Foreign Office who later became a leading historian remarked in 1937 that "the important difference between the Versailles Treaty and the previous peace treaties providing for payment to the victors by the defeated Power was that, on this occasion, no sum was fixed by the treaty itself" (Carr 1937). Soon after the Armistice, Germany was stripped of its gold reserves, most of its merchant navy, and whatever equipment (such as rolling stock) that might have been of use to the victors. Deliveries of coal were also required. In the following months, preliminary reparation payments were required, pending a final settlement.

In March 1921, the German failure to fulfill part of those preliminary requests prompted Allied troops to occupy the towns of Dusseldorf, Duisberg, and Ruhrhort on the east side of the river Rhine. Needless to say, this move did not contribute to a stable international environment. Only one month later, the London Schedule of Payments for the first time formally established Germany's reparation obligations. Germany, however, dragged its feet, so the Allies again entered its territory in 1923, this time occupying the mining district of the Ruhr.

It was not until 1924 that an agreement was reached that created the preconditions for a reasonably stable system of international payments, allowing private capital to flow into Germany. This agreement, the Dawes Loan, made it possible for reparations to be smoothly transferred to France (which was due to receive 52 percent of the payments made), the British Empire (which would receive 22 percent), Italy (10 percent), Belgium (8 percent), and the other minor Allies.

The mechanism by which the postwar international payment system was allowed to work will be the subject of further discussion in the next chapter. Here we wanted to stress the immediate adverse repercussions of the postwar settlement on the world economy. While the sum finally agreed upon, and the schedule of payments, might not have been significantly above what Germany could reasonably have paid without crippling its economy, the manner in which the whole problem was dealt with between 1918 and 1924 added an enormous further element of uncertainty to an already unstable postwar international economy. At the same time, the reparations issue made international relations difficult, acrimonious, and full of damaging potential for revenge.

Chapter 3

The 1920s: Crises and Currency Stabilizations

We have now set the scene by placing the interwar performance of the international economy in its historical perspective and discussing in some detail the economic and political consequences of the First World War and the postwar settlements. To begin our study of the period itself, we look first at some of the critical financial developments in the 1920s. These include the problems of inflation and hyperinflation, which afflicted almost all the European economies, and the related instability of many of their banking systems. We then focus on the issue of exchange rates, and we analyze the different routes followed by the main countries in their attempts to stabilize their currencies and return to the gold standard. Our final theme in this chapter is the operation of the gold standard during this decade and the reasons that it failed to provide the benefits in international trade and growth its advocates had anticipated.

3.1 Accelerating Prices and Hyperinflation

During the war years, prices rose rapidly in all the belligerent countries as demands increased and supplies were disrupted. Neutral countries could not remain immune to this process. The extent to which prices surged upward between 1914 and 1918 is shown for a selection of countries in the first column of table 3.1. There was a brief respite immediately after the Armistice, when commodity prices fell, but from the spring of 1919, inflation resumed its course during a production boom that lasted until the spring or summer of 1920. The boom was especially strong in the United Kingdom and some of the neutral countries, and in the United States. As can be seen in the second column of table 3.1, the extent of inflation in 1920 varied widely, but price increases were common to all countries.

From the middle of 1920, the boom gave way to a worldwide slump that continued until 1921 or, in some cases, a year later. The depression was

Table 3.1 Consumer price indices, 1918–1926 (1914 = 100)

	1918	1920	1922	1924	1926
Countries with hyperinflation until 1922 or 1923					
Austria	1,163	5,115	263,938	86[a]	103
Germany	304	990	14,602	128[a]	141
Countries in which inflation continued after 1920					
Belgium	1,434	—	340	469	604
Finland	633	889	1,033	1,055	1,078
Italy	289	467	467	481	618
France	213	371	315	395	560
Countries in which inflation was controlled after 1920					
Norway	253	300	231	239	206
Sweden	219	269	198	174	173
Switzerland	204	224	164	169	162
UK	200	248	181	176	171
Denmark	182	261	200	216	184
Netherlands	162	194	149	145	138

[a] Linked to base year via gold price. For Austria, the index for 1923 on this basis was 76. For Germany, hyperinflation continued until late in 1923, and the price index for that year (1914 = 100) was 15,437,000,000,000.

Source: Maddison (1991), 300–303.

particularly severe in the United Kingdom and the United States, but few countries escaped. During this downturn and in the subsequent years, nations' economic experiences diverged sharply. Three distinct trends can be identified. In one group of countries, represented in the upper panel of table 3.1 by Germany and Austria, the decline in activity had no effect, and inflation gave way to hyperinflation. In a second group, represented by Belgium, Finland, Italy, and France in the middle panel, inflation continued but was not allowed to get completely out of control. The third group, consisting of the Scandinavian countries, Switzerland, Britain, and the Netherlands, imposed strict deflationary policies of dear money and fiscal restraint, and by this means these countries succeeded in actually reducing prices and wages until 1922 or 1923. Thereafter, prices in this group of countries were broadly stable or falling.

Five countries proved totally unable to contain the war and postwar pressures and were ravaged by hyperinflation: Austria, Hungary, Poland, Russia, and Germany. The latter was by far the most remarkable case, culminating in wholesale prices rising at the astronomical rate of 335 percent per month from August 1922 to November 1923 (Holtfrerich, 1986, 17). Even as the inflationary spiral was gathering momentum, there was heated controversy over its causes. Within Germany, almost all officials, bankers, and industrialists, and a great many economists, adopted the balance-of-payments theory, according to which the root cause of the hyperinflation was to be found in the burden of reparations and occupation costs imposed on a defeated Germany. It was claimed that the costs of occupation and reparations were primarily responsible for the magnitude of the deficit on the balance of payments and that this deficit in turn caused the extraordinary depreciation in the external value of the mark, forcing up import prices. As the accelerating costs and prices spread through the economy, the authorities were compelled to expand the issues of paper money, thus fueling inflation. This analysis was supported by some foreign scholars, notably Williams (1922) and Graham (1930).

Opponents of this view reversed the causal chain and advocated a quantity-theory explanation. They argued that it was the excessive issue of paper money that had initiated the vicious circle, and they traced the origin of hyperinflation back to the size of the massive budget deficit. An authoritative interwar exposition of the quantity-theory explanation was given by Bresciani-Turroni (1937), who argued that the crux of the problem was not to be found in the Treaty of Versailles and the reparation payments but in the enormous increase in state spending arising both from the heavy reliance on borrowing during the war and from the huge outlays required by postwar economic and social programs.

Such programs were essential for the very surival of the new Weimar republic, which was under great pressure from both left- and right-wing extremists. The vested interests on either side were too bitterly divided to reach any agreement on how the necessary taxes should be allocated between labor and capital. The printing of paper money thus provided the only acceptable way out of the dilemma. Initially, at least, many of the contending social groups could argue that the resulting inflation brought more benefits than costs.

The headlong expansion of the money supply in turn reduced the external value of the currency and added further to inflationary pressures. To make matters worse, the unexpectedly rapid pace of the inflation itself undermined attempts to balance the budget, because the real value of any revenue received was always less than had been anticipated when the taxes were imposed. Assessment of many taxes was also made more difficult in conditions of rapid inflation.

The effect of the expanded note issue was then intensified by a steep rise in the velocity of money circulation. From the outbreak of war until the summer of 1921, the currency in circulation and the internal price level had increased broadly in line (apart from a brief "flight from the mark" in 1919). But then expectations were changed by what were seen to be excessive demands for reparations and the London Ultimatum (May 1921) threatening the occupation of the Ruhr in case there were no compliance by Germany. From the summer of 1921, the flight from the mark became continually quicker as first Germans and then foreigners lost confidence in the mark's value. By the second half of 1922, the demand for real-money balances was falling steeply (i.e., there was an abrupt rise in the velocity of circulation), and the acceleration in the rate of price increase outpaced even the exceptionally rapid growth of the money supply (Bresciani-Turroni, 1937, 162–75; Holtfrerich, 1986, 184–93).

The enormous difficulties faced by postwar governments in coping with the abnormal fiscal problems created by the First World War and the socioeconomic conditions that followed the Armistice were responsible for the inflationary trends not only in Germany and the other hyperinflation countries, but also in many of the other countries in the second and third groups mentioned above. Apart from the huge costs of the war and postwar restoration, the years of conflict had transformed social and political attitudes, weakening the old order and accelerating the rise in influence of the working classes. In the tense and difficult situation created by devastation and financial disorder, the political parties in countries such as France, Belgium, and Italy could not agree on how the burden of taxation should be shared among the different social classes. As in Germany, conflicts over the distribution of incomes and the burden of taxation stand out as a principal source of financial instability in most other European countries.

3.2 Stability and Crisis in the European Banking Systems

As noted above, the boom that followed the Armistice came to an end in the middle of 1920, and output, employment, and incomes began to fall in almost all European countries. In a number of cases, the recession proved to be fairly severe. Of the large countries of Europe, only Germany escaped a postwar slump due to the temporarily beneficial effects of hyperinflation: exports were stimulated as long as the value of the mark depreciated more rapidly than the relative rise in German prices, and investment was stimulated by the fall in real interest rates. A number of countries also experienced a banking crisis in this period.

Whether or not such a crisis developed in a given country, and the extent of its severity, depended on several factors: the severity of the depression in the real economy, the policy stance of the central bank, and the organization of the banking system. Banks were more likely to fail in countries where the real slump was more severe and was accompanied by a price deflation, where the central bank was unwilling or unable to act as a swift lender-of-last resort, and where banks established close financial links with their industrial clients, on the German model of "universal banking." Where banking crises occurred, they in turn produced feedback effects on output and employment, the real side of the economy.

Britain showed the highest degree of stability in the banking system in 1920. There had been no panic or financial crisis in Britain since 1890. The separation between bank and industry was, by the early 1920s, quite securely established, so that banks did well in terms of profitability and currency/deposit ratios during the postwar depression; the depression itself was rather mild; and the Bank of England had developed such a strong reputation as a lender of last resort that it could defuse the possibility of banking panics by its very presence. The Irish system also remained stable, both because of factors similar to those in Great Britain and because of the close links between the two financial systems.

The French case is perhaps less clear-cut, but the reasons for the overall stability of its banking system may nevertheless be traced back to the three factors mentioned above. During and after the war, most French enterprises continued in their time-honored tradition of self-financing from retained profits. Universal banking existed in France, but it was normally confined to small provincial banks. The crisis of 1921 made some enterprises less reluctant than before to resort to long-term bank credit, but this was, on average, a rather limited phenomenon. Deposits fell in real terms during the first part of the 1920s as a response to inflation and to the high yields of state bonds, but the reaction of banks was prudent: they increased the liquidity of their portfolios. The Banque de France favored this process by encouraging the placement of government securities with banks. The real recession was rather mild and, importantly, was not coupled with price deflation.

The stability of the postwar German financial system is particularly interesting, providing a sharp contrast with the collapse of 1931. From this point of view, inflation was a blessing, because it resulted in growth rather than a slump in the output and employment, and it caused the economy to be oversupplied with liquidity. Given that central bank credit financed most of the government's expenditure, there could be no question about lending-of-last-resort to financial institutions, which obviously proved to be unnecessary. Inflation also ensured the postwar stability of the Austrian and Polish banking systems. In Austria, however, the stabilization of the currency was internationally supervised and engineered, with strong deflationary monetary and fiscal measures that produced a stock-exchange crash in 1924. The resulting crisis in the real and financial sectors of the economy caused widespread failures among small- and medium-sized banks.

Elsewhere, bank failures were more common; they characterized the postwar economies of Italy, Spain, Portugal, and Norway. In Italy, the third- and fourth-largest universal banks became insolvent between 1921 and 1923, partly as a result of overtrading during and soon after the war, and the difficulties were exacerbated by the cyclical downturn of 1920–1921. One of these banks was declared bankrupt at the end of 1921, but deposits were to a large extent guaranteed by the central bank, which also saved a metal-making and engineering concern—probably the most important of its kind in the country—owned by the bank. In the following year, fearing a run on deposits if another large bank went under, the central bank staged a large lending-of-last-resort operation in favor of the fourth-largest bank in the country. Thus, the active policy stance of the central bank, which privileged bank stability over other policy goals such as currency stabilization, prevented the insolvency of two large banks from spreading to other financial institution and to the real economy, which by 1922 was rapidly expanding.

The Spanish central bank was not as ready as its Italian counterpart to accommodate the liquidity needs of credit institutions in serious difficulty. It, therefore, remained on the sidelines in 1920 when an early recession in manufacturing made a number of Catalonian universal banks insolvent. The crisis hit the most developed region in the country, with the eventual failure of the oldest and most prominent Spanish credit institutions. The crisis was very severe in Barcelona, but its effect on Madrid and Bilbao, the two other financial centers in the country, was relatively mild.

A new wave of runs on bank deposits unfolded in Spain in the second half of 1924. After years of persistently falling prices, both for goods and for financial assets (industrial shares), during which industrial companies required continuous assistance from credit institutions, a number of banks were dragged into insolvency. Again, the central bank remained passive; only in the case of the Banco Central, one of the largest in Spain, was it forced to yield to pressure from the government of Primo de Rivera and provide enough assistance so that the Banco could actually overcome its problems.

In the Netherlands and in Scandinavia, bank failures followed the slump of 1920. In Denmark, the central bank took a fairly active stance and was able to avoid a major confidence shock. The Bank of the Netherlands seems to have been less successful in this respect, and the failure of one of the largest commercial banks shook public confidence. The Norwegian case stands out for the length of its banking troubles, which lasted from 1923 to 1928. As the wartime boom in the real sector was particularly buoyant, the slump in Norway was relatively more serious than elsewhere, particularly given the strong deflationary policy imposed to stabilize the currency and return to gold. Given the links between manufacturing firms and banks, and the unwillingness of the central bank to let lending of last resort jeopardize its monetary stance, it is not surprising that bank failures followed one after the other for a longer period in Norway than anywhere else. It is likely that institutional innovation embodied in the Bank Administration Act made things worse rather than better.

To sum up: the postwar slump in the real economy resulted in financial panics and runs on banks whenever (1) the central bank decided to refrain from providing the necessary liquidity either for policy reasons or for sheer prejudice, and (2) the central bank had established close long-term relationships with client firms of the kind that characterized the so-called universal banks. The story repeated itself on a larger scale ten years later. The lesson of the early 1920s was not learned mainly because the gold standard prevented central banks from responding to the needs of banks—and economies—in the early 1930s.

3.3 Stabilization and the Return to Gold

As long as postwar fiscal problems persisted, prices continued to increase and currencies continued to depreciate. Eventually, however, even those social groups who found some benefit in inflation began to fear its continuation, and the compromises necessary to reduce spending, raise taxes, and restrict the creation of credit were agreed. In many cases, the process was assisted by foreign stabilization or reconstruction loans and by temporary credits, both mainly from London and New York, but in some cases arranged through the League of Nations.

The issue of domestic loans to fund excessive short-term debt was also important, notably in the French and Belgian stabilizations. At various dates between 1922 and 1927, the major countries in the first and second groups mentioned above achieved the necessary degree of financial stabilization to restore the gold standard, with its commitment to sound money and fixed exchange rates. By the end of the decade, in Europe, only the Spanish peseta remained to be stabilized. The dates at which this was achieved de facto (legal restoration was sometimes delayed for various reasons) are given in table 3.2, together with a measure of the extent to which the foreign-exchange value of each currency had depreciated as compared with its prewar parity. The countries are again grouped in three panels corresponding to those in table 3.1. The extreme cases of inflation and hyperinflation leading to currency depreciation of 10 percent of prewar parity or less are shown in the upper panel. In the middle panel are examples of countries that allowed serious inflation to continue after 1920 and experienced depreciation of their currencies to between 10 percent and 30 percent of the prewar rate. The six countries that imposed deflationary policies after 1920 and were able to return to gold at the prewar parity are covered in the lower panel.

The First World War I had imposed heavy costs on Britain, but the nation had been less adversely affected than the continental belligerents by physical destruction and financial disruption. Despite Keynes's forceful dissent, prevailing opinion strongly favored a return to gold at the prewar parity. The objective, the method, and the price to be paid were clearly set out early in 1920 in a memorandum by the Bank of England to the Chancellor of the Exchequer (quoted in Howson, 1975, 18):

> The first and most urgent task before the Country is to get back to the gold standard by getting rid of this specific depreciation of the currency. This end can only be achieved by a reversal of the process by which the specific depreciation was produced, the artificial creation of currency and credit, and for

Table 3.2 Postwar stabilization of currencies, 1922–1929

	Year of de facto restoration of gold standard	New parity as percentage of prewar parity
Currency depreciation to less than 10 percent of prewar parities		
Germany	1923	0.0000000001
Poland	1926	0.000026
Austria	1922	0.00007
Hungary	1924	0.0069
Romania	1927	3.1
Bulgaria	1924	3.8
Portugal	1929	4.1
Greece	1927	6.7
Yugoslavia	1925	8.9
Currency depreciation to between 10 percent and 30 percent of prewar parities		
Finland	1924	13.0
Belgium	1926	14.5
Czechoslovakia	1923	14.6
France	1926	20.3
Italy	1926	27.3
Return at prewar parity		
Sweden	1922	100
Netherlands	1924	100
Switzerland	1924	100
United Kingdom	1925	100
Denmark	1926	100
Norway	1928	100

Source: Brown (1940), I, 393–402; II, 919, 1028; Nurkse (1944), 116; Nötel (1986), 181–83.

this the appropriate instrument is the rate of interest. The process of deflation of prices which may be expected to follow on the check to the expansion of credit must necessarily be a painful one to some classes of the community, but this is unavoidable.

None of the other belligerents shared this determination, but among the neutrals the Scandinavian countries, Switzerland, and the Netherlands were similarly committed to the restoration of the prewar parity of their currencies. In Denmark, voices were raised among politicians, businessmen, and economists recommending stabilization at about 75 percent of the old parity, but they were unable to win the struggle for public opinion against the slogans of the deflationists, who demanded a return to "our old, honest krone," and there was a parallel debate in Norway, where an even greater appreciation of the currency was required.

A very high price had to be paid for this belief in the virtues of the return to gold at the old parity. In Britain, the collapse of the export industries and the sustained downward pressure on wages, employment, and working-class living standards have frequently been seen as the sacrifice that financial interests imposed on industry in order to preserve the gold standard. In 1928 Keynes (1972, 85) commented on the contrasting fortunes of Great Britain, which had been financially conservative and responsible, and France, which had "'offended so grossly against all sound principles of finance" and was "avoiding the sacrifices of deflation." He noted that despite this, the Bank of France had emerged much stronger than the Bank of England, and he concluded with asperity: "Assuredly it does not pay to be good."

In Denmark and Norway, the return to the gold standard caused a depression from 1925 to 1928 that was almost as severe as the one in 1929–1933, with sharply falling production and prices, an increased number of business failures, and very high unemployment. Sweden similarly experienced considerable difficulties at the beginning of the 1920s, in contrast with Finland, which chose not to follow the deflationary path.

Italy and the two other "late stabilizers," France and Belgium, initially enjoyed a brief period when their exports benefited from exchange rates more favorable than those of the countries that followed orthodox deflationary policies. However, once Mussolini had decided that the lira should be stabilized at the *quota novanta*, representing a substantial upward revaluation of the prevailing rate, it became necessary to impose painful deflationary measures, resulting in slower growth of output and exports, and higher unemployment.

Once stabilization was achieved, further problems were created by the extent of the relative over- and undervaluation of currencies resulting from the independent and uncoordinated process by which each country selected its parity. Some currencies, notably those of Britain, Italy, Denmark, and Norway, were probably overvalued; in other cases, including France, Belgium, and Poland, the rate selected provided a degree of undervaluation. These disparities had important consequences for competitiveness in foreign trade. In addition, other powerful forces were also at work, and these too contributed to the highly variable pattern of export performance in the 1920s. These data are given in table 3.3, listed in order according to the level achieved by 1929, relative to 1913.

In the case of Britain, it has been generally accepted that the decision to return to gold at the prewar parity of $4.86 resulted in an overvaluation of the currency by about 10 percent. However, it would be wrong to see this as the primary reason for the decline of the export sector shown in table 3.3. Coal, textiles, shipbuilding, and other major export industries were already confronted by an extremely difficult structural problem created by technological change, the growth of substitute products, and the opportunity that the war had created for import substitution and for foreign competitors outside Europe, particularly the United States and Japan, to capture a large share of Britain's traditional markets. Nevertheless, the overvaluation of sterling

Table 3.3 Volume of merchandise exports, 1924–1929 (1913 = 100)

	1924	1925	1926	1927	1928	1929
Denmark	142	138	147	170	179	181
Netherlands	125	135	140	161	166	171
Norway	111	122	130	141	143	167
Finland	125	139	142	160	156	161
Sweden	96	106	114	136	131	156
France	119	124	134	146	148	147
Italy	117	127	123	116	118	123
Belgium	—	73	76	96	108	107
Switzerland	87	90	87	98	101	101
Germany	51	65	72	73	82	92
Austria	76	82	77	87	92	86
United Kingdom	76	75	67	77	80	81

Source: Maddison (1991), 316–19.

undoubtedly added significantly to Britain's fundamental structural weakness, as did the high interest rates necessary to sustain the currency.

As table 3.3 indicates, the 1929 volume of British exports was still 19 percent below its 1913 level. Of the other European countries that reestablished their currencies at the prewar parity against gold, only Switzerland was unable to expand exports above the prewar level. The Scandinavian countries and the Netherlands all increased the volume of their exports substantially relative to 1913, despite the probable overvaluation of their currencies. However, these increases consisted largely of specialized foods and raw materials that were less subject to competitive pressures than manufactured goods and coal. Some of the factors underlying differential movements in exports in the 1920s are discussed in section 4.2.

3.4 The "Rules of the Game"

One consequence of the sequence of postwar financial developments and policies that contemporary accounts of the period heavily emphasized was the short-term and long-term destabilizing effect of the massive flows of capital. The process gained its initial momentum early in the 1920s, with the flight from currencies such as the German mark, the French franc, and the Italian lira, as those who could transferred their financial assets to what they perceived to be safer currencies. With the high interest rates necessary to defend the pound, London was a favored haven.

Once confidence in the stability of the French and other continental currencies—and in their underlying public finances—was restored, speculative funds flowed back in again in eager anticipation of capital gains when the new parities were legally established. For example, Italy was the recipient of a considerable capital inflow of this nature during the 18 months preceding the de jure stabilization of the lira in December 1927. There was a similar burst of speculation in 1925 and 1926 when the Danish and Norwegian krone appreciated sharply in anticipation of the legal restoration of these currencies in January 1927 and May 1928 respectively.

The Flow of Gold to France

From a British perspective, the loss of gold as flight capital rushed back to France after the success of the Poincaré stabilization at the end of 1926 was always mentioned—and often resented—as a major cause of the weakening in Britain's external financial position. In the first place, France had elected to stabilize the franc at one-fifth of its prewar value, whereas Britain had accepted the discipline necessary to restore sterling at the prewar parity; this disparity was seen as a major source of balance-of-payments disequilibrium. Second, there was a dramatic increase in French reserves, accumulated at first in foreign exchange and later in gold, but the French authorities did not respond to this increase by inducing a corresponding increase in the money supply. Such a move would have stimulated the rise in prices that might have restored equilibrium.

In June 1928, French gold reserves were only 29 billion francs; by the end of 1932, they had increased by 53 billion francs, but the increase in note circulation over the same period was only 26 billion francs (Mouré, 1991, 55–56). Instead, the returning French capital was mainly used for the purchase of government securities, either directly by the private sector or by commercial banks as their deposits increased. The government, in turn, was able to repay a substantial part of its debts to the Bank of France. As a result, the large increase in the central bank's holdings of gold and foreign currency was, to a considerable extent, neutralized.

Thus, as seen from London, the gold standard in France was not operated according to the rules, and the necessary adjustment process was frustrated. The position was exacerbated by the very low level of French foreign investment. With their pre-1913 assets largely wiped out by the war and the Russian revolution, French rentiers had become extremely reluctant to trust any more of their capital to foreign governments and enterprises.

Treasury and central bank officials in Paris and London argued bitterly in public and private over the reasons for the movement of gold to France, what action should or could be taken in order for the flow to be reversed, and whose responsibility it was to take the corrective measures. Even when it was recognized that the final outcome was not the result of a French policy willfully designed to maximize the inflow of gold, it was still regarded as a failing in the system leading to a serious maldistribution in international holdings of gold.

Eichengreen (1986) emphasized that the Bank of France could in theory have reduced its high reserve ratio by means of expansionary open-market operations, but it was effectively precluded from doing so by statutory restrictions. These had been imposed by the 1928 stabilization law specifically to prevent a recurrence of the lax monetary policies that were held responsible for the searing inflation of 1922–1926. The British thought these restrictions should be relaxed in the interests of international monetary cooperation; the French were determined to protect their currency from any possibility of renewed inflation.

The United States and Japan Give Priority to Internal Policy

Similar issues were debated with respect to the United States, the other country to show a substantial increase in its gold holdings during the 1920s. Gold convertibility of the dollar was restored as early as 1919, and in the early part of the following decade, the American banking authorities considered that gold inflow into the United States was the result of the abnormal postwar conditions in Europe, and that most of the gold would in due course return to Europe and therefore should not be used as the basis for domestic credit creation in the United States. Neutralization was thus a deliberate policy, for which there were "sound and compelling reasons" (Nurkse, 1944, 73–75).

In the subsequent period, 1925–1929, the United States continued to neutralize any changes in the stock of gold, though on a less extensive scale. In 1928 and 1929, the Federal Reserve Board actually initiated a progressive increase in interest rates in order to prevent what it saw as an alarming rise in speculation on the stock exchange, regardless of its implications for the requirements of international stability. Countries such as Britain, which were running balance-of-payments deficits at this time, might well have asked the following question, as did the author of an official history of the United States in the world economy (Lary, 1943, 166),

> whether a more aggressive policy of credit expansion could have been safely followed with a view to supporting a higher level of prices and money incomes in the United States, thus helping to meet the foreign demand for dollars and relieving the strain on foreign exchanges and the general world deflationary pressure that developed in the latter part of the twenties.

Lary's answer was that, as was so often the case in the interwar period, considerations of internal policy were given far higher priority, and "the threat to international stability, although not overlooked, was regarded as a regrettable but necessary risk to be run in rectifying an unsound domestic situation."

The Japanese economy was largely unaffected by a conflict predominantly fought in Europe. In the postwar period, however, banking crises and an earthquake of catastrophic magnitude required an expansion of the supply of liquidity to the economy incompatible with the restoration of the gold standard, which therefore did not take place until January 1930 (Faini and Toniolo, 1992; Metzler, 2006).

Did the Gold Standard Help to Restore Equilibrium?

These controversies over the policies of the two surplus countries, France and the United States, are a special case of the more general debate about the degree to which the crises in the international monetary system in the interwar period, particularly from 1931 onward, could be attributed to the alleged failure of countries to operate the gold standard according to the rules followed in the pre-1914 era, thus depriving the system of its fundamental equilibrating mechanism. On a strict interpretation, the traditional policy required not merely that changes in holdings of gold should be automatically reflected in corresponding changes in the domestic currency, but that further purchases or sales of domestic assets should be made by the monetary authorities so that the impact of movements in gold was magnified in proportion to the central bank's reserve ratio.

In his League of Nations study of the behaviour of 26 countries during the years 1922–1938, Nurkse (1944, 68) found that "from year to year, central banks' international and domestic assets, during most of the period under review, moved far more often in the opposite than in the same direction." The extent of the inverse correlation was even greater in the five-year period of fixed exchange rates when the restored gold standard was in operation. For 1927–1931, international and domestic assets changed in the same direction in only 25 percent of possible cases, compared to 32 percent for the interwar period as a whole.

Various qualifications to this finding need to be noted, such as the possibilities that responses to flows of gold might have been delayed or that movements of private short-term capital might have distorted the pattern. It must also be recognized that even the classical gold standard was not quite as simple and automatic as the textbook models suggested. Nevertheless, the broad conclusion was that there was an increasing tendency in the interwar years to use gold reserves as a buffer to protect countries from the transmission of external shocks, rather than as the means by which fluctuations originating abroad were automatically transmitted to the domestic credit base, thereby easing the restoration of exchange-rate and balance-of-payments equilibria.

In terms of the four factors noted in section 1.3, the war and the postwar settlements caused the dislocation that produced the capital and currency flows that put the gold standard under strain. The continuing controversies over the gold standard during the 1920s gave evidence both of a failure of leadership and of the absence of international cooperation. All these discussions, of course, were undertaken within the framework of the gold standard, the presumed anchor of economic stability.

Chapter 4

Output, Productivity, and Technical Progress in the 1920s

In this chapter, the focus moves away from the financial policies and flows that were the dominant theme of Chapter 3, although we will have to return to those matters in subsequent chapters. Our aim here is to concentrate on developments in the "real" economy, particularly to examine what was happening to output and output per worker during the 1920s.

After the massive economic problems caused by the First World War, some European countries, the United States, and Japan achieved relatively rapid improvements in industrial production; however, other countries around the world struggled to regain their prewar levels of output and had advanced only a little by the late 1920s. Despite these difficulties, a number of factors helped to promote more rapid growth in productivity (output per hour worked), and this acceleration was a highly significant feature of the decade. In agriculture, conditions were generally much less satisfactory than in industry, and what little progress was made at the beginning of the decade was soon interrupted. For most primary-producing countries, the second half of the 1920s was an acutely difficult period of falling farm prices and stagnant output.

We begin with an overview of the structures and stages of development of various economies, and then we analyze the movements in output in industry and agriculture. The final sections examine the developments in productivity and the underlying sources of technical progress. We emphasize this feature of the 1920s as support for our fundamental proposition that the depression that overwhelmed the world at the end of the decade was the result of the policies that had been adopted during and after the war; it was not the uncontrollable outcome of a slowdown in technical progress or some other natural phenomenon.

4.1 The Structure of European Economies

In 1913, the United Kingdom, Germany, and France had less than half of Europe's population but accounted for 72 percent of Europe's output of manufactures and a slightly higher proportion of its manufactured exports. This superiority had been slightly eroded by the end of the 1920s as a result of the big three's economic and political misfortunes and the more successful performance of the Netherlands, Czechoslovakia, Spain, Italy, and the Scandinavian economies, but the United Kingdom, Germany, and France were still the overwhelmingly dominant European economic powers.

The best guide to the economic structure of the European economies in the interwar period is provided by the distribution of the labor force. The size and composition of the working population in the main European countries around 1930 is analyzed in table 4.1. The number and proportion of occupied workers are classified in three sectors: (1) agriculture; (2) industry, including mining, manufacturing, and building; and (3) transport, finance, distribution, and other services. The twenty-two countries are listed in diminishing degree of industrialization as indicated by the share of the working population in agriculture, noted by the figures in the second column.

This ranking is also very strongly inversely correlated with economic prosperity as indicated by levels of per capita income. As can be seen in figure 4.1, the lower a country's share of agricultural labor, the higher its per capita income. There were, however, a few countries (notably Switzerland, Denmark, and the Netherlands) with unusually high agricultural productivity, and they enjoyed a better standard of living than would be expected given the proportion of their labor force engaged in farming.[1]

The European economies fall broadly into four groups. In the top group were five highly industrialized countries. In the United Kingdom, Belgium, Switzerland, and Germany, at least 40 percent of the labor force was working in industry; in the Netherlands, the proportion was slightly lower than this, reflecting the larger size of the service sector. All these countries had less than 30 percent of their working population still on the land; the proportion was exceptionally low in Britain and Belgium and relatively high in Germany.

A second group of countries, including France, Czechoslovakia, Austria, and three Scandinavian countries, had also made considerable progress in the development from primary to secondary and tertiary activity, and by 1930 the working population was distributed in roughly equal proportions among the three sectors. Together the eleven countries in these top two tiers accounted for more than 70 percent of all the workers in industry and services in Europe.

The third group comprised the southern European countries of Italy, Portugal, Greece, and Spain, together with Ireland and Hungary. The share of the labor

---

[1] In some other cases (such as Portugal), income is below the expected level. The probable reason for this is the classification of female farm servants as working in services, with a corresponding understatement of the proportion in agriculture relative to other countries.

Table 4.1 Occupational distribution of the working population, 1930

	Working population (millions) (1)	Percentage in			Total (5)
		Agriculture (2)	Industry (3)	Services (4)	
1. Less than 20 percent in agriculture and more than 40 percent in industry					
United Kingdom	21.65	6	46	48	100
Belgium	3.74	17	48	35	100
Switzerland	1.94	21	45	34	100
Netherlands	3.18	21	36	43	100
Germany	32.30	29	40	31	100
	62.81	20	43	37	100
2. About 35 percent in agriculture and in industry					
Austria	3.17	32	33	35	100
Denmark	1.59	35	27	38	100
Norway	1.17	35	27	38	100
France	21.61	36	33	31	100
Sweden	2.89	36	32	32	100
Czechoslovakia	6.72	37	37	26	100
	37.15	36	33	31	100
3. About 50 percent in agriculture and 20–30 percent in industry					
Italy	17.26	47	31	22	100
Portugal	3.95	48	18	34	100
Ireland	1.34	48	15	37	100
Hungary	3.83	53	24	23	100
Greece	2.75	54	16	30	100
Spain	8.10	56	21	23	100
	37.23	50	25	25	100
4. More than 65 percent in agriculture and less than 20 percent in industry					
Poland	15.00	65	17	18	100
Finland	1.72	64	15	21	100
Yugoslavia	6.48	79	11	10	100
Romania	10.46	79	7	14	100
Bulgaria	3.43	80	8	12	100
	37.09	73	12	15	100
Total Europe	174.26	41	30	29	100

Source: Bairoch (1968).

force in agriculture was still around half, and—except for Italy—the share in industry still less than 25 percent. A final group of five countries in central and eastern Europe were still overwhelmingly agricultural and rural. They had 65–80 percent of their labor force in farming and less than 20 percent in industry.

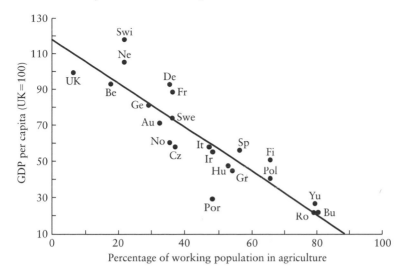

Figure 4.1. Per capita income and share of the labor force in agriculture, 1929.

Together these two lower tiers accounted for almost two-thirds of all the workers in agriculture in Europe and only a quarter of the workers in industry.

There was thus very considerable diversity in the structure of economic activity and in the vulnerability to changes in external conditions. The economic experience of the countries in the two upper groups of table 4.1 was primarily dependent on developments in industry, though the absolute numbers occupied in farming was still large in France and Germany, and the primary sector was important for Denmark and Norway. These countries, as well as Italy, were very exposed to the general state of world trade. The health of their economies could be strongly influenced by trends in competition from abroad and by changes in economic conditions in their customary markets and in exchange rates and tariffs. Conversely, the prosperity of the countries in the two lower groups rested almost entirely on conditions in agriculture and the price of food and raw materials, and most of them were much less vulnerable to external developments.

We have already emphasized the powerful and long-lasting economic effects of the war and the postwar settlements. A striking variety of patterns of growth can be discerned in the main industrial economies, even over the relatively short period from 1913 to 1929. The fourteen countries divide into three distinct groups.

Six countries increased level of industrial output by at least 50 per cent compared to the prewar level. For the three most successful of these economies, Finland, the Netherlands, and Czechoslovakia, the overall increase was more than 85 percent. A second group, which includes France, Belgium, and the United Kingdom, achieved only modest growth, raising output by 30–40 percent over prewar levels by 1929. For the third group, including Germany and Austria, this was a most dismal period, with additions to industrial output of 20 percent or less over prewar levels. A substantial part of these marked contrasts can be explained by the two factors that we stressed in previous chapters: the very great variations in the impact of the First World War and its immediate aftermath on economic and political conditions in the different regions, and differences in the nature and timing of the exchange-rate policies adopted in the postwar period.

The direct and indirect consequences of the 1914–1918 war affected economic activity in numerous different ways in individual countries (see Chapter 2). By 1920, those nations that had remained neutral (the Netherlands, Spain, and the Scandinavian countries) and those that avoided occupation (Italy and the United Kingdom) were able to produce at least as much as they had in 1913, and considerably more than that in the Netherlands and Denmark. In stark contrast, the devastation and disorganization in the belligerent countries that were defeated or occupied caused tremendous losses and a deep decline in production. In France and Germany, output in 1920 declined by roughly one-third compared to the prewar level; in Austria, Hungary, and Poland, output plunged to less than half of what it had been before the war.

Some industries, such as steel, electricity and electrical engineering, motor vehicles, and chemicals, were strongly stimulated by wartime military require-ments or by shortages caused by the interruption of prewar trade flows. Not all of this increased production could find a market once the fighting ended, and certain industries were left with considerable excess capacity. In other sectors, as in the Swedish case discussed below, the spur created by the war continued to have very positive effects.

The direct effects of the war continued to be felt long after hostilities ceased in November 1918. As a rule, a natural catch-up process operated, so that once recovery began, growth was most rapid in those countries that had suffered most in the war years. France, Austria, Poland, Czechoslovakia, Hungary, and Belgium all achieved a very rapid increase in output between 1920 and 1924. By this standard, the German recovery was well below par, principally because of the continued disruption of activity due to disputes over reparations, culmi-nating in the occupation of the Ruhr and the hyperinflation of 1923–1924.

For Germany, Austria, Hungary, and Poland, the initial postwar expansion was insufficient to offset wartime destruction and disruption. These countries had not regained their prewar level of output by 1924, and their recovery con-tinued at a brisk pace in the late 1920s, though Poland had still not reached the 1913 level by 1929. Developments in the Soviet Union deprived Poland of an important prewar trade partner, and the expiration of agreements providing for large quantities of coal and other duty-free exports to Germany was fol-lowed from 1925 by a tariff war and a sharp fall in trade with Germany. The iron and steel industries and coal mining were particularly hard hit.

The very slow recovery in Austria was a direct consequence of the demise of the Austro-Hungarian Empire. Each new independent country wanted to locate varied production within its borders, and Austria's favoured position as the economic center of southeastern Europe disappeared.

4.2 Industrialization outside Europe

The data in table 4.2 extend the view from Europe to several other large countries for which we have data. It can be seen easily that the larger European economies included in this table do not fall at the top of the table but rather are scattered throughout it. It was not only in Europe that countries had moved far from their reliance on agriculture as the primary source of income. The United States, of course, was the leader in this transformation. Despite the abundant land that made the United States a major exporter of agricultural products, less than 10 percent of the American workforce was engaged in agriculture by 1930.

The United States had not suffered economically from the war; they had been involved only in the later stages and had fought far from home. Even though the share of production allocated to the war effort was never very large in the United States, the cessation of wartime production led to a sharp recession in 1921. Production fell rapidly, but it recovered equally rapidly. Industrial production rose at a rapid rate during the rest of the 1920s. Inflation was not stimulated by this ebullient activity; prices drifted downward during the decade.

Consumer durables made their debut in economic life in the United States during the 1920s. Electric machines entered American households, making

Table **4.2** Structure of national economies, 1930–1934 (percentages)

	Agriculture	Manufacturing*	Service**
UK	4	34	62
USA	9	26	65
South Africa	13	31	56
Japan	19	28	53
Germany	20	41	39
France***	22	36	42
Mexico	22	20	58
Argentina	24	27	49
Brazil	24	13	63
Italy	30	28	42
India	61	n.a.	n.a.

* Includes Industry and Construction
** Includes Other (Transportation, Communication, Commerce)
*** Data for 1930–34 unavailable. Numbers listed are from 1935 to 1939.

Source: Mitchell (2003)

life more pleasant for women and allowing them to live comfortably without servants. By 1929, radios were in more than half of American households, vacuum cleaners were in more than 40 percent of households, and washing machines were in one-third of households. Refrigerators spread more slowly; they were in more than 10 percent of American households in 1929 and in more than half of American households by 1939. England and Wales, which appear to be more advanced in Table 4.2, lagged far behind the United States in the diffusion of consumer durables. Less than 20 percent of British households had vacuum cleaners and less than 1 percent had washing machines in 1929 (Bowden and Offer, 1994).

American households lacked the resources to purchase these durables out of current earnings. The spread of consumer durables in America was hastened by a great expansion of consumer credit. Companies followed the lead of McCormick and Singer, who had extended credit to purchasers of reapers and sewing machines in the nineteenth century. They advertised their products in national magazines, and they offered liberal terms for consumers to borrow and purchase their products (Olney, 1991). The United States, always prosperous because of its abundant land, began in this era to draw away from Europe and the rest of the world in the quality of its urban life as well.

The most notable new machine was used outside the house. Internal-combustion trucks had made their debut on farms before the war, and luxury cars were an occasional sight. Henry Ford introduced the Model T in 1914, making cars available to a wide spectrum of American families. The growth of automobiles would remake the landscape of America, just as the growth of consumer durables was remaking the operation of households.

Ford was able to produce cars so cheaply for several reasons, the most important being his innovation of the assembly line. He introduced mechanized production—later satirized by Charlie Chaplin in *Modern Times*—that made it possible for workers to produce many more cars per hour than before. In order to convince workers to work under these repetitive conditions and not to sabotage the line of production, Ford introduced the "five-dollar day," offering a high wage to those workers who were willing and able to endure the discipline of the assembly line (Raff and Summers, 1987). This combination of rapid production and high wages has been known ever since as Fordism.

A second reason that Ford could produce so cheaply was that he standardized his product. The famous statement attributed to Ford—"You can have any color you want, as long as it's black"—may be apocryphal, but it captures Ford's intent succinctly. The change to mass production was both an increase in the quantity of goods available and in the standardization of these goods. A third reason was that he offered credit for automobile purchases, as the producers of other durables were doing.

The expansion of automobile production led to a change in company organization as well. Ford revolutionized the production line, but General Motors was the locus of vast internal change in organization. William Durant formed General Motors in 1908, but both he and the company faced financial collapse in the recession that followed the war. Pierre du Pont had invested much of the wartime profits from the manufacture of gunpowder in General Motors, and he bought Durant out at the end of 1920. Du Pont brought Alfred P. Sloan, Jr., into General Motors, and Sloan became the company's president by 1924. He created what became known as the multidivisional structure of the modern corporation, which spread widely among large American business enterprises.

The essential feature of the multidivisional structure was the distinction between line and staff. The line officers made day-to-day decisions in running the firm's operations; the staff concerned itself both with the enterprise as a whole and with the longer run. General Motors was organized into several divisions, each of which made cars for a certain income class of customers, plus a few other divisions for trucks, accessories, and other purposes. The staff function initially was restricted to an executive committee that oversaw the operations of the divisions. The committee enlarged its ability to gather information about the activities of the divisions, and it began to allocate resources among them. The committee became the general office of the company. No longer were decisions made by bargaining among the heads of divisions. Decisions were made instead by general executives who had the interests of the corporation at heart and the time and information needed to make sound decisions for the future (Sloan, 1963; Chandler, 1977).

South Africa and Japan were not as industrial as the United Kingdom and the United States, but their agricultural sectors shrank below the level of France and Germany during the 1920s. Despite the similarity of the sectoral divisions of these two economies, they were based on very different kinds of economic activities. South Africa was prospering on the basis of its gold mines, operated by black African workers. The government moved in the late 1920s to construct a two-tier labor system. "Civilized" workers—that is, Afrikaners—were to be paid more than "uncivilized" workers when they did the same work, and skilled jobs were reserved for the former class. The government was not worried that black Africans could not perform well in skilled occupations. In fact, the opposite was true; the government was afraid that black Africans would do well and would force wages for skilled white workers down. In order to prevent that adverse outcome, they imposed labor rules that developed into apartheid (Feinstein, 2005).

Japan was developing at this time into a standard emerging economy. After the Meiji Restoration in 1866, Japan had moved from an agricultural economy to one based on light manufacturing, particularly textiles. Light manufactures accounted for two-thirds of Japanese exports in the 1920s, and cotton textiles were the largest part of those exports. Japan had been an importer of cotton cloth before starting its own cotton industry in 1890, after which it moved quickly into being a net exporter (Ito, 1992).

Elsewhere in the Japanese economy, *zaibatsu*—that is, sets of interrelated and interlocked companies held closely by families—grew on the basis of large profits during the war. The four largest zaibatsu—Mitsui, Mitsubishi, Yasuda, and Sumitomo—were active in many parts of the economy, ranging from banking and insurance to steel and machinery. They remained active long after the 1920s, and the presence of interlocked firms was as much a characteristic of the Japanese economy as the growth of large firms was in the United States (Flath, 2000).

During the war, Japan had gone off the gold standard, as the major European countries had, and it followed them also in adopting a firm resolve to return to gold at prewar parity. This policy stance resulted in continuous deflation during the 1920s, which has been blamed for the lackluster performance of the economy. Recent research suggests, however, that the deflation was caused by anticipation of the resumption of the gold standard, while growth was encouraged by fiscal and monetary expansion. Japan finally went back on gold in January 1930, after the beginning of the depression in America and Europe. This miracle of bad timing was offset by the rapid abandonment of gold in December 1931. Thus, the decision to resume gold at prewar parity, however misguided, does not appear to have done major harm to the Japanese economy (Faini and Toniolo, 1992).

4.3 Britain and Germany in the 1920s

We return to the two main industrial economies of Europe for two reasons. They were important in the early stages of the Great Depression, and controversies about their lack of progress in the 1920s abound. The growth of industrial production in the United Kingdom was painfully slow throughout the 1920s. Unemployment was very high, and severe depression in the major industries pulled down the economy's overall performance. The four large staple industries—coal mining, iron and steel, shipbuilding, and textiles—found themselves unable to compete in world markets during the 1920s, and all of them produced less in 1929 than in 1913. There is no reason to doubt that these industries suffered from the decision (effectively made as early as 1918) to return to gold at the prewar parity of $4.86. It is generally accepted that this represented an overvaluation of about 10 percent against the dollar. Against a number of European currencies, notably the French and Belgian francs, the German mark, and the Italian lira, the margin by which sterling was overvalued in the early 1920s was considerably larger.

However, there were other, more powerful, structural forces that were responsible for the depth and persistence of the problems facing British industry. "Although the bulk of discussion about the problems of British industry in the interwar period stressed British mistakes, faults, and short-comings, there can be no doubt that the basic causes were secular, impersonal and inevitable" (Kahn, 1946, 72). The First World War dealt British overseas trade a savage blow from which it never recovered. In 1920, the volume of UK exports of all kinds was about 30 percent less than it had been in 1913. Even in 1929—the best year for British exports in the entire interwar period—export volumes still languished at almost 20 percent below their prewar level. A detailed classification of United Kingdom exports of manufactures reveals a devastating loss of market share in all types of products and in all markets (Maizels, 1965).

Before the war, Britain had exported a much larger proportion of its output of manufactures than any other country in Europe. British manufacturing as a whole depended on overseas sales for 45 percent of its markets; cotton textiles for an extraordinary 75 per cent; woollen and worsted products, shipbuilding, and many types of machinery for about half; and iron and steel for roughly one-third. These high ratios made the United Kingdom especially vulnerable to external changes. The country's markets shrank as a result of several features of this period, including the growth of import substitution in many traditional markets such as Canada, Australia, India, and western Europe; the imposition of higher tariffs; and the increase in competition from Japan, the United States, and other foreign manufacturers. This vulnerability was enhanced by the dominant position that the large export-dependent staples occupied in the British economy, accounting for roughly half of industrial output and employment.

Certain long-term trends had already started to weaken Britain's position in export markets before 1913. If exports had continued at a normal peacetime pace, it might have been possible for British exporters to respond by searching for new markets and developing new products and processes. Instead, the war severely curtailed British exports. Workers were recruited for the armed forces, production was diverted to meet military requirements, imports of raw materials for civilian products were severely restricted, and shipping was unavailable to bring in supplies or to deliver goods to foreign customers.

This forced withdrawal from the market accelerated the growth of import substitution and compelled importers to look elsewhere for the cotton cloth, machinery, shipping, and other goods and services they needed. While the United Kingdom was out of action, nonbelligerents were able to expand their output in ideal conditions. The war thus presented rival manufacturers with a marvelous opportunity and simultaneously prevented Britain from adjusting to these deeply detrimental developments. The war compressed what might otherwise have been a long, drawn-out process of change into a few years, and made it difficult—in some cases impossible—for British industry to find a satisfactory answer to the challenge.

The inevitable results of this constraint on adaptation to foreign competition were excess capacity, heavy losses, and high unemployment. In sectors such as iron and steel and shipbuilding, still further damage was caused by the huge increase in productive capacity undertaken in 1914–1918 to supply armaments and other temporary military requirements. When peace came, all these industries were left with excessive capacity built at inflated wartime prices, and they suffered from high unit costs and depressed markets. The resulting combination of financial weakness and unemployment in turn acted as a major constraint on the elimination of inefficiencies in industrial structure, organization, and practice, which were essential if the economy was to prosper in the new conditions.

1914–1918 was also a massive misfortune for the coal industry. Before 1914, Britain had enjoyed a substantial trade in exports of coal to Europe. The war and the short-lived postwar boom encouraged further expansion, often of old and inefficient mines. When the fighting ended, it proved impossible to restore the previous level of exports. The Netherlands, Spain, and other former importers had developed their own mines during the war, and Britain also faced increasing competition from Germany and Poland. At the same time, demand was reduced as a result of technical advances in fuel conservation and the growing use of substitutes, particularly in shipping, where oil replaced coal as the principal source of fuel. These trends were temporarily concealed by the disruption of German production and the closure of the Ruhr coalfields in 1923, but once Germany resumed production, British coal exports dropped to four-fifths of what they had been in 1913. Domestic sales were also restricted by the depressed state of the major coal-using industries, and total output of coal thus remained well below the 1913 level throughout the 1920s.

It was widely recognized that Britain's early lead in industrialization had enabled it to build up a monopoly position in the supply of industrial goods that was not sustainable in the long run. As other countries developed their own resources, Britain's grossly disproportionate share of world trade and production would inevitably be eroded. However, the heavy commitment to the staple industries made adjustment more difficult, and no one expected the process to occur as abruptly as it did between 1913 and 1920.

Neither employers nor workers proved adept in adjusting to the scale and speed of the transformation made necessary by the war and the sudden deterioration in Britain's position. A difficult situation called for flexibility, intelligence, and vision, but the responses from the staple industries were typically stubborn, stupid, and short-sighted. Lord Birkenhead, a member of the cabinet, is reported to have said during the dispute that culminated in the general strike of 1926: "It would be possible to say without exaggeration that the miners' leaders were the stupidest men in England if we had not had frequent occasion to meet the owners" (Mowat, 1955, 300). Capital and labor together aggravated the extant problems and impeded the necessary modernization and rationalization of industry.

Of course, there were exceptions to the generally doleful British pattern. New science-based industries developed that were largely independent of export markets. Those that expanded rapidly in the 1920s included electric power supply, electrical machinery, and electrical goods and appliances; motor vehicles; rayon; and certain parts of the chemical industry, such as synthetic nitrogen, dyestuffs, drugs, and photographic chemicals. Some of these trades benefited from the first small steps taken in the direction of tariff protection at the beginning of the decade. The share of these industries in industrial output roughly doubled between 1913 and 1929, but they were still too small to compensate for the lack of progress in the old staples.

Another feature that differentiated the expanding industries from the old staples was the scale of their operation. The old industries typically consisted of very large numbers of small firms, whereas the new businesses tended to have their output concentrated in a few large producers and were thus able to enjoy important economies of scale. One significant example was the dominant role of Courtauld's in the production of rayon; a second was the formation of Imperial Chemical Industries (ICI) in 1926. According to Chandler (1990, 358), this merger "provides one of the very few examples of systematically planned, large-scale, organization building in British industry." It was the result of several factors: the earlier centralization of a major participant in ICI, Nobel Industries; the problems of British Dyestuffs, formed during the war to replace imported dyes; and the recent formation of IG Farben in Germany. The creation of ICI was followed during the later 1920s by administrative centralization. Although broadly following the American model, Chandler suggests that the centralization at ICI was due more to the British tradition of personal leadership.

German producers were cut off from many export markets during the war and were hampered after the war by the monetary chaos described in section 3.1. However, the chaos did have the advantage of clearing many firms of their debt and lowering the costs of new physical capital formation. After stabilization in 1924, German industry rapidly regained the international position it had held before the First World War.

German industry made extensive use of cartels. Antitrust legislation was passed in 1923 but proved to be of little consequence. Many cartels evolved into trust companies or IGs (*Interessengemeinschaften*). IGs were prevalent in chemicals, steel, railroad equipment, and other heavy industries. The chemical IGs were merged into a single giant firm, IG Farben, shortly after German stabilization. The resulting company dominated the chemical industry in Germany and rapidly became a major competitor on the world scene.

The expansion of the Weimar economy after 1924 has been labeled unhealthy by many historians. One accusation is that wages were too high to be sustained. Borchardt (1979) argued that real wages outran productivity growth, taking 1913 as a standard. This view, which makes the depression in Germany the result of structural problems in the German economy rather than of German economic policies, has become known as the Borchardt thesis.

Holtfrerich (1986) responded that Borchardt's result was an artifact of the way he did his calculations; when hourly wages are compared with labor productivity per hour, no imbalance can be detected. Dimsdale, Horsewood, and Van Riel (2006) used econometric tools to argue that the influences cited by Borchardt were offset by other factors such as cartel pricing.

Whatever the resolution of this calculation, everyone agrees that wages were a larger share of national income in the 1920s than they had been before the war. If this was not due to wages outrunning productivity, then it was due to an increasing number of higher-paid salaried jobs and a rise in the participation rate. In any case, the profit or rent share of income was reduced.

It is plausible to see such a change in income distribution as a constraint on investment. Smaller capital income, in the absence of changes in workers' propensity to save, led to smaller investment funds. However, this inference is incomplete. Other critics of the Weimar economy point to the capital inflows to be discussed in the next chapter as a source of unhealthy capital expansion. The problem, according to this contrary view, is that much Weimar investment was unproductive. Capital imports financed construction, particularly public construction, which is said to have increased German foreign indebtedness without enhancing its productive capacity. The problem, in other words, was not that the supply of capital in Weimar Germany was deficient; it was rather that the demand for investment was skewed toward unproductive purposes.

4.4 Agriculture in the 1920s

As we saw earlier (see table 4.1), there were more than 70 million men and women in Europe who were dependent on farming for their livelihood. In the immediate postwar years, they enjoyed a fleeting period of prosperity, as prices soared while output was recovering from the ravages of the war. However, a crisis followed swiftly in 1920 when the postwar boom was brought to an end (see section 3.1), and for the great majority of Europe's farmers, the remainder of the decade was one of growing difficulty and deteriorating conditions.

Farmers in the New World faced similar problems. It did not matter that Canada, the United States, and Argentina were major agricultural exporters. Their farmers were subject to the same world market, where low prices created hardship. In the United States, farmers had borrowed freely to expand during their glory days before and during the war. Their debts loomed ever larger as prices fell, because the debts had been contracted when farm prices were high. Farmers everywhere tried to escape the grip of the world market, whether through government or private actions.

A popular measure was the formation of cartels for various products. Both countries and private groups participated in attempts to avoid market pressures for wheat, sugar, rubber, coffee, wool, and other products. The pattern was clear and similar: in each case, governments or international cartels bought the product to raise its price above what competition would have made it. They succeeded in slowing the decline in agricultural prices in the late 1920s, but only at the cost of accumulating rising stocks of unsold product. This pattern, observable in commodity after commodity, was unsustainable, and it shows the difficulty of finding a remedy for unfavorable economic developments. An ominous sign for the future was the rising cost of holding these inventories, a cost that was dependent on the interest rate. As interest rates rose at the end of the decade, the ability of the cartels to continue their policies was increasingly at risk (Kindleberger, 1986).

The root cause of these problems was the excess supply of foodstuffs on world markets, created by continuous expansion of acreage outside Europe by countries able to produce competitive grains and other food crops at much lower cost. Most producers were unwilling or unable to compensate for this excess by making a corresponding reduction in their output. Given that there was also no prospect of a commensurate growth in consumption, markets became progressively weaker. The downward trend in prices was briefly interrupted by crop failures in the mid-1920s but then continued with renewed momentum. The final collapse came with frightening speed in 1930 and 1931. The two commodities that were most adversely affected were wheat and sugar. Both were especially important as a source of export earnings.

For wheat, the fatal interaction of increasing acreage and falling prices is illustrated in figure 4.2.[2] As can be seen in the upper panel, the long-run expansion of the area under cultivation by the four large overseas exporters—the United States, Canada, Australia, and Argentina—continued remorselessly. During the war and immediate postwar years, a big reduction in European output and the collapse of Russian exports stimulated further expansion. Between 1909–1913 and the mid-1920s, the four large overseas exporters increased their output by almost 50 percent. In contrast, acreage and output of wheat both in Europe and in the other producing countries was broadly the same in these two periods.

Unfortunately, however, this stability on the part of European producers was not sufficient to prevent supply running ahead of demand on the world markets. Consumption of wheat was not increasing in step with rising incomes, and in the richer countries consumption was actually falling as consumers switched their spending to higher-quality foods, such as meat and

---

[2] The data on wheat production and consumption used in figure 4.2 and the following paragraphs are from Malenbaum (1953). The price of wheat imported by Britain (Svennilson, 1954, 246) is taken as a satisfactory measure of trends in the world price in light of London's free market and its role as the world's clearinghouse for wheat.

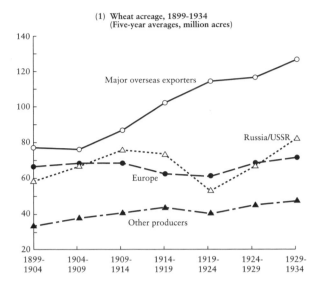

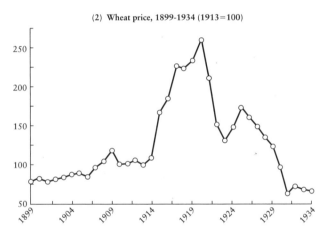

Figure 4.2. Trends in the world wheat market, 1899–1934.

dairy products, fruit, vegetables, and eggs. In the United States, for example, wheat consumption per head of the population was approximately 15 percent lower in 1924–1928 than it had been in 1909–1913. In France, it dropped by 12 percent, and in the UK by 8 percent.

This imbalance between supply and demand was quickly reflected in mounting stocks of unsold wheat, with inevitable consequences for prices (see the lower panel of figure 4.2). The steep fall in prices was temporarily reversed in 1924 and 1925, but only because of crop failures in each of these years in one or more of the main New World producers. As soon as overseas harvests recovered, the decline continued. The prices of most products were falling in the late 1920s, but farmers suffered because the prices they received for their produce fell more sharply than those they paid. This adverse "scissors" effect applied both to the relative prices of the equipment, fertilizers, and other goods purchased for use on the farm, and to the prices of the goods and services they and their families consumed.

The one policy that might have prevented the deterioration in relative prices was a significant reduction in acreage by all the major producers. The issue was the subject of much discussion at international conferences, but it proved impossible to reach agreement. Each country found persuasive reasons why its production should be preserved while others curbed theirs.

Instead, several European governments, including such major wheat importers as France, Germany, and Italy, resorted to higher tariffs and other protectionist measures in a vain attempt to protect their farming communities from the damaging trends in world markets. The initial postwar tariff barriers were erected against imported wheat in the mid-1920s, easily predating the precipitate fall in prices in 1930. These nationalistic policies not only failed to restore prosperity; in the long-run, they also precluded the gains in productivity and income that could have been achieved by increased regional specialization and a higher level of intra-European trade. Furthermore, by artificially raising the domestic prices for agricultural products, the policies helped to restrict consumption and thus exacerbated the fundamental problems.

The crisis would have been worse if output per unit of land had also been increasing, but this did not happen. For the world as a whole, there were only modest fluctuations in yields around a broadly level trend. In Europe, the yield averaged 18.8 bushels per acre in 1909–1914, declined during the war, and then recovered; but by 1924–1929, yields had only reached 18.3 bushels per acre. These averages conceal very large differences in productivity. In Denmark and the Netherlands, prewar output already exceeded 40 bushels per acre, and in Belgium, the United Kingdom, Germany, Sweden, Norway, and Switzerland, prewar yields were above 30 bushels per acre. However, in Austria, France, Romania, Hungary, and Poland, the yield was only about two-thirds of this; and in Italy, Spain, Bulgaria, and Yugoslavia, yields were no more than half this level.

While a large part of these disparities can be explained by soil and climate, they indicate the potential improvements in yields that could have been reaped in the more backward countries by increased inputs of fertilizers, better seeds, crop rotations, and greater mechanization. Countries at a higher level of agricultural technology might also have been expected to make further advances. In fact, however, most countries made little or no progress in the 1920s, and in several countries yields actually declined. In the more developed regions of western Europe, innovation was retarded by the slow recovery from the war, the generally unfavourable economic conditions in agriculture, and the adverse movements in the farmers' terms of trade. In eastern and southern Europe, rural overpopulation, fragmentation of landholdings, and low levels of education and organization represented additional obstacles to the spread of better practices.

Land reforms were introduced in many parts of central and eastern Europe and in Greece by governments that saw land reform as a prudent response to rural unrest and the Bolshevik revolution, but the effect on production was generally small. The most beneficial results were achieved in Czechoslovakia, where holdings of medium size increased in importance, raising the efficiency of production and marketing. In Poland, Bulgaria, and Hungary the reforms were extremely modest in scope, and their effects were correspondingly limited.

Even where the scale of redistribution was more radical, it had often had little impact on efficiency. In a number of countries, the reforms essentially transferred ownership from landlord to tenant without changing the conditions of production, though it is argued that uncertainty regarding ownership rights discouraged investment and sales of land to more efficient farmers in Romania and Yugoslavia (Lampe and Jackson, 1982, 352). The reforms also tended to reduce the marketable surplus because the peasants preferred to increase the production of staple subsistence crops such as corn, and the sharp fall in wheat production and yields in Romania has been attributed to peasants' greater interest in cattle-rearing and fodder crops (Royal Institute of International Affairs, 1932, 149).

The problems faced by sugar producers were very similar to those just described in relation to wheat, except that in this case the destructive competition came from the tropical countries, especially Cuba and Java. During the First World War, the output of European beet sugar fell sharply, both because labor was not available and because of the closing of the British market. Production of cane sugar in the tropics expanded to take advantage of the new opportunities. When the fighting finished, there was a temporary shortage of sugar and a rise in prices, which encouraged further extension of the cane area in the tropics, but as soon as European production recovered to its prewar level, the boom came to an end. In 1913, beet sugar accounted for 45 percent of a total supply of twenty million tons; in 1924, it accounted for only 33 percent of an increased supply of twenty-five million tons.

By this point, more sugar was being produced than could be consumed, and prices tumbled. In 1924, the price of sugar in London was still 80 percent higher than it had been before the war; one year later, it collapsed with catastrophic speed to the prewar level, and continued to fall. The producers nevertheless attempted to maintain their output, and they looked to their governments for assistance. The American government responded with protection for its domestic producers. The expansion of Florida sugar production under this umbrella is one cause of current environmental problems in the Everglades. Farmers drained the swampy lands, as farmers have done since time immemorial, and increased the flow of water out to sea. They either didn't understand or didn't care about the process that created wetlands in southern Florida, often miles away from their farms; they merely responded to the inducements created by sugar tariffs. Only many decades later did people realize how harmful the expansion of American sugar production had been.

The constraints that had been agreed to at the 1902 Brussels Convention were quickly abandoned, and Europe returned to an era of protection and of bounties and subsidies for output and exports. These measures could work successfully for one or two countries, but when all producers attempted to rely on them, they were self-defeating and simply served to aggravate the problems of overproduction.

No country escaped the world crisis in agriculture at the end of the 1920s, but some suffered sooner and more deeply than others. The countries that were most affected by the decline in farm prices and conditions were the cereal and sugar-beet exporters in eastern Europe and the rest of the world. Other regions were able to escape the worst effects by increasing their output of products that were less vulnerable to competition from low-cost overseas producers, and those countries that were large importers of food, notably the United Kingdom, gained from the relative fall in food import prices.

In Italy, Spain, Portugal, and Greece, farm incomes were partially sustained by sales of citrus fruits, wine, and tobacco. For Denmark, the Netherlands, and some of the other countries of western Europe, increasing consumption of meat and dairy products provided some shelter from the worst effects of the depression, and their farmers also gained from the steep fall in the costs of the fodder crops fed to their livestock. Nevertheless, the overall impact of the farm crisis was a severe setback to economic progress and a retardation of both industrial growth and international trade.

4.5 Aggregate Productivity Growth

Despite all the problems caused by the war and by postwar financial instability, there was a significant improvement in productivity in the 1920s. Table 4.3 portrays the rate of growth of both production per head of population and of productivity (measured by GDP per hour worked) from 1890 or 1870 to 1913, and from 1913 to 1929. Before the war, there was a clear difference in the rates of growth of industrializing countries versus other countries. The advanced countries had entered the process of modern economic growth, with increases in GDP per capita of more than 1 percent per year, while the other countries had not yet made the transition from more stagnant economies. Outside of Europe, Argentina and Japan had joined the United States and Europe in this process of industrialization and growth.

Table 4.3 Growth of GDP per head, 1890–1929, and per hours worked, 1870–1929 (annual percentage rate of growth)

	GDP per head		GDP per hour worked	
	1890–1913	1913–1929	1870–1913	1913–1929
France	1.7	1.9	1.7	2.3
Germany	1.8	0.8	1.8	1.4
Italy[a]	1.9	1.2	1.6	2.0
United Kingdom	0.9	0.3	1.2	1.4
Turkey	—	−0.1		
Argentina	2.5	0.9		
Brazil	0.4	1.7		
India	0.4	0.0		
China	0.5	0.8		
Japan	1.4	2.4	1.9	3.4
USA	2.0	1.7	1.9	2.4

[a] 1899–1913.

Source: Maddison (1995), 194–204, 249.

The picture is far more complex in the 1920s. There was considerable disparity in the progress of European countries, as noted already, and other countries fared unequally as well. Economic growth in Germany slowed down in all of the disruptions of the Weimar period. The United Kingdom, which was growing slowly already before the war, grew even more slowly in the 1920s. Argentina and India had similar reductions in the rate of growth. Only Japan had an acceleration of growth in the 1920s.

The economy of Turkey stagnated between 1913 and 1929. This lack of progress is not surprising in light of the political turmoil in that part of the world. The economy of the Ottoman Empire was predominantly agrarian at the start of the war. Despite this orientation, Istanbul and other large cities were supplied by imports before the war as a result of transportation costs in the global economy. The war interrupted this trade and also drained labor from the countryside as farmers became soldiers. The result was food scarcity in the cities, which led in turn to difficulties and political change. Turkey fought a war of independence from 1920 to 1922. The demise of the Ottoman Empire, like the disappearance of the Austro-Hungarian Empire, led to a proliferation of new states and borders, with consequent economic difficulties (Pamuk, 2005).

The second part of the table contrasts changes in productivity, measured here by labor productivity in the absence of good data on capital. These data are available only for the most advanced countries, and they are reported here for a longer prewar period. In the period before the First World War, there was normally very little difference between the growth of GDP per capita and labor productivity, but this ceased to be true after 1913. In the later period,

GDP per hour worked increased much more rapidly than GDP per head (compare the second and third columns of table 4.3).

While the performance of individual countries varies considerably, it is clear that in almost every case, in Europe as well as in the United States and Japan, productivity growth accelerated between 1913 and 1929. The few countries that did not participate in this process of productivity improvement included Germany, Austria, and Hungary, all of which suffered great changes and hyperinflations in the 1920s. For Europe as a whole, the average rate of growth of GDP per hour of labor input was a little more than 2 percent per annum over the years from 1913 to 1929, compared to about 1.5 percent per annum between 1890 and 1913.

It may at first seem odd that labor productivity grew more rapidly than production per head of population. This apparent paradox exposes one of the dominant trends of the twentieth century: the labor input from each person declined, while at the same time product per hour worked increased more than proportionally. The dominant explanation for the persistent tendency of total hours worked to rise more slowly than the increase in population—and thus for productivity to rise more rapidly than production per head of population— was the reduction in working hours that occurred in almost all industrialized countries in the years following the war. The working week was typically reduced from around fifty-four hours to about forty-eight hours in most industries and countries, and many more workers were able to take paid holidays.

This fall in hours worked reflected the universal and long-standing desire to take some part of the benefits of increased productivity in the form of more time for leisure rather than more consumption of goods and services. Further moves in this direction were made possible in the postwar period by the increases in the strength of the trade unions and the left-wing political parties, and also by the existence of favorable economic conditions for workers to exercise their greater bargaining power. The trend was thus in part a response to increases in productivity already achieved, but it also acted as a stimulus for firms to make further advances to compensate for the fall in labor input. Higher productivity also permitted increases in real wages, and in most countries the worker's lot improved due both to higher disposable incomes and increased leisure.

However, as we shall see in Chapter 7, not all leisure was the result of free choice. Involuntary unemployment was generally quite high during the 1920s, and this rise above prewar levels also helped to raise the rate of growth of GDP per hour worked above that of GDP per capita. Changes in the proportion of the population seeking work were a further contributory factor. For example, the larger-than-average gap in 1913–1929 between the two measures for Denmark is accounted for by a fall in the participation rate; the small difference for Sweden and Germany is accounted for by a sharp rise in this rate.

The growth of labor productivity is evidence not only that capital continued to be accumulated throughout this period (albeit with interruptions) but also that there was no interruption in the incorporation of new knowledge into production techniques and in the formation of new human capital through better education. In fact, when economic historians of the interwar years discuss supply factors and technical progress, they portray a much more dynamic picture than when they focus on aggregate demand.

The distinguishing feature of modern economic growth identified by Kuznets, the "extended application of science to problems of production," was not impaired during the 1920s. Just as life continues in the midst of great hardship, so modern industrial economies continued to introduce new products and production techniques, improve managerial skills, educate scientists and engineers, and diffuse literacy, even during the macroeconomic chaos of the period. If anything, the process of the expansion of scientific and technological knowledge was encouraged by spillovers from wartime technical progress. Seen in this light, the Great Depression at the end of the 1920s and the high unemployment rates of the interwar decades seem to be an even greater tragedy, in that there was nothing "natural" about them. They were entirely man-made.

4.6 Technical Progress and Organization in the Industrial Sector

How can we account for the acceleration in technical progress achieved in the 1920s? One distinguished contemporary observer (Ohlin, 1931, 66) referred to the decade in the following terms:

> The rapid technical development during this period and the deep-going changes in organisation, commonly called "rationalisation," were factors which increased the need for adaptability. There would seem to be reason to believe that this rationalisation movement proceeded at a more rapid rate than before the war . . . . New machinery was introduced on a larger scale than before, as shown by the enormous expansion of the machine-producing industries. The growth in output of manufactured goods took place in many countries with no, or only small, rise of the number of workers.

It was a process of innovation, modernization, and mechanization that began in the late nineteenth century and proceeded most rapidly in the United States. The methods of production gave rise to the large companies described earlier. Europe made some headway before the war, but European countries still had a long way to go: in 1913, the average industrial worker in the United States produced roughly twice as much as his or her counterpart in the United Kingdom and Germany (Broadberry 1993). Many of the crucial advances made after 1919 had their origins in the earlier period but were greatly improved and more widely disseminated in the years between the wars. In addition, technical progress in sectors such as chemicals, motor vehicles, and aviation was strongly stimulated by the war, and this too created huge possibilities for increases in productivity in the interwar period in both Europe and the United States.

Of the numerous technological developments in this period, two were of quite exceptional importance: electricity for power, lighting, and communications, and the motor vehicle for transport. These two advances had the potential to bring about an immense increase in economic efficiency. They could dramatically reduce the cost and increase the flexibility of production, and their great benefits could be enjoyed across the whole economy, in the workplace and in the home. Cheap electric motors revolutionized the motive power for industry and agriculture and stimulated the mechanization of production; cheap motor cars, trucks, and tractors transformed transport costs for goods and people. Together these innovations made possible the introduction of new products and new methods not only in large, centralized factories but also in small workshops and remote villages.

The spread of electricity provided a boost to industrial productivity, but only with a lag. Electric motors replaced steam engines and even water power in many factories before the war. The older forms of energy had economies of scale such that one large engine or water wheel powered an entire factory. Electric motors could be small enough for each machine to have its own motor. It took several years, however, for industrialists to understand the implications of this change. They initially simply replaced the power source, and it wasn't until after the war that they realized they now had much more flexibility in organizing production. Only at this point did productivity rise, as labor was used more efficiently. Even though electricity was introduced before the war, the effects on productivity only became apparent in the 1920s (David, 1991).

Although small firms shared in the benefits of the new technology, the dominant tendencies favored large plants with substantial economies of scale achieved by the application of techniques of mass production and standardization, introduced together in a way that gave producers much more control over the pace and continuity of the effort exerted by the labor force. Rationalization was, perhaps, just a fashionable buzzword; it is indisputable, however, that considerable "industrial restructuring" took place in the 1920s, often with the direct or indirect aid of the state. In Italy and Germany this "restructuring" was also promoted and sustained by the "universal banks." Such restructuring meant the creation of the cartels and combines to which we referred earlier, but it did not stop there. Measures to cut costs were adopted on a large scale.

These changes in turn allowed firms to lower prices dramatically and thus increase still further the market for their products. In Britain, for example, fifty-five employee weeks were required to produce a car at the Austin Motor Company in 1922, but only ten were necessary in 1927 (Lewchuk, 1987, 174). As a result of productivity improvements of this magnitude, it was possible to bring the price of an average passenger car down from £550 in 1922 to less than £300 in 1929. At the Bat'a works in Czechoslovakia, the introduction of American-style techniques of mass production in 1924–1927 increased the annual production of shoes from 3.5 million pairs to 15.2 million pairs, with huge increases in labor productivity. These improvements permitted enormous reductions in price and created vast new markets for the firm at home and abroad (Teichova, 1985, 275).

It is not possible to discuss each breakthrough separately, but it may help to convey the scale and significance of the process if we list some of the most important new products and processes that became available for widespread application in the years immediately before, during, and after the First World War. The selection made by Svennilson (1954) is reproduced in table 4.4.

Striking gains in productivity were made in the production of capital goods, such as electrical and mechanical machinery, which helped to promote investment in a wide range of other industries, and also in goods purchased by consumers, including clothing, radios, refrigerators, and other household appliances. Some innovations transformed the distribution and packing of goods; others made their impact on the operation of financial and commercial offices.

Many of the advances were interdependent, and progress in one field was stimulated by, and contributed to, developments in other fields. The expansion of production in the car industry needed not only the improvements to the internal-combustion engine and the use of electric power, but also modern high-speed machine tools, which in turn depended on ball bearings, new alloy steels for the body, and new plastics for the interior fittings. Increased sales of cars and commercial vehicles then encouraged the construction of better roads.

Table 4.4 New products and processes developed immediately before, during, or immediately after the First World War

Alloy steels (e.g., stainless steel); nonferrous alloys; electric furnace technique; continuous
  rolling mills for steel production
The rotating cement kiln
New electrochemical processes
New methods for the fixation of atmospheric nitrogen
New methods for bleaching of wood pulp; the use of pulp in chemical production
Rayon
New methods of oil refining (cracking); hydrogenation of carbon; other synthetic methods
  for production of heavy organic chemicals
Synthetic solvents, plastics, and rubber
Ball bearings
Use of diesel motors for large ships
Electronic tubes; domestic radios
Aircraft
More efficient office machinery
New machinery in clothing industry
New methods of canning
Prefabricated material for packing; machinery for packing

Source: Svennilson (1954), 21.

Table 4.5 Innovations in the 1920s

USA	Europe	Other
Wireless telephone[1]	KLM is the world's first airline	Atom splitting
First nonstop flight across the	company (Netherlands)[15]	(New Zealand)[21]
Atlantic[2]	Electric kettle (UK)[16]	Insulin
Thompson submachine gun[3]	Self-winding watch	(Canada)[22]
Band-aid[4]	(Switzerland)[17]	Quartz crystal
First 3D movie[5]	Mechanical television (UK)[18]	clock (Canada)[23]
Traffic signal[6]	Aerosol can (Norway)[19]	
Frozen food[7]	Penicillin (UK)[20]	
16 mm home movie camera[8]		
Dynamic loudspeaker[9]		
Complete TV system[10]		
First talkie movie[11]		
First transatlantic phone call[12]		
Car radio[13]		
Credit card[14]		

Sources:
1. "History: The 20th Century." Did You Know? http://www.didyouknow.org/history/20thcentury.htm.
2. Ibid.
3. Encyclopedia Britannica Online. http://www.britannica.com/eb/article-9072197.
4. "BAND-AID BRAND Adhesive Bandages Story." http://www.bandaid.com/brand_story.shtml.
5. "Cinematic Terms: A Film-Making Glossary." *The Greatest Films.* http://www.filmsite.org/filmterms1.html.
6. U.S. Department of Transportation. http://education.dot.gov/aboutmorgan.html
7. Birds Eye Foods. http://www.birdseyefoods.com/corp/about/clarenceBirdseye.asp.
8. "Chronology of Motion Picture Films." Kodak. http://www.kodak.com/US/en/motion/products/chrono1.jhtml?id=0.1.4.38&lc=en.
9. Rice, Chester W. and Kellogg, Edward W. (1925). "Notes on the Development of a New Type of Hornless Loudspeaker." *Transactions of the American Institute of Electrical Engineers*, 44, 461–75.
10. "Inventor Profile: Philo Taylor Farnsworth." National Inventors Hall of Fame. http://www.invent.org/hall_of_fame/56.html.
11. "The Jazz Singer." *The Greatest Films.* http://www.filmsite.org/jazz.html.
12. "1927: Transoceanic Telephone Service." AT&T. http://www.att.com/attlabs/reputation/timeline/27atlan.html.
13. "Paul Galvin, Motorola." American National Business Hall of Fame. http://www.anbhf.org/laureates/pgalvin.html.
14. Mowery, D. C., and Rosenberg, N. (1998). *Paths of Innovation: Technological Change in 20th Century America.*
15. "History: The 20th Century." Did You Know? http://www.didyouknow.org/history/20thcentury.htm.
16. "Inventors: The History of Kitchen Innovations." About.com. http://inventors.about.com/library/inventors/blkitchen.htm
17. The UK Patent Office. http://www.patent.gov.uk/media/pressrelease/2003/0406.htm.
18. "Historic Figures: John Logie Baird." BBC. http://www.bbc.co.uk/history/historic_figures/baird_logie.shtml.
19. "History." Aerobal. http://www.aerobal.org/12.html.
20. "Sir Alexander Fleming: Biography." The Nobel Foundation. http://nobelprize.org/medicine/laureates/1945/fleming-bio.html.
21. Ernest Rutherford and the Splitting of the Atom. Science Museum. http://www.sciencemuseum.org.uk/on-line/atomicfirsts/page2.asp.
22. "Frederick G. Banting: Biography." The Nobel Foundation. http://nobelprize.org/medicine/laureates/1923/banting-bio.html.
23. "Inventors: Clock and Calendar History." About.com. http://inventors.about.com/library/inventors/blclock.htm#quartz.

Not everyone gained from this process. Productivity gains in one industry could damage another; for example, large economies in the amount of fuel consumed in the generation of electricity severely harmed the coal industry. Old products such as gas lamps, woollen stockings, and horse-drawn carriages were displaced by new ones that were better and cheaper. There was also the danger that new methods of production and labor-saving equipment would reduce the demand for labor, and much was written about the threat of "technological unemployment." As it happened, however, this did not normally become a reality, because lower demand in some sectors was more than offset by increased requirements in those that were expanding. The main causes of unemployment lay elsewhere (see Chapters 6 and 7).

A more detailed list of innovations is shown in table 4.5. Svennilson, writing a half-century ago, was impressed with many industrial processes that led to more efficient production. We have become aware more recently of the many changes in consumption that resulted from innovations of the 1920s. Insulin improved the life chances for many diabetics, while mass-produced adhesive bandages made small cuts more tolerable. Penicillin was discovered at the end of the decade but would not affect the lives of people until after the Second World War. Many other innovations in consumer goods are easily recognizable. That the Thompson submachine gun is on this list reveals the sad fact that not all innovations improve the quality of life; it is possible for specific innovations to make civilized life more difficult.

It is interesting to note that the World Economic Conference held in Geneva in 1927 "unanimously recognized the benefits of rationalisation and scientific management and it asser[ted] the need of greater, more far reaching and better co-ordinated efforts in this field" (League of Nations, 1927, 48). The statement reflects the intellectual climate of the time. On the one hand, it expresses the positivist faith in progress and technology; on the other, it voices the belief—also widespread outside the planned economies—that such progress requires an enlightened "visible hand."

Chapter 5

International Capital
Movements in the 1920s

Our aim in this chapter is to ascertain the part that movements in international capital played in the drama of the 1920s. We investigate the initial role of these capital flows in helping to promote the measure of stability achieved in the mid-1920s, and then their contribution to the detrimental developments that culminated in the crisis of 1931. We begin with an overview of the scale, origins, and destinations of foreign lending during this decade, based on recently compiled estimates that provide a more comprehensive picture than hitherto available. We then consider in more detail the special relevance of the inflow and withdrawal of these external funds to the position of Germany (including their relationship to the amounts paid in reparations) and to the position of the producers of food and other primary products in central and eastern Europe and overseas.

5.1 An Overview of Foreign Investment

Capital Flows in the 1920s

The major sources of international finance and the destinations to which it went in the period 1924–1930 are shown in figure 5.1. In these seven years, the flow of capital from the creditor nations, as measured by their records, amounted to at least $9 billion (equivalent in present-day prices to around $100 billion) and may have been appreciably more than that, perhaps between $10 and $11 billion.[1] Almost 60 percent of this sum came from the United

[1] For a more complete account of the estimates discussed in this chapter, and of the sources from which they are derived, see Feinstein and Watson (1955). They compiled independent estimates from the balance-of-payments records of both the creditors and the debtors. In principle, these should agree; in practice, it was found

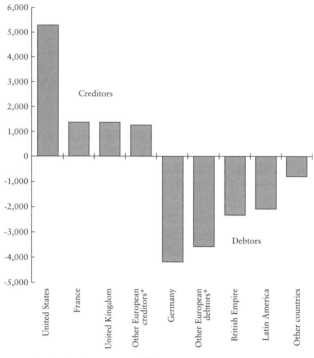

*For list of countries see Table 5.2

Figure 5.1. Sources and destination of international capital flows, 1924–1930.

States; about 15 percent each came from the United Kingdom and France; and the balance, on a much smaller scale, came from the other European creditors: Switzerland, the Netherlands, Czechoslovakia, and Sweden.

About one-third of this massive outflow was invested in Germany, and a further one-fourth was invested in the other European countries. The four British dominions and India together received a little less than one-fifth, as did the countries of Central and South America. Much of this was intended as long-term investment, but changes in bank deposits and other forms of short-term investment also made a significant contribution to the increased indebtedness of the

that the former were consistently lower. Feinstein and Watson argue that there are probably two major reasons for this discrepancy. First, there are errors in the data, including a systematic tendency of the major creditors to overstate their deficits and understate their surpluses. Second, the flight of private capital evaded exchange controls and other restrictions on the free movement of capital in ways that distorted the current-account statistics. Feinstein and Watson suggest a very arbitrary 15 percent as the likely size of the addition required to the estimates, based on the creditors' records.

borrowing countries. Indeed, within Europe, the net addition to the two types of capital were of approximately equal magnitude over the period 1924–1930.

The high point of this international migration of capital occurred in 1928; it then fell off very rapidly, and after 1930, there was no further net investment abroad by the major creditors as a whole. This aggregate movement conceals an apparent difference between the United States, which maintained a small net outflow for three more years, and the major European creditors, all of whom became net importers of capital in 1931. However, the outflow from the United States consisted predominantly of the withdrawal of foreign short-term assets in response to fears that the dollar would depreciate (as it did from April 1933 until the formal devaluation announced by Roosevelt at the end of January 1934); on long-term capital, the United States was also a net recipient.

Interest rates in Europe were appreciably higher than in the United States, and those in Germany were among the highest in Europe. Capital flowed to selected European borrowers on a massive scale once stabilization had been achieved, and the adoption of the Dawes Plan provided at least a temporary settlement of the dispute over reparations. In Europe, as elsewhere in the 1920s, it was the United States that was the dominant creditor, but the United Kingdom and France were also substantial net lenders.

The total inward flow (long- and short-term) to the thirteen principal European borrowing countries amounted to approximately $10 billion in the seven years from 1924 to 1930, with more than $7 billion going to Germany, and the balance going in much smaller sums to a number of other countries, notably Austria, Poland, Greece, and Hungary. At the same time, many of these borrowers were themselves lending to others, and there was an outflow from them amounting to some $3 billion in the case of Germany, and about $750 million for all the other countries.

This movement of American capital to Europe in the 1920s initially contributed to international monetary stability by recycling the funds that flowed out to pay for Europe's current account deficits with the United States. In comparison with the pre-1913 period, Europe's trade balance had deteriorated because of the weakening in her relative industrial competitiveness. The net receipts on invisible account were also greatly reduced. The loss of overseas assets as a result of the war and the Bolshevik revolution eliminated a large part of the prewar inflow of interest and dividends from abroad, while the inter-Allied debts increased the payments that had to be made to the United States. The inflow of foreign capital after stabilization thus helped to preserve the external value of the mark and other currencies. It also helped sustain Europe's commitment to the gold standard.

But the gold standard that had worked so well before World War I would not work nearly so well afterward. The capital flows of the 1920s masked many of the structural changes that had taken place during the war. As we saw in section 3.3, Europe attempted to regain stability in the 1920s by reviving the previous rigid system of international exchange. Capital flows were the lubricant that allowed people to ignore structural changes in the world economy for a few more years.

Long-Term Foreign Investment in 1914 and 1938

On the eve of the First World War, long-term foreign investment in Europe amounted to about $12 billion, a little more than a quarter of the total foreign assets accumulated by the world's creditor nations. Britain's interest in the Continent had declined in the late nineteenth century, as her investors switched their attention to the empire and the developing regions of North and South America. By 1914, Britain's holdings of European securities were little more than $1 billion, only 5 percent of the UK total, and half what it had been forty years earlier. (See table 5.1.)

In sharp contrast to this situation, the other European creditors had allocated some 40 to 50 percent of their much smaller total foreign investment to Europe. France was by far the largest source of foreign capital on the continent, with European holdings amounting by 1914 to some $5.4 billion. Almost $2.5 billion of this was invested in Russia, with loans both to the tsarist government and

Table 5.1 Long-term foreign investment, 1914 and 1938 ($ million to nearest $50 million)

	1914		1938	
	Total investment	Of which in Europe	Total investment	Of which in Europe
Creditors:				
United Kingdom	20,000	1,050	22,900	1,750
France	9,700	5,400	3,850	1,050
Germany	5,800	2,550	700	250
Netherlands	1,200 ⌐		4,800	1,650
Belgium	⌐		1,250	300
	├ 4,300	├ 3,000		
Switzerland	⌐ ⌐		1,600	800
Sweden	⌐		400	350
Italy	├ 1,400		400	100
Other Europe[a]	⌐		650	150
Total Europe	42,400	11,300	36,550	6,400
United States	3,500	700	11,500	2,350
Other countries	200	—	4,750	600
Total	46,100	12,000	52,800	9,350

[a] For 1938 includes $400 million for Portugal, $100 million for Spain, and $150 for Czechoslovakia (all of it in Europe).

Source: Feinstein and Watson (1995).

to joint-stock banks and industrial companies. The total German investment outstanding on the continent in 1914 was about $2.5 billion, with the largest share allocated to Austria-Hungary, and with less than $500 million allocated to Russia. The remaining countries, including Belgium, the Netherlands, Switzerland, and Sweden, had total holdings in Europe of some $3 billion, but there is no information about the countries in which that money was invested. The United States had only ventured into Europe on a modest scale, with assets of some $700 million, almost all in the form of direct investment in manufacturing, oil distribution, and other commercial activities.

World War I and its immediate consequences played havoc with these investments. France and other holders of Russian securities lost their entire capital when the tsarist regime was overthrown. Investments in enemy countries either became worthless or were very severely depreciated. According to one estimate, only a quarter of the nominal value of France's pre-1914 foreign securities in Europe survived to 1919 (Meynial, quoted in Royal Institute of International Affairs, 1937, 131). German losses were even more striking, and by the end of the war, almost nothing remained of Germany's previous holdings of foreign securities. Britain was left with little more than a third of its investments in Europe and was also compelled to sell more than $3 billion of its prewar dollar securities in order to meet wartime obligations for equipment purchased in the United States. In total, the foreign assets lost by the three main European creditors may have exceeded $12 billion, over one-third of the investments they had accumulated abroad over the preceding century (Royal Institute of International Affairs, 1937, 131; United Nations, 1949, 4–5; Woytinski and Woytinski, 1955, 199–200).

While European assets were thus being sharply diminished by these wartime losses and sales, the United States greatly strengthened its economic position. In 1914, long-term private foreign borrowing by the United States exceeded her investments abroad by more than $3 billion. By 1919, the United States emerged from the war with foreign long-term assets of $6.5 billion and liabilities of only $2 billion. America was from then on a substantial net creditor with respect to private long-term capital. The United Kingdom and the Netherlands also showed a small nominal increase, but the transwar changes were dominated by the rise in the long-term external assets of the United States. Despite this, the United Kingdom remained the largest overall creditor, with long-term foreign assets double those of the United States.

Some two decades later, on the eve of the Second World War, the amount invested in Europe was a little more than $9 billion, less than one-fifth of the world total. Of the pre-World War I European creditors, only the United Kingdom showed any advance, even in nominal terms, over the 1914 level. However, Europe remained of limited interest to British investors. As in the pre-1914 period, the greater part of the long-term capital outflow from the United Kingdom was directed to the dominions and India. United States capital in Europe had increased to more than $2.5 billion by 1938, outstripping investments of about $1.7 billion each for the United Kingdom and the Netherlands. The principal European borrowers from the United States were Germany, the United Kingdom, Poland, and Italy.

The 1938 figures in table 5.1 provide a useful record of the level of foreign investment as it stood at the end of the period. However, the net change between the two benchmarks actually conceals some of the most crucial features of the capital flows in the interwar period. First, it relates only to long-term investment. In 1914, short-term liabilities (and corresponding assets) were small, even for the United Kingdom, and were closely related to the financing of trading activities and to London's central position as banker for much of the world. During the interwar period, the extent and character of these short-term investments changed enormously: they grew very much larger and became far more volatile. The changes indicated by table 5.1 omit all record of these developments and thus give no indication of the violent fluctuations in short-term capital that occurred during the interwar years.

Second, the character of the capital flows, both short-term and long-term, differed markedly between the 1920s and the 1930s, with radical changes in their origin, direction, motivation, and effect. Estimates of the stock of capital at the beginning and end of the period are thus a very inadequate basis for a full appreciation of the nature and causes of international capital movements in the intervening years.

5.2 European Lending and Borrowing

Relevant balance-of-payments statistics for the individual European borrowers and lenders for the periods 1924–1930 and 1931–1937 are summarized in the first and second columns of table 5.2.

In the first period, the records of the debtors show an immense net inflow of some $7.8 billion, an average rate of more than $1.0 billion per annum—though, as noted above (see footnote 1), the true figures might be roughly 15 percent lower than this. The movement of capital was dominated by foreign lending to Germany, which received more than $4 billion, which was more than 50 percent of the gross flow to Europe. Most of this capital came from the United States, and for a while it seemed that there was no limit to the appetite of American issuing houses and their investors for German bonds—regardless of the purposes for which the loans were raised—or for the interest to be earned from placing money on short-term deposit with German banks. The next-largest destinations, a long way behind, were Austria and Italy, which together obtained about $1.5 billion. Roughly $1.3 billion was invested in eastern Europe, especially Romania, Poland, and Hungary. These were quite large sums relative to these countries' national economies, giving foreign capital a significant role in their interwar economic and political history.

Table 5.2 Balances on current account, gold, and foreign currency, European creditors and debtors, 1924–1930 and 1931–1937 ($ million to nearest 10 million)

	1924–1930	1931–1937	1924–37
Europe: Creditors			
United Kingdom	1,300	–4,000	–2,700
France[a]	1,340	–690	650
Netherlands	380	–290	90
Switzerland	370	–340	30
Czechoslovakia	250	90	340
Sweden	180	–20	160
Total	3,820	–5,250	–1,430
Europe: Debtors			
Germany	–4,190	1,010	–3,180
France[a]	—	2,190	2,190
Austria	–860	–150	–1,010
Italy	–710	–50	–760
Romania	–440	–110	–550
Poland	–400	70	–330
Hungary	–320	20	–300
Greece	–310	–120	–430
Belgium	–240	230	–10
Norway	–140	0	–140
Yugoslavia	–80	–50	–130
Bulgaria	–50	20	–30
Finland	–40	150	110
Denmark	–40	60	20
Estonia, Latvia, and Lithuania	0	40	40
Ireland	30	–130	–100
Total	–7,790	3,180	–4,610
Total Europe	–3,970	–2,070	–6,040

(+) = net capital export, (–) = net capital import
[a] France is included with the creditors for 1924–1932 and with the debtors for 1933–1937; the estimates cover the French overseas territories, except Indochina for 1924–1930.

Source: Feinstein and Watson (1995).

On the other side, the payments accounts of the principal European creditors show a capital export of $3.8 billion, with France and the United Kingdom each contributing approximately $1.3 billion and the Netherlands and Switzerland each a little less than $400 million. As in the nineteenth century, Europe was a relatively unimportant outlet for British investors, most of whose funds were still directed to the empire and South America. Europe accounted for a larger share of the foreign lending by France and other European creditors. Taking the figures as they stand, there appears to have been a net inward flow for Europe as a whole during these seven years of about $4 billion; but, as suggested earlier, it is likely that the estimates are subject to a bias tending to understate the outflow from the creditors and overstate the inflow to the debtors, so that the actual net import of capital to Europe from the United States was probably considerably lower than this.

For Germany, the peak year for the inflow of capital was 1928, when it reached $1 billion; capital inflow then dropped very sharply. Wall Street stock prices, which had started to climb in 1927, were surging upward in 1928, luring more American investors away from foreign lending, in hopes of making a quick fortune at home. Also, there were growing doubts in the United States about the rapid expansion of Germany's external obligations and the unproductive purposes for which some of the foreign capital had been raised— doubts partly stimulated from within Germany by those concerned about the increase in the country's indebtedness. From 1930, with the accession of Brüning, the adoption of deflationary policies intensified the economic depression, and after the success of the National Socialists in the general elections in September of that year, the sense of impending political crisis was a major deterrent to further foreign investment.

For the other European debtors, the peak came a year earlier, when Austria, Italy, Poland, and Yugoslavia all raised large sums in the United States. Sizable new bond issues were still possible for a few countries in 1928, including Denmark, Norway, and Italy in New York, and Greece and Hungary in London, but the boom was over, and new lending fell away very rapidly during the following years. Economic conditions in many areas were already deteriorating, particularly in the agricultural regions of central and eastern Europe. A sharp decline in prices of wheat, sugar, and other farm products drove down export revenues and drastically weakened the ability of these countries to service their foreign debts. For the European debtors as a whole, the capital inflow dropped from about $1.7 billion in 1927 and 1928 to $1 billion in 1929, and less than half that a year later.

A Classification of European Borrowing in the 1920s

Examination of alternative data sources provides a useful supplement to the story told by the balance-of-payments data. The alternative data cover separate categories of foreign investment in either direction: new issues of long-term shares and bonds for foreign borrowers, purchases and sales of existing securities and real property, amortization and repayment of debts, direct investment, and changes in short-term international indebtedness. There are serious gaps in these data that make it impossible to cover all items as fully or as accurately as would be desirable, but they provide more details about some items. (See table 5.3.)

Table 5.3 Comparison of the balance on current account, gold, and foreign currency, with direct estimates of capital transactions, European debtors, 1924–1930 ($ million to nearest $10 million)

	Germany	Other European debtors[a]	Total
Balance of payments			
1. Current account balance	–3,620	–2,810	–6,430
2. Gold and foreign currency	–570	–790	–1,360
3. *Total Capital Movement*	–4,190	–3,600	–7,790
Capital transactions			
Long-term capital			
4a. New bond issues abroad			
Central and provincial governments	470	1,030	1,500
Municipalities	160	210	370
Corporations	980	550	1,530
Total	1,610	1,790	3,400
4b. New share issues abroad	90	240	330
5. *Less:* Repayments of debt	–260	–530	–790
6. Direct inward investment	120	200	320
7. Foreign purchases of domestic securities and real property	1,350	0	1,350
8. Other capital inflows	30	420	450
9. *Less:* Investment abroad by debtors	–1,050	–150	–1,200
Net long-term capital movement	1,890	1,970	3,860
Short-term capital			
10. Increase in assets	–1,050	n.a.	n.a.
11. Increase in liabilities	3,450	n.a.	n.a.
Net short-term capital movement	2,400	1,150	3,550
12. *Total Capital Movement*	4,290	3,120	7,410
Errors and omissions	–100	480	380

Balance of payments: (–) = Deficit or increase in assets = net capital import

Capital transactions: (+) = Decrease in assets/increase in liabilities; (–) = increase in assets/decrease in liabilities

Note: Rows 4–6 cover the import of capital from the six main creditors; row 8 covers all forms of capital import from other countries, e.g., by Austria from Germany (offset by the increase in Germany's assets in row 9) or by Romania from Czechoslovakia.

[a] See table 5.2 for list of countries.

Source: Feinstein and Watson (1995).

Estimates on this alternate basis were compiled for each of the seventeen European debtors for the period of massive inward capital flow from 1924 to 1930. The results are given in the first column of table 5.3 for Germany and in the second column for the other European debtors as a group. Total capital movement as measured by balance-of-payments data is given in row 3, and as measured by capital transactions in row 12. The difference is shown in the final row as errors and omissions. The remarkably small size of this residual must be partly the fortuitous outcome of compensating errors in various components of the two estimates, and, in the second column, in the estimates for the different countries. It is nevertheless an encouraging result, suggesting that the overall results are broadly reliable despite the numerous uncertainties in the two sets of figures.

Row 4a shows that almost $3.5 billion of new long-term financing was obtained by European debtors from external bond issues in the capital markets of the major creditors. The lion's share of this money, 58 percent, came from the United States; the United Kingdom provided 18 percent, the Netherlands 9 percent, Sweden 7 percent, and Switzerland and Sweden 4 percent each.

This classification of the origins of long-term bond finance must, however, be qualified by the observation that it is possible to identify only the immediate source of the funds, not the ultimate source. Thus, if a loan was issued in Switzerland but the shares were mainly purchased by French or German investors, our statistics would still show this as capital from Switzerland. For Germany, about 40 percent of these loans were floated for governments and municipalities, and 60 percent were loaned to private corporations. In the other countries, corporate borrowing was responsible for only 30 percent of loans issued, and most of the loans were made by central and local governments.

Investment in Germany by countries other than the six major creditors (for example, loans from Belgium or Italy) and in other European countries by Germany and Czechoslovakia are shown in row 8. The $450 million we have allowed for the estimated inflow under this heading is very uncertain. The entry relating to long-term capital in row 9 covers the estimated outward movement of capital from these debtors, for example, investment elsewhere in Europe by Germany and in Africa by Belgium or Italy. (Foreign lending by Germany is offset by row 8 to the extent that it was a movement of capital to the other European debtors.)

The enormous sums involved in short-term capital movements over this period are indicated in rows 10 and 11. There was a substantial outflow as banks and other concerns in the creditor countries built up their private external holdings of floating assets. In the case of Germany, this amounted to more than $1 billion. This increase in net short-term finance was significantly more important for Germany than the supply of long-term capital, accounting for about 55 percent of the total inflow in 1924–1930. For the other countries, the proportion was rather smaller, but short-term capital still made up about 37 percent of the total inflow.

5.3 Reparations and Capital Flows to Germany

The huge sums that poured into Germany were frequently portrayed by German politicians and financiers as the inward transfer necessary to permit the payment of reparations. In reality, however, reparations amounted at most to one-third of the gross receipts from abroad. In the period 1924–1930, the total amount paid in reparations amounted to approximately $2.4 billion (about 2.3 percent of Germany's aggregate national income over these years), whereas the gross inflow of capital during the same period amounted to approximately $7,000 million, or 6.6 percent of national income (Schuker, 1988).

As long as United States bankers and investors remained eager to invest their capital in Germany, the much-debated transfer problem created by the demand for payment of reparations to the Allies was effectively solved. There were, of course, expressions of concern both within Germany and outside it that at a later date these loans would have to be repaid, and Germany would then face an impossible double burden. But the hunger for external capital was too powerful to be stemmed by such remote considerations.

A number of recent American studies have developed the theme originally stated by Mantoux (1946) in criticism of the campaign fought at the time by Keynes (1919). They have argued that the domestic burden involved in raising the necessary sums through taxation was also considerably exaggerated, and that after the downward adjustment made under the Dawes Plan—and perhaps even before it—the reparations amounts were well within Germany's capacity to pay.

However, this analysis does not allow sufficiently for the fact that it was envisaged at the time that payments would be progressively raised as the German economy expanded, or for the extreme reluctance of Germans to accept even a modest increase in taxation to meet what was universally regarded as an unjustified and oppressive imposition by hostile antagonists. Thus, even if the economic aspects of the problem were not as crippling as had been assumed in the 1920s, the exaction of reparations was still of deep political and psychological significance for Germany. The issue thus remained a paramount cause of instability and a barrier to international economic cooperation.

The figures quoted above show that the average annual capital flow to Germany net of reparations was equivalent to more than 4 percent of Germany's national income. Given the low level of domestic savings, the willingness of foreigners to fund German capital expenditure enabled the country to live well beyond its means. There were several reasons for the acute shortage of domestic capital. The years of war and hyperinflation had wiped out virtually all liquid capital, including most of the reserves of the banking system, and fear of inflation remained a deeply inhibiting factor, even after stability was restored. There was also considerable misallocation of available funds to unprofitable industries, including agriculture, and to social amenities that were desirable but that produced no revenue.

Foreign capital thus permitted a higher level of investment and consumption in Germany than domestic resources would have supported. It enabled central and local governments to spend more and tax less, it caused the supply of imported goods to be greater than it would otherwise have been, and it allowed the Reichsbank to add substantially to its reserves of gold and foreign exchange.

The liquidity of the banking system was also greatly improved by the funds received from abroad, although the banks were following a risky strategy to the extent that they relied on short-term deposits to make long-term loans. The massive foreign borrowing contributed to Germany's industrial rationalization and revival, notably in the coal, iron and steel, electrical, and chemical industries. However, only about 60 percent of the long-term foreign capital issued in Germany in 1924–1930 was taken by private enterprises; the remainder went to various public and semipublic bodies, such as local governments. This enabled the local bodies to make substantial investments in public utilities, urban transport, housing, and social, cultural, and sporting facilities.

This position was stable only for as long as the necessary imports of funds could be maintained. The underlying problems and social conflicts within Germany meant that the economy was extremely vulnerable to any change in the preferences of American investors. The flow of long-term capital from abroad fell sharply in the first half of 1927, following a bitter attack on foreign borrowing by the Reichsbank president, Dr. Schacht, and the withdrawal of the tax concessions previously enjoyed by foreign subscribers to German bonds. This subjected the economy to great pressures, and after a decline in gold reserves, the tax exemption was reinstated and the bond flotations quickly revived. They reached a peak in the second quarter of 1928, then fell abruptly and virtually ceased by the spring of 1929. The flow of capital from abroad recovered in 1930, but in 1931 the situation was transformed, and there was actually a net outflow of more than $600 million.

Several factors contributed to America's unwillingness to continue sending capital to Europe on the scale of earlier years. Internally, the tightening of monetary policy by the Federal Reserve raised interest rates sharply, thus weakening the incentive to lend abroad. With the stock-exchange indices soaring upward through 1927 and 1928, there was further strong encouragement to keep funds at home in the hope of more substantial gains from speculation on Wall Street. On the external side, there was sharply growing concern about the rising total of Germany's foreign liabilities and her ability to continue to meet the obligations these imposed.

Did the End of the Capital Inflow Cause the German Slump?

In the late 1920s, Germany went into a slump of unparalleled severity. Between 1929 and 1932, real domestic production fell by 16 percent, industrial production fell by more than 40 percent, and the value of exports fell by almost 60 percent. Unemployment raced from 1.3 million in 1927 (less than 4 percent of the labor force) to 5.6 million in 1932 (more than 17 percent). The sudden contraction of capital imports from the United States has often been cited as the critical factor that precipitated this catastrophe (Lewis, 1949; Falkus, 1975; Sommariva and Tullio, 1987). However, other scholars have argued strongly that the source of Germany's economic troubles was primarily domestic in origin (Temin, 1971; Balderston, 1983; McNeil, 1986).

The domestic-origin account is supported by the fact that nominal short-term interest rates were stable through the second half of 1928, fell in the first quarter of 1929, and only moved up in the second quarter. If the external-origin view of the depression was correct, it might have been expected that nominal short-term interest rates would have risen sharply as soon as the foreign inflow was cut off; but the observed pattern is easily explained if the German economy was already moving into recession before the import of capital from the United States dried up.

German industrial production recovered strongly in 1927 after the depression of 1925–1926, but then industrial production showed virtually no further growth in 1928 or 1929. Similarly, unemployment dropped to 1,600,000 in the six winter months October 1927 to March 1928, and then increased sharply to 2,400,00 in the corresponding period of 1928–1929. The same pattern is evident in the investment data. Gross fixed investment at current prices in the public sector (government and railways) expanded until 1927, and in other sectors the rise continued for a further year, though even at its peak in 1928 the investment ratio was low by comparison with the prewar period. Moreover, information on investment intentions shows that both nonresidential building permits and new domestic orders for machinery had already turned down in late 1927 or early 1928, well before the cessation of foreign lending.

Balderston (1983) attributes the low level and early decline of foreign investment primarily to an acute and persistent shortage of domestic capital, claiming that this provides a "thoroughly endogenous explanation" for the decline in fixed investment. Borchardt (1979) also finds a domestic explanation for Germany's great depression, but as noted in section 4.2, he argues that the root of the trouble was an excessive increase in wages relative to the growth of productivity. The sociopolitical distributional conflicts that emerged in the aftermath of the Great War are the focus of his analysis.

Although the virtual cessation of capital imports from the United States and the subsequent net outflow did not initiate the depression, it undoubtedly added greatly to the problems facing German policy makers and contributed to the adoption of measures that exacerbated the initial decline in activity. In principle, their options were either to abandon the gold standard, boosting activity by allowing the mark to depreciate, or to follow orthodox policies of retrenchment, reducing imports and expanding exports by deflating the economy.

From late 1929, long-term American capital was no longer available to sustain German budget deficits. German investors—with the experience of

1922–1923 still deeply etched in their memories—displayed great reluctance to purchase long-term government bonds. The government and the Reichsbank were thus inexorably driven to resort to short-term borrowing. The more the short-term debt increased, the greater the perceived threat to stability, and the more energetic the efforts of domestic and foreign asset-holders to withdraw their capital from Germany. The deterioration in the political situation provoked by the steadily deepening depression and the opposition to tax increases gave added grounds for distrust of the currency.

The first of a succession of waves of capital flight occurred in the spring of 1929. There were further massive losses of gold and foreign exchange in late 1930 and on an even bigger scale in 1931. The authorities were thus forced to adopt restrictive policies at precisely the point when the economy was in urgent need of counter-cyclical measures to stimulate revival. Short-term interest rates were raised in the second quarter of 1929, and the federal government, cities, and states initiated a succession of increasingly desperate efforts to raise revenues and restrict spending. From the end of 1930 and through 1931, Brüning introduced a succession of austerity decrees imposing progressively harsher increases in direct and indirect taxation accompanied by reductions in civil-service pay and in state welfare benefits. The descent was cumulative and catastrophic.

5.4 Capital Flows to Central and Eastern Europe and to Overseas Primary Producers

Elsewhere in central and eastern Europe, the end of the foreign lending boom was an even more significant factor helping initiate the depression and contributing to its severity. Unlike Germany, most of these countries—Czechoslovakia was the exception—relied primarily on exports of agricultural products for their foreign revenues, and they were in trouble as soon as export prices began to tumble. They had borrowed heavily during the 1920s, frequently in the form of loans at fixed interest, and even when the funds had been productively invested (by no means always the case), they found themselves unable to service their debts from the rapidly diminishing proceeds of their exports. Thereafter, they could only meet their external obligations for as long as they could continue to attract fresh capital. After 1929, when the inflow of foreign capital ceased, the combined pressures proved intolerable, and painful adjustment was inescapable.

Hungary was more deeply affected than the other agrarian producers in this region, and this country provides a good illustration of the difficulties the region confronted. Together with Poland, Hungary had been the largest of the east European borrowers in the mid-1920s, and by the end of 1930 had an accumulated external debt of some $700 million, a great part of which had gone to unproductive expenditure. The export revenues on which Hungary depended to service these debts came overwhelmingly from agricultural products, particularly wheat and corn. As the prices for these products plunged, export proceeds went down with them; by 1931, their value was barely half the 1929 level, and by 1932, it had fallen to less than one-third the 1929 level.

The resulting balance-of-payments problem was insuperable. In a period of some ten weeks from the beginning of May 1931, the central bank was compelled to pay out more in gold and foreign exchange than it had possessed in April, a drain only made possible because rescue credits of $50 million were obtained from abroad. With bankruptcy threatening, urgent measures were required.

By mid-1931, Poland, Romania, Yugoslavia, and Bulgaria were in a similarly untenable position. Yet all five countries were inhibited by fear of inflation from following the example of other primary producers such as Australia and Argentina and depreciating their currencies. The deep prevailing fear of inflation in the minds of both politicians and the public is well indicated in the comment of a contemporary Polish economist, Edward Lipinski (quoted by Nötel, 1986, 228): "After this [repeated] collapse [of the Polish currency] its preservation became a sacrosanct principle of popular belief . . . . It was duly realized that any devaluation could easily lead to panic, price manipulation, ruin of saving institutions, and a further sharpening of the crisis . . . . Stability of the currency thus was turned into a popular myth." Deprived of this solution, countries turned increasingly to moratoria, rigorous exchange controls, and commercial policy restrictions.

The Role of the Agricultural Crisis in the Great Depression

The problems that beset the agrarian producers emerged early in the cycle of events culminating in the Great Depression, and they were particularly severe in the case of the two agricultural crops grown in central and eastern Europe, wheat and sugar (see section 4.3 for a detailed account). By 1925, it was impossible to find markets for the products coming both from the restoration of output in Europe and from the recently expanded producers in North and South America. It thus seems clear that a strong case can be made for the overproduction of agricultural foodstuffs and for a downturn well before the break in activity in the industrial countries. For cotton, rubber, tin, and other industrial raw materials, however, as argued by Fleisig (1972), the causal sequence ran from the decline in industrial activity to the fall in prices.

If all economic adjustments took place automatically and without friction, this fall in agricultural prices would hardly matter from the standpoint of global economic stability. Any fall in the incomes of the producers of wheat would be offset by the rise in (real) incomes of the consumers of bread, and there would be no net effect on aggregate world demand. Unfortunately, this is not what happens in practice. The primary producing countries were forced to respond immediately to the deterioration in their international-payments position by contracting activity and cutting their imports. By contrast, the consuming nations were slow to appreciate the improvement in their purchasing power and were under no urgent pressure to expand their activity.

The loss of income to the food-growing countries and the cessation of foreign lending had substantial adverse consequences for others as well as for themselves. In the sphere of trade, the decline in export revenues for food-growing countries undermined their ability to purchase manufactured goods from abroad, significantly reducing the exports of their customary suppliers, especially Britain. In the financial sphere, many of them were forced to devalue their currencies in 1929 and 1930, thus precipitating the period of instability on the foreign exchanges. Others turned to tariffs, exchange controls, and bilateral trading agreements, contributing to the contraction in world trade. Countries with strong links to sterling—both those within the British Empire, such as Australia and New Zealand, and those in Latin America, such as Argentina and Brazil—had traditionally kept their surplus balances in London; but now that they were in difficulty, they were forced to run down these balances, thus adding to the pressures on United Kingdom reserves.

Chapter 6

The Onset of the
Great Depression

From the late 1920s, the descent into the depression gathered pace in Europe and in much of the rest of the world. Bankers, politicians, industrialists, farmers—all were seemingly helpless in the face of successive currency and banking crises, growing stocks of unsold food, falling prices, collapsing export markets, abandoned factories, and ever-lengthening queues of men and women waiting desperately for work or for relief payments. In this chapter we first outline the general course of the depression as reflected in the contraction of both output and international trade. We then trace the movement into the crisis as it developed in Austria and Germany and spread to other parts of central and eastern Europe, to Britain, to the United States, and to the primary producing countries; and we examine the breakdown of the gold standard in the course of this process. We also look at the position of the banks in countries where the crisis was less severe than in Austria and Germany.

In the concluding part of the chapter, we analyze the critical factor that eventually brought the slump to an end: the abandonment of the gold standard, accompanied by a strong and public declaration of the change.—We examine the working out of this change in the policy regimes in Britain and the United States, and we consider whether a similar policy could have been adopted in Germany, thus forestalling the change in regime that Hitler introduced in 1933, with all its attendant costs for Germany and for the world.

6.1 The Course of the Crisis

A broad overview of some of the principal features of the world depression and of the magnitude of the crisis is given in tables 6.1 and 6.2. As table 6.1 shows, the collapse of international trade was extraordinarily swift and steep. The imposition of deflationary policies in pursuit of financial orthodoxy in the leading gold-standard countries forced world trade into a vicious

Table 6.1 World trade, 1929–1932 (index numbers, 1929 = 100)

	1929	1930	1931	1932
1. Value at current prices[a]	100	80	57	39
2. Export volume	100	93	85	74
3. Export price	100	86	67	52

[a] Index of the value of exports by seventy-five countries measured in pre-devaluation U.S. gold dollars.

Source: League of Nations (1939a), 8.

Table 6.2 World production and prices, 1929–1932 (index numbers, 1929 = 100)

	1929	1930	1931	1932
1. Industrial production				
a. World[a]	100	87	75	64
b. Europe[a]	100	92	81	72
c. North America	100	81	68	54
2. Primary production—food				
a. World	100	102	100	100
b. Europe[a]	100	99	102	104
c. North America	100	102	103	100
3. Primary production—raw materials				
a. World	100	94	85	75
b. Europe[a]	100	90	82	73
c. North America	100	90	80	64
4. World prices				
a. Food	100	84	66	50
b. Raw materials	100	82	59	44
c. Manufactures	100	94	78	63

[a] Excluding the Soviet Union.

Source: Rows 1–3: League of Nations (1939b), 423–24. Row 4: League of Nations (1939a), 61.

downward spiral. The problem was exacerbated by growing resort to tariffs and exchange controls, and by the impoverishment of food producers resulting from the downward slide in agricultural prices (as discussed in sections 4.3 and 5.4).

As restrictive monetary policies reduced output, causing exports to contract, producers of manufactured goods naturally cut back their purchases of coal, cotton, metal ores, and other industrial raw materials. The primary-producing countries were in turn forced to react to this deterioration in their exports by further restrictions on their imports of manufactured goods. The depression rapidly embraced both the advanced industrial countries and the producers of food and raw materials. Falling prices interacted with falling quantities, with catastrophic results (Bernanke, 1995).

As can be seen in the first row of table 6.1, the value of world trade fell by 20 percent in 1930, by a further 29 per cent in 1931, and by 32 percent in 1932. At the end of this staggering collapse, the volume of goods traded (row 2) had fallen by a quarter, and their price (row 3) had fallen by half, reducing the gold value of international trade to barely 40 percent of what it had been three years earlier. The international economy was suffering the most severe contraction of demand it had ever known.

The movements in the output of industrial and primary products are shown in the first three panels of table 6.2. These series all measure the quantities produced. Falling prices are shown in the final panel. In the world as a whole (row 1a), output plummeted in three years to less than two-thirds of the 1929 level. The descent was slightly less severe in Europe but more catastrophic in North America. The volume of food produced (row 2) was not affected and remained broadly stable during this period; but as noted above, the output of industrial raw materials (row 3) inevitably fell as industrial production declined, and again the reduction was worse in North America than in Europe.

The remarkable fall in world prices of all products is measured in row 4 of table 6.2, with prices of primary products dropping most steeply. By 1932, prices of industrial raw materials had collapsed to only 44 percent of their 1929 levels, foodstuffs to 50 percent, and manufactures to 63 percent. By implication, a unit of raw materials exported in 1932 bought only 70 percent of the industrial products it had fetched in 1929. Primary-goods-producing countries were therefore severely affected.

As is immediately apparent from table 6.3, no European country escaped the contraction in output and in world trade and prices between 1929 and 1932. The fall in industrial production in 1932 relative to 1929 is given in the first column, and the corresponding fall in the value of exports is given in the second column. In general, 1932 was the trough year for output, but in many countries the value of exports continued to drop for two or three more years. For eleven of the nineteen countries listed in the second column of table 6.3, including the United Kingdom and France, the value of exports plunged by more than 60 percent between 1929 and 1932. In six others, including Germany, Italy, Belgium, and the Netherlands, the decline was only slightly less severe, with exports falling by 1932 to well below half their 1929 values. For the continent as a whole, the value of its exports was reduced from $15.6 billion in 1929 to $6.3 billion in 1932. Every country was thus subject to a massive decline in demand.

The contraction of industrial production in individual European countries between 1929 and 1932 can be seen in the first column of table 6.3,

Table 6.3 The collapse of European industrial production and exports from 1929 to 1932 (1929 = 100)

	Industrial production	Value of exports[a]
Poland	58	38
Germany	61	45
Austria	62	32
Belgium	63	47
France	74	39
Czechoslovakia	75	36
Yugoslavia	76	35
Finland	84	44 (72)
Netherlands	84	42
Hungary	86	32
Italy	86	44
Romania	88	58
Spain	88	35
Sweden	89	36 (52)
United Kingdom	89	36 (50)
Denmark	90	47 (67)
Norway	94	51 (75)
Greece	101	39
Switzerland	—	38
Total Europe	72	40

[a] Values measured in old U.S. gold dollars; the higher values in national currencies are shown in parentheses for those countries that had devalued by 1932. Devaluation reduced the foreign-exchange proceeds of a given quantity of exports but made the exports more competitive in foreign prices and so increased the volume of sales.

Source: For industrial production figures (excepting Yugoslavia), Maddison (1995), 194–204, 249. Yugoslavia: Kaser (1985), 573. For export-value figures, League of Nations (1937), 53.

where the countries are listed according to the severity of the depression. In the four countries that were most badly affected—Poland, Germany, Austria, and Belgium—industrial output plunged almost 40 percent in three years. In France, the decline was delayed until 1931 but was then equally precipitous: 26 percent in two years. Industrial production fell almost as steeply in Czechoslovakia and Yugoslavia. The Czechoslovakian case was unusual in that industrial production continued to fall in 1933, finally coming to a halt at 59 percent of the previous peak. Elsewhere in Europe, the fall in industrial activity was more moderate, but in the majority of countries industrial production still fell between 10 and 20 percent. Of the eighteen countries covered in table 6.3, there is only one, Greece, in which output in 1932 was above the 1929 level, and then by only 1 percent.

The decline in industrial output, in primary product prices and in world trade drove unemployment to unprecedented heights, and we will devote the whole of Chapter 7 to a discussion of this aspect of the economic tragedy, which entailed major social costs and in some cases bore significant political consequences. We turn first to closer examination of the ways in which the gathering crisis affected currencies and banking systems, and of the reactions of governments and central bankers as the world economy made its final descent into the abyss.

6.2 The U.S. Banking Crisis of 1930

The United States had the longest banking crisis in the world, starting in late 1930 and lasting until early 1933. Banking crises were confined to countries on the gold standard in the 1930s (Grossman, 1994). Most of the crises, however, were short, typically occurring near the time when the gold standard was abandoned. In the United States, the final stage of the banking crisis preceded the abandonment of the gold standard by six weeks.

The crisis began when the Bank of United States, a New York bank with a grandiose name, failed in December 1930. A southern bank, Caldwell and Company, also failed, but it was small by comparison. The Bank of United States had expanded recklessly in the late 1920s, making many investments in New York real estate. As the depression reduced the prices of these buildings, the bank was in increasing trouble. Friedman and Schwartz (1963) labeled the failures in late 1930 as a banking crisis, but the rise in failures was largely composed of the failure of these two banks. There was no evidence of the credit stringency and high interest rates that normally accompany a banking crisis (Temin, 1989; Wicker, 1996).

At around this same time, Americans began to shift their money holdings from bank deposits to cash. Because banks expand the money supply by creating deposits, this change in preferences decreased the supply of money. The shift in preferences started slowly and continued for the next two years. While it must have been caused by fears for bank solvency, there is no evidence that the bank failures of late 1930 initiated the decline in the money stock. Only after the United Kingdom abandoned the gold standard in September 1931 did enough banks fail to accelerate the fall in the money stock (Temin, 1989).

Bernanke (1983) argued that bank failures had another effect on economic activity, one that added to the effects of a falling money supply. He noted that banks are credit intermediaries, bringing potential lenders and borrowers together by pooling assets and eliminating the need for individual borrowers and lenders to meet and evaluate each other. As banks failed, remaining banks could not fulfill this function as well as before, both because there were fewer banks and because people were suspicious of them. In Bernanke's terms, bank failures raised the "cost of credit intermediation." In the terms of modern macroeconomics, a fall in the stock of money is a demand shock, while a rise in the cost of credit intermediation is a supply shock.

American banks continued to fail through 1931 and 1932, with a peak in the failure rate in the fall of 1931. Weak banks failed continuously, apparently without infecting neighboring banks; the fragmented American banking structure was unable to weather the strains of the depression as the British and Canadian banks did. The banking problems in Germany came all at once and were offset by government action; only in America did a steady stream of bank failures lead customers to withdraw their funds, raise the cost of credit intermediation, and decrease the stock of money (Temin, 1976; Wicker, 1996; Calomiris and Mason, 2003).

6.3 The Currency Crises in Austria and Germany

In 1929, the United States ceased to supply capital for Europe on its previous lavish scale, and from 1931 was actually a net recipient of long-term capital. The only other country in a strong financial position was France, which attracted ever-larger quantities of gold and foreign exchange. Both the American and the French authorities refused to take any steps to relieve the mounting crisis of confidence and liquidity in the rest of the world. National currencies and banking systems were drawn inexorably into the gathering storm.

The crisis that ultimately undermined the currencies of central Europe began in Vienna in 1929 with the failure of the Bodencreditanstalt, the second-largest Austrian bank. Under pressure from the government, the Rothschilds' Creditanstalt agreed to a merger, but the rescuing bank was itself in a very weak position, and the enlarged institution could not provide a long-term solution. The Creditanstalt, Austria's largest bank, had unwisely operated during the 1920s as if the Habsburg empire had not been broken up. In fact, the Viennese banks had been cut off from a good share of their original industrial base, especially in Czechoslovakia. There was never a sound basis for their business in the 1920s, and their heavy commitment to unprofitable industries meant that failures and losses were inevitable.

In May 1931, after an auditor's report revealed its true position, the Creditanstalt went under and was forced to reorganize with the help of international credit and a partial standstill agreement with its foreign creditors. This collapse set off a run on the bank that spread to the Austrian schilling. The government quickly ran through its foreign-exchange reserves in a vain attempt to adhere to the gold standard and only belatedly imposed foreign-exchange controls.

While the Austrian crisis was the first in 1931, it did not cause the subsequent German crisis and those that followed from it. The German crisis of July 1931 was due to exclusively German causes (see section 5.3). The German crisis was a twin crisis, similar in some ways to the Asian crises of 1997 (Schnabel, 2004). Both the German banks and the German mark collapsed in the summer of 1931, eventually setting off runs on the British pound and the American dollar. The traditional view of the German crisis was taken from the preceding Austrian crisis: banking problems caused by overextended lending brought down the currency. More recent work, however, suggests that the budgetary problems of the Weimar Republic brought down the currency and with it the banks (Ferguson and Temin, 2003). If banking problems initiated the crisis, then bankers are to blame; if the currency was key, politicians are the villains. A small detail can determine a whole view of the Great Depression.

The Weimar budget was severely out of balance by 1931. Tax revenues had fallen, and unemployment expenses had risen. It proved impossible to agree on a budget, and Chancellor Brüning governed by decree. Loans from the United States and France covered the deficit in early 1931, but Brüning then championed a customs union with Austria and cast doubt on his commitment to pay reparations. His statements exacerbated tensions left over from the First World War and dried up loans to Germany. Gold reserves at the Reichsbank and deposits at the large German banks held up until Brüning's statement on reparations in early June, after which they quickly fell apart.

Banks appealed to the Reichsbank for help, particularly the Danat Bank, which was heavily invested in a major failed firm. But the Reichsbank ran out of assets with which to monetize the banks' reserves as its gold reserves shrank. Despite some credits from other central banks, the Reichsbank had fallen below its statutory requirement of 40 percent reserves by the beginning of July, and it was unable to borrow more. The Reichsbank could no longer purchase the Berlin banks' bills by mid-July.

The Reichsbank tried to replenish its reserves with an international loan, but Brüning's attempts to shore up his domestic support had choked off international capital flows, as shown in table 5.2. The French offer of help came with political strings that were unacceptable to the Germans, while the Americans pulled in the opposite direction to isolate the German banking crisis from any long-run considerations. The absence of international cooperation was all too evident; no international loan was forthcoming. There was no hegemonic lender of last resort.

Germany abandoned the gold standard in July and August 1931. A series of decrees and negotiations preserved the value of the mark but eliminated the free flow of both gold and marks. In one of the great ironies of history, Chancellor Brüning did not take advantage of this independence of international constraints by expanding. He continued to contract as if Germany were still on the gold standard. Brüning's actions at this time are vivid testimony to the power of ideology: leaders like Brüning felt compelled to cling to orthodoxy even as the world economy collapsed. He continued to advocate gold-standard policies after abandoning the gold standard itself. He ruined the

German economy—and destroyed German democracy—in the effort to show once and for all that Germany could not pay reparations.

As a consequence of the German moratorium, the withdrawal of foreign deposits was prohibited, and huge sums in foreign short-term credits were frozen. As other countries came to understand that they would be unable to realize these assets, they in turn were compelled to restrict withdrawals of their credits. Many other European countries suffered bank runs and currency crises in July, with especially severe crises in Hungary, where the banks were closely tied to those in Austria, and in Romania. As a result of the extensive foreign withdrawals from the Budapest banks, it was again necessary to impose a partial moratorium on external obligations and to declare a three-days "bank holiday."

In the same month, a leading Swiss bank had to be rescued by a takeover. In contrast, French banks were generally in a strong position by the end of the twenties, and they largely avoided the crisis of 1929–1931, with only mild failures in 1930–1931. The British commercial banks were also largely unscathed, finding strength in their branch structure and security in their traditionally cautious policy toward involvement in industry.

6.4 Disintegration of the Gold Standard

Sterling under Pressure

The stability of the British banks did not extend to the position of sterling. Almost immediately after Germany abandoned the gold standard, the British pound was under pressure. Sales of sterling increased steadily after July 14, and the Bank of England raised bank rates on July 22. The British troubles were accentuated when the standstill agreements froze some £70 million of British bankers' loans to Germany.

Although the currency crises on the continent had added to Britain's problems by simultaneously provoking a flight from sterling and freezing her foreign short-term assets, the extremely weak balance-of-payments position on both current and capital accounts was a more fundamental cause of Britain's inability to sustain the gold standard. Britain's external financial position in the 1920s was undermined by several factors. On the current account, these included the abrupt transwar collapse of export markets for coal, cotton, and other staple products; the forced sale of a substantial fraction of Britain's overseas investments to help meet the costs of World War I; the overvaluation of sterling as a result of the decision to return to gold at the prewar parity of $4.86; and the adverse impact that the calamitous fall in primary-product prices had on Britain's traditional empire and Latin American markets in the late 1920s.

The capital account was a further source of weakness. Britain had attempted to maintain its pre-1914 role as an exporter of long-term capital to the developing countries, but by the 1920s, the country could no longer achieve this by means of a surplus on current account and was forced to offset the outflow by substantial borrowing from abroad. Much of the capital attracted to London was short-term, as described in Chapter 5, leaving Britain vulnerable to any loss of confidence in sterling. The increasing deficits on the current accounts of Australia and other primary producers who normally held a large part of their reserves in London compelled them to draw on these balances, further weakening Britain's position.

By mid-1930, the United Kingdom's gold and foreign-exchange reserves amounted to some £175 million, and other liquid assets were approximately £150 million. Because the corresponding short-term liabilities amounted to some £750 million, this was only an adequate defence against withdrawals as long as confidence in the pound remained high. When confidence drained away in the course of 1931, it seemed to the British authorities that sterling's parity could no longer be sustained. After borrowing reserves from France and the United States in July and August, Britain abandoned the gold standard on September 20.

As was so often the case in financial developments during the interwar period, the influence of history was of critical importance. Foreign concern about the scale of Britain's budget deficit increased markedly with the publication of the Report of the May Committee in July 1931 and was the paramount reason for the final collapse in confidence in sterling. As Sayers observed (1976, 390–91), it is difficult today to understand this obsession with the deficit, given the relatively trifling sums under discussion:

> The explanation lies . . . in memories of the currency disorders of the early twenties, which were, after all, less than ten years behind. In those troublesome times it had become accepted doctrine that an uncorrected budget deficit is the root of forced increase in the supply of money and depreciation of the currency, and that such depreciations become almost if not quite unmanageable. This view was not a mere academic fetish: it permeated the atmosphere in all financial markets . . . . The Bank [of England] itself, in all the advice it tendered to the struggling central bankers of recovering Europe, year after year preached the gospel. It was not to be wondered at, that in 1931 the physician should be expected to heal himself—and that when he seemed unwilling to set about it, his life should be despaired of.

Even so, it has been argued that the suspension of the gold standard was not inevitable and could have been averted if the authorities had been more resolute in their defence of the parity adopted in 1925 (Balderston, 1995). This would have required a much more aggressive policy to raise interest rates and reduce the level of domestic activity. Such a policy might have involved severe damage to employment and enterprise, and perhaps to political stability, but if firmly implemented would have shown speculators that the United Kingdom was determined to maintain the gold standard. However, international economic organization is intended to be a means to an end, not an end in itself, and it is not surprising that the British government was unwilling to persist with its commitment to the gold standard regardless of the cost exacted in terms of lost output and increased unemployment.

In considering the factors underlying Britain's departure from gold, much contemporary and subsequent British comment attributed considerable significance to the undervaluation of rival currencies, especially the French franc. Research has shown that the importance of this factor was greatly overstated (Eichengreen and Wyplosz 1990). It was not the exchange-rate policy that was the basis for France's prosperity at the end of the 1920s, or for her successful resistance until 1931 to the slump from which almost all other countries were suffering; and France's share of exports in GDP was actually falling after 1927. Instead, the strength of the French economy should be attributed to the crowding-in effect of Poincaré's fiscal policies, which induced an upsurge in domestic investment. Similarly, in the case of Belgium, export growth on the back of a depreciated currency was not maintained after 1926, and the main sources of prosperity are to be found in the domestic economy, associated with the expansion of the banking sector.

The Bank of England, after an initial delay to rebuild its gold reserves, sharply reduced interest rates in 1932. As in Germany, British monetary authorities continued for a time to advocate gold-standard policies even after they had been driven off the gold standard. But while the grip of this ideology was strong in the immediate aftermath of devaluation, it wore off within six months. British economic policy was freed by devaluation, and monetary policy turned expansive early in 1932. The British devaluation, however, was hardly the basis for international cooperation. The British did not seek international leadership; they did not champion their policies as hegemonic activity. Instead, they backed into devaluation, arguing that they had no alternative. While many smaller countries followed the British lead, the other major financial centers sought instead to protect themselves from British policy. The British devaluation was a good policy—it broke the suffocating grip of the gold standard on economic policy—but it did not point the way toward international cooperation.

The British government had relinquished its prewar role as steward of the international gold standard. More properly, it acknowledged in 1931 (however backhandedly) that this leadership role could no longer be sustained. The domestic cost had become too great relative to Britain's diminished resources. If the international economic orchestra needed a conductor, it would have to be found outside London—presumably in America.

The Dollar under Pressure

The financial panic spread from Britain to the United States, jumping instantaneously over the Atlantic Ocean in September 1931. Bank failures rose, and the Federal Reserve banks lost gold. There were both internal and external drains. In one of the most vivid acts of poor monetary policy in history, the Federal Reserve raised interest rates sharply in October to protect the dollar, in the midst of the greatest depression the world has ever known. This was not a technical mistake or simple stupidity; this was the standard response of central banks under the gold standard. It shows how the ideology of the gold standard transmitted and intensified the Great Depression.

The pressure against the dollar eased, but the American economy accelerated its decline. The Federal Reserve had chosen international stability over domestic prosperity, a choice the Bank of England had not made. The result was intensified deflation and accelerated economic decline. Unlike Britain, which arrested the decline in 1932, the United States had to wait an additional painful year. This delay was not only costly for America; it added to the deflationary forces in Europe, delaying European recovery and putting pressure on the fragile Weimar political system as well. If there was one decision that turned a bad recession in 1930–1931 into the Great Depression, the decision by the U.S. Federal Reserve to preserve the gold value of the dollar instead of promoting domestic prosperity was it.

Collapse of the Gold Standard

By the time Britain was forced to abandon the gold standard, seven other countries, including Australia, New Zealand, and Argentina, had already done so. After Britain's departure, another twenty-four countries followed rapidly, including Sweden, Denmark, Norway, Finland, the Irish Free State, Greece, and Portugal. As a British writer noted mournfully (Waight, 1939, 1): "If the foundations of the citadel of financial probity were unsound and the structure about to tumble, other centres could not remain for long unaffected." In many other countries, there was no formal suspension, but the gold standard was made ineffective by the imposition of a range of exchange controls and restrictions. This applied ultimately to Germany, Austria, Hungary, Bulgaria, Czechoslovakia, Romania, Estonia, and Latvia.

By the middle of 1932, the institution that had been generally accepted as the best guarantee of international stability, trade, growth, and prosperity had been completely shattered. Only the United States and, in Europe, only France, Belgium, the Netherlands, Switzerland, Italy, Poland, and Lithuania remained on the gold standard. Only the first four of the European countries listed here were truly committed to its spirit, refraining from the imposition of exchange controls and allowing relatively free movement of gold. The inability to make the gold standard function successfully in the interwar era was widely regarded as a symbol of failure, even though the actual consequences for the real economy were highly favorable. Those countries that remained committed to gold did much more poorly subsequently than those that abandoned it.

At the same time as the gold standard was disintegrating, there was also a renewed outbreak of tariff warfare provoked by the deterioration in economic conditions and by the introduction of the Hawley-Smoot tariff in the United States in 1930. Britain finally abandoned her longstanding commitment to free trade at the end of 1931, and numerous countries—including France, Italy, the Netherlands, Norway, Spain, Portugal, and Greece, and many others outside Europe—increased their tariffs in a desperate attempt to protect themselves from the deepening depression and the collapse of any attempt at international cooperation. In the judgement of the League of Nations (1933, 193–94): "There was probably never any period when trade was subject to such widespread and frequent alterations of tariff barriers. . . . Currency instability has led into a maze of new protectionist regulations and private trading initiative generally has given way to administrative controls."

6.5 Currencies and Banks in Other Countries during the Depression

Spain stands as the prime example of a country that avoided the worst excesses of the Great Depression by staying off the gold standard (Choudhri and Kochin, 1980). There was an attempt to fix the peseta in the late 1920s as France and Italy stabilized their currencies, but the deflationists lacked the political muscle. The government continued to run deficits that were monetized by healthy banks. There was a run on Spanish banks contemporaneous with the failure of the Creditanstalt in Austria. Martin-Aceña (1995) cites internal causes, but the peseta was under pressure as well. Very few banks failed, and the experience is not thought of as a panic. The Bank of Spain acted as a lender of last resort, enabled to do so by two factors. Unlike the Reichsbank, the Bank of Spain was not bound by the inflexible standards of the gold standard. It did have to raise Spanish interest rates to protect the value of the peseta, but it continued to lend freely, as Bagehot (1873) had advised. The banks also held large portfolios of government debt that could be sold for cash.

In Greece and Portugal, the impact of the economic depression was relatively mild, and with minor exceptions, the banks in each of these countries came through the period in reasonably good health. Where banking failures occurred in these countries, it typically owed more to banks' involvement as universal banks with unsound or loss-making industries than to inherent financial difficulties. In Greece, as in Britain and other countries in which mixed banking was not the normal practice, the banks were much better able to sustain their liquidity and solvency, although problems were aggravated where the central bank was unable or unwilling to act as lender of last resort.

There were no general banking crises in Italy and Poland, even though they were on the gold standard. Differences in banking policy between them and other gold-standard countries may well be the cause of the difference in financial outcomes. On the assumption that the direction of causality runs in this direction, it is tempting to ask whether Austria and Germany could have adopted the Italian and Polish policies.

The Credito Italiano, one of two large German-style universal banks in Italy, found itself illiquid in 1930 as the economic downturn began. A holding company was formed to take the industrial assets of the bank, disguising its universal character without changing the fundamental financial status of the bank. This cosmetic change was not enough to deal with the problem. More action was needed at the start of 1931. The government reached an agreement with the Credito Italiano in February 1931 in which the bank gave up its holding company and its investment activities in return for a substantial grant of money from the government. The Credito Italiano was transformed from a universal bank to a commercial bank, but it was not allowed to fail.

Banca Commerciale, the other universal bank, needed help later in 1931, and a similar agreement was reached with them in October. In return for an even larger infusion of cash, this bank too allowed itself to be restricted to short-term activities. The banks were transformed. The government became actively involved in the finance of industry. But there was no banking crisis.

Secrecy was absolutely critical to the success of this policy. Depositors did not panic or move into cash; they did not spread difficulties from bank to bank in a contagion of fear. The lira was not subjected to unusual pressure. The policy decisions had been undertaken by a small group of men, and no word leaked out to the financial community. Such secrecy was possible in the Fascist government that ruled Italy; we can only speculate on why the secrecy did not result in the kind of self-serving policies usually associated with this kind of restricted decision making.

The story in Poland is similar, although less spectacular. There was no secrecy, and there were no secret agreements in the face of collapse. Instead, there was a gradual state takeover of troubled private banks. The first test of Polish banking policy came in 1925 as the result of an agricultural crisis. The state responded by taking over troubled banks. Another crisis came in 1929, at the start of the economic downturn. The world agricultural crisis caused prices to fall in Poland, threatening banks who had loaned on the security of crops. Again, the government stepped in and took over troubled banks.

A third crisis in 1931 followed the failure of the Austrian Creditanstalt, in which the pattern of government expansion continued. Private banks held 40 percent of Polish deposits and investments in 1926, but only 20 percent by 1934. The Polish policy was not undertaken by a small group of secret financiers. It was not composed of a few large grants to banks. It was instead a policy stance extended to a large number of banks over a period of years. Its effectiveness came from the knowledge of its existence, that is, from the government's commitment to keeping credit markets stable.

Italy and Poland, therefore, were similar in the interwar period in that their governments directly supported banks in trouble. The form in which this overall policy was implemented was vastly different—almost diametrically opposite—in the two countries. But government takeovers were common to both. Their common policies contrast sharply with those of Austria and Germany, in which failing banks were merged with other banks. This was a far less effective measure, because the amalgamated banks then found themselves in trouble.

It would be comforting to report that Italy and Poland were spared the worst excesses of the depression as a result of their banking policies, but such was not the case. These countries were on the gold standard, and the gold standard was the primary transmission mechanism of the Great Depression. Unlike Spain, Italy and Poland experienced both deflation and falling production at about the rate of other gold-standard countries. Only by breaking the "golden fetters" of the gold standard, to use Eichengreen's term, was it possible to break the deflationary spiral.

The Japanese showed how to do this, although perhaps not with any forethought. They had gone onto the gold standard in 1930 after substantial deflation in the 1920s. Their attempts to get onto the gold standard had resulted in domestic economic troubles not too different from those in Britain, but they were equally determined to restore the value of their currency. Alas, their success was even more short-lived than the that of the British; they abandoned the gold standard in late 1931 and depreciated the yen sharply. As a result of this quick shift in policy, Japan—like Spain—avoided the worst of the depression (Eichengreen, 1992a, 308–10).

Latin American countries had similar experiences, although slightly earlier and without avoiding a deep depression. Argentina was the leading economy of Latin America, and it managed to rejoin the gold standard in 1927, not much later than the British and French. The cessation of capital flows to Latin America at the end of the 1920s, however, produced currency strains there even before the European crisis of 1931. Argentina went off gold again in December 1929, signaling a regime change in monetary policy that produced recovery by 1935. The rapid abandonment of the gold standard reduced the impact of the depression in Latin America, but the cessation of capital exports to that region made the downtown severe nonetheless. Almost all South American countries, although not Argentina, defaulted on their international bonds in 1931, reducing capital flows further (Eichengreen, 1992a, 236–41; Della Paolera and Taylor, 2001).

People in Africa and Asia suffered greatly during the depression, and the suffering was compounded by political upheavals in many countries. Most of the people in these areas were farmers, and they were hard hit by the fall in world agricultural prices. Nascent industrializing countries like Turkey and Egypt found their plans frustrated by lack of foreign capital and even of markets, because the high tariffs added to the burdens imposed by the fall in aggregate demand. Some countries, like Australia, tried to alleviate the pain by depreciating their currencies; some colonies, like India, had currency policies imposed on them. It was hard for agricultural countries to avoid the depression emanating from North America and Europe, although Spain and Japan successfully moderated their suffering by their devaluations (Rothermund, 1996).

6.6 The End of the Contraction

Unhappily, it took a change of leadership to bring about a change in the policy regime. We now can see that restoration of the postwar gold standard was the problem in the 1920s, not the solution, because it imposed monetary constraints that prevented the authorities from taking the action necessary to contain the banking panics and failures. These crises amplified relatively modest initial disturbances and undermined the financial stability of the leading centers.

The ideology of the gold standard was very strong, and it was extremely difficult for leaders to abandon it in this time of crisis. Not recognizing that this ideology was a large part of the problem, they instead held on to it as a drowning person holds on to a life raft. These golden chains only dragged the European economy farther under water. Only when national economies were freed of these constraints could the economic contraction be halted.

The change in policy regime can be seen most clearly in the United States. The Hoover administration followed a policy regime that became more orthodox in 1931 and 1932. It was highly traditional in its support for the gold standard and its focus on efforts to bolster the credit markets rather than the economy directly. Although not initially deflationary, Hoover drew exactly the wrong lesson from the currency crisis of 1931 and became a strong deflationist.

The Federal Reserve maintained a passive stance in the early stages of the Depression, replaced by active contraction in response to the run on the dollar in 1931. The Federal Reserve's steps toward expansion in March to July of 1932 were halted when the open-market purchases alarmed other central banks and threatened the solvency of member banks by lowering returns on bank portfolios. The Glass-Steagall Act of 1932 reiterated support for the gold standard at the same time.

The first sign that a new policy regime was on the way came after the election, in December 1932, when President-elect Roosevelt torpedoed Hoover's efforts to settle war debts and reparations multilaterally, signifying his opposition to continuation of the existing meager international financial cooperation. A change in regime became more tangible in February 1933, when Roosevelt began a serious discussion of devaluation as part of an effort to raise commodity prices.

This talk led to a run on the dollar and helped cause the "bank holiday" in March. The New York Federal Reserve Bank found its gold supplies running dangerously low at the start of March. It appealed to the Chicago Federal Reserve Bank for help, but the midwestern bank refused to extend a loan to its New York cousin, its different view of the world echoing the contrast between the German and French attitudes when the Reichsbank appealed for a similar loan in July 1931. The New York Federal Reserve Bank then appealed to Roosevelt to shut down the entire national banking system, a draconian way to force cooperation among the Federal Reserve banks.

No longer London, not yet New York. The Hoover administration had not been willing to lead the world economy out of trouble. Hoover had remained committed to the policies that were depressing both the American and European economies. There was no chance for new leadership to emerge in America during the long contraction of the early 1930s. And when a change in leadership took place, in 1932–1933, it happened slowly and with great confusion that magnified the problem. Without domestic leadership, the United States could not be a leader of the world economy.

Once inaugurated, Roosevelt responded by declaring a "bank holiday." He also imposed controls over all foreign-exchange trading and gold exports. He ended private gold ownership and took control over the sale of all domestic gold production. These controls allowed Roosevelt to avoid speculative disequilibrium when he began to devalue the dollar. At the same time, he prohibited the private export of gold by executive order. The dollar, freed from its official value in April by the Thomas Amendment to the Agricultural Adjustment Act, began to fall. It dropped steadily until July, when it had declined between 30 and 45 percent against the pound.

The clarity of the change in policy was unmistakable. The United States was under no market pressure to devalue. Despite the momentary pressure on the New York Fed, the United States held one-third of the world's gold reserves, ran a chronic foreign trade surplus, and dominated world trade in modern manufactures like automobiles, refrigerators, and other consumer durables. The devaluation was a purely strategic decision that appeared to have no precedent. Orthodox financial opinion recognized it as such and condemned it.

This was a change of regime of the type described by Sargent (1983) in his account of the end of several hyperinflations. It was a dramatic change, clearly articulated and understood. It was coordinated with fiscal and monetary policies. The new regime clearly was designed to increase both prices and economic activity. It was supported by a wide degree of consensus—professional, public, and congressional—despite the vocal opposition of some financial leaders.

As with the British devaluation, the United States's action was the key to breaking free of the deflationary policies of the gold standard. It also was a national decision, taken without consultation or cooperation with other nations. Sequential devaluation was the best policy under the circumstances, but it was hardly a coordinated international response to the economic crisis. Devaluation was only one dimension of a multifaceted new policy regime.

During Roosevelt's First Hundred Days, the passive, deflationary policy of Hoover was replaced by an aggressive, interventionist, expansionary approach. The New Deal has been widely criticized for internal inconsistency (Hawley, 1966; Lee, 1982); there was, however, a steadily expansionary bias in policy that added up to a marked change from the Hoover administration (Temin and Wigmore, 1990).

German Deflation—Was There an Alternative?

The story is similar, although not as clear-cut, in Germany. As noted above, Chancellor Brüning continued to deflate the German economy through 1930, 1931, and the beginning of 1932, even though Germany had effectively gone off the gold standard in July 1931. The modern debate over Brüning's deflationary policy dates from 1979, when Knut Borchardt presented a case that Brüning had no alternative. (The original paper and two successors have been translated in Borchardt, 1991).

Borchardt argued in three steps. First, there was no perception that the contraction was going to be more severe than those of 1921 and 1926 before the German banking crisis in July 1931 and Britain went off gold in September 1931. There consequently was no incentive to undertake any alternative economic policy before then. Second, there was no way to finance any expansionary measures. International capital flows could not have been increased, as discussed in section 5.3, and the Reichsbank was barred by international agreement from extending domestic credit. Finally, expansionary measures would not have worked because the structural problems of the Weimar economy, discussed in section 4.2, were too severe.

The question of whether Brüning could have acted differently actually has two parts. On the one hand, there is the historical question of whether other plans were available for Brüning to choose. Holtfrerich has identified several proposals of expansionary measures. Prominent among these is the famous WTB (Woytinsky, Tarnow, and Baade) Plan of December 1931 to increase public works in what we would now call Keynesian "pump priming" (see section 7.4). Borchardt and his followers have responded that none of these alternative plans was in fact politically viable. The WTB Plan, for example, was not even accepted by the Social Democrats for whom it was created. It was so watered down by the time it was formally adopted as party policy in April 1932 that it was not significantly different from Brüning's policies.

Another actual proposal was the cabinet discussion of devaluation following the British devaluation. It is clear that this devaluation, like all devaluations in a gold standard, would have violated previous agreements. It is less clear whether anyone would have held Germany to its international obligations so soon after Britain had defaulted on its obligations. And the credit controls initiated by Brüning after the banking crisis of July 1931 violated the spirit, if not the letter, of Germany's gold-standard commitments. As noted above, these controls represented the abandonment of the gold standard just as clearly as a devaluation would have done. They gave Brüning the freedom to expand without risk of capital flight.

On the other hand, there is the philosophical question of whether any historical figure can step out of historical context to do something different. No one, for example, expected Roosevelt to go off gold in 1933. Nothing that he had said in his previous career or his campaign for the presidency indicated a preference for this policy. There also was no extensive discussion of devaluation as an option—no "WTB Plan" for an American devaluation. Nevertheless, as noted above, Roosevelt went off gold soon after taking office.

The second step in Borchardt's argument is that there was no way to finance a German public works program in 1931–1932. This also has been subject to extensive debate. One issue is whether the Reichsbank could extend credit to the government. Another is whether the bond market—if the government had tried to borrow directly from the public—would have responded well to a policy like the WTB Plan. If the public would have been cheered and would have bought the bonds eagerly, financing would not have been a problem. But if the public were to decide that this expansion was the first step down the crimson path toward a repetition of the 1923 inflation, then selling these bonds at any reasonable interest rate could have been a problem.

The third step in the Borchardt thesis is that the Weimar economy was "sick" beyond recall. This was discussed above in section 4.2. Here we need only note that all three steps in Borchardt's argument remain unresolved.

Chancellor Brüning was replaced by Papen in late May 1932. The Lausanne Conference in June 1932 effectively ended reparations and cleared the major political hurdle from Germany's path. Brüning said later that he had fallen "fifty meters from the goal"—the goal, that is, of ending reparations, not ending the disastrous economic contraction.

Brüning's deflation was replaced by Papen's first steps toward economic expansion. Brüning had initiated a small employment program that had little effect in the context of his deflationary policy regime. This program was expanded by Papen and complemented by some off-budget government expenditures. In addition, Papen introduced tax credits and subsidies for new employment. These were steps in the right direction, but they did not alter the perception of the policy regime. They still appeared to be isolated actions, not regime shifts.

The new policy measures (like the Federal Reserve's open-market purchases earlier that year) nevertheless produced some effects. There was a short-lived rise in industrial production and shipments. The recovery was only partial, and the data are mixed, but there was a definite sign of improvement .

These tentative results seem to have had an immediate political impact as well. The Nazis had leapt to prominence in the 1930 election, increasing their seats in the Reichstag from 12 to 107. They then doubled their large representation in the Reichstag in the election of July 1932. But that was their high point in free elections. They lost ground in the second election of 1932, in November, garnering 33 percent of the vote instead of 37 percent and reducing their representation in the Reichstag from 230 seats to 196 (Hamilton, 1982; Childers, 1983).

Further economic improvement could well have reduced the Nazi vote even more. If so, we need to ask whether the recovery begun under Papen could have continued. For if it had, then the political courage to hold out a little longer with the Papen or Schleicher governments might have spared Germany and the world the horrors of Nazism. The question then is not simply about the recovery. It is also whether Germany—and hence the world—was balanced on a knife edge in 1933 between the continuation of normal life and the enormous costs of the Nazis.

There is, however, only a slim case for believing that the recovery could have been sustained. The instability of politics mirrored the instability of the economy. The policy regime was in the process of changing, but there was no clear signal of change like the American devaluation. There was no assurance that Papen's tentative expansionary steps would be followed by others. The recovery of 1932 consequently was neither sharp nor universal. Even though a trough can be seen in some data, other series show renewed decline into 1933. The economy fell back to its low point in the brief Schleicher administration, and it appeared that the Papen recovery was abortive.

For Nazism to have been a transitory aberration, the recovery would have had to resume in early 1933. It would have had to be strong enough to repair the damage to the political fabric caused by the social and political effects of extensive unemployment. The expansive policies already undertaken would have had to have further effects—which they probably did—and the American recovery would have had to spill over into Germany. Both factors are possible, but neither was very strong, and the latter could not have come for several more months. One can argue that the future course of the German economy under elected governments would have limited the Nazis to continued minority status, but it is harder to argue that an upturn would have led to a rapid decline in Nazi support.

Hitler was appointed chancellor at the end of January 1933, and sustained economic recovery began only thereafter. The advent of the Nazi government heralded the presence—as in the United States—of a new policy regime. Instead of focusing on the clear political discontinuity in 1933, we need to expose the clear change in economic policy. The Nazi government was truly a new regime, both politically and economically. The Nazis set out immediately to consolidate their power. They obliterated democratic institutions. They turned away from international commitments to the restoration of domestic prosperity, and they gave their highest priority to the reduction of Germany's massive unemployment. Hitler conducted a successful balancing act. He reassured businessmen that he was not a free-spending radical at the same time as he expanded the job-creation programs and tax breaks of his predecessors. Hitler's Four-Year Plan embodied many of the new measures and enhanced their visibility as a new policy direction in 1936.

Employment rose rapidly in 1933. The new expenditures must have taken time to have their full effects. The immediate recovery therefore was the result of changed expectations when the Nazis took power. It was the result of anticipated as well as actual government activities. Even though the specifics of the Nazi program did not become clear (and in fact were not formulated) until later, the direction of policy was clear. As we now can see more clearly than contemporaries did, the Nazi expansion was based from the first on rearming Germany (Tooze, 2006). Hitler had been criticizing the deflationary policies of his predecessors for years, and the commitment of the Nazis to full employment was well known. As in the United States, a change in policy regime was sufficient to turn the corner, although not to promote full recovery.

Contemporaries had trouble distinguishing the new administrations in the United States and Germany. Both Roosevelt and Hitler looked like "new men" who were taking charge from the paralyzed old guard. But it soon became clear—if it was not at the start—that the two leaders came from opposite ends of the spectrum. Roosevelt acted to preserve democracy in an economic crisis; Hitler, to destroy it. The evils of the Nazi regime must be accounted among the worst effects of the Great Depression.

Chapter 7

Unemployment

7.1 The Changing Meaning of Unemployment

In 1909, when William Beveridge, the future mastermind of the welfare state, published his book *Unemployment: A Problem of Industry*, the word "unemployment" itself was relatively new; it had first appeared in the *New English Dictionary* only twenty years back, in 1888. According to Keynes, Alfred Marshall's 1890 book *Principles of Economics*, the definitive nineteenth-century economics treatise, mentions unemployment only once. Before 1913, one finds just a handful of articles dealing with unemployment in serious economic journals; by the 1930s, a constant flow of scholarly publications was produced dealing with the measurement, determinants, and effects of unemployment. More important is the fact that before the First World War, issues such as monetary policy, tariffs, taxes, and the regulation of monopolies dominated political debates and electoral campaigns; in the 1930s, unemployment had definitely taken center stage. Some would say that unemployment was "discovered" in the last decades of the nineteenth century but became a relevant economic, social, and political issue only in the 1920s and much more so during the Great Depression.

There are two reasons why the unemployment received such an overwhelming attention in the 1930s. To be sure, the slump in output, investment, and prices was of a magnitude never seen before. None of the nineteenth-century depressions had produced such a high number of "out of work" persons. At the same time, however, labor markets in the most advanced industrial countries had considerably changed over the previous fifty-odd years, with most changes taking place after 1914. A brief survey of the new labor-market conditions allows us to understand the impact of unemployment on the daily life of the most affected individuals and communities, as well as to intuitively perceive what difference it made to be unemployed in western Europe and North America instead of in less developed, predominantly agrarian societies.

At different times in the nineteenth century, a number of countries made their transition from being an agrarian society to being an industrial society.

Labor markets were also affected by the transition, and they showed two distinct, yet related, features. On the one hand, the seasonal component of the demand for labor declined over time yet remained relatively high. A good number of workers were hired and laid off according to the ebbs and flows of agricultural activity, which remained of paramount importance. When idle, workers would typically consider themselves as "out of work" rather than "unemployed." The difference between the two terms was sociological and psychological rather than just semantic. Workers, particularly unskilled ones, expected to be "out of work" for a certain number of weeks every year, but they also expected to be hired again sometime in the future. During the downward phase of the business cycle, spells of involuntary inactivity were longer than at times of cyclical expansion, but expectations of getting back to work remained. People's lives adjusted accordingly, particularly by savings to cover out-of-work periods and by inter- and intrafamily mutual support (which may be considered as informal insurance). The most enterprising people would travel long distances to find a job when they were out of normal work closer to home. Southern Italian peasants went so far as to take advantage of the different harvest season to temporarily migrate to Argentina for the winter harvest. The term "underemployment" would later be coined for those who could not work full time over the year or even the life cycle.

A second feature of labor markets during the long transition from an agrarian economy to an industrial economy derived from the link many first-generation industrial workers kept with the countryside. Industrial unskilled employment typically began with the expansion of the cities' demand for ever-increasing numbers of construction workers. Construction was also seasonal and highly cyclical, and it suited workers who did not want to risk leaving the security of food provided by the extended family on the farm. Workers would thus typically move either daily, weekly, or seasonally from country to city and back again without severing personal and economic links to either setting. Work time over the life cycle may have increased with industrialization, but "underemployment" remained the key feature of industrialized labor markets, its social cost being somewhat cushioned by the option of going back to the rural environment in idle times. When demand for unskilled work increased in industries other than construction, worker turnover was considerable, making for a continuation of situations of underemployment. When demand for urban industrial work increased to the point of making it reasonable for workers to take the risk of permanently distancing themselves from the countryside in order to take full advantage of higher urban wages, only then did unemployment became a main feature of labor markets as well as a major social problem, due to its duration and to increased uncertainty about if and when it might end.

The nineteenth century did have its chronically unemployed people who were looked down upon with a mix of pity and of the moral stigma that is attached to lazy, immoral, or utterly inept people. It was for churches and charitable institutions to take care of such hopeless cases of long-term unemployment, rather than the government. Things began to change in the last decades of the century, with changing employment patterns as well as the emerging class struggle that would lead to organized labor in the form of trade unions and socialist parties. Both these developments were accelerated by the war. Large factories became common for the mass production of arms, vehicles, and uniforms, while life in the trenches provided a fertile ground for working-class propaganda.

7.2 Measures and Kinds of Unemployment in the 1930s

Even today, unemployment is notoriously difficult to measure, and it is almost impossible to compare unemployment statistics across countries for the 1930s. What we said in the previous section shows that it was not easy to have a uniform definition of unemployment. Underemployment was an even fuzzier concept for statisticians. Moreover, in an era when sample surveys and polls were just making their first timid appearance, one had to rely on official head counts of unemployed workers. Most industrial countries published statistics of the number of people officially registered as unemployed, but registration depended on the amount and duration of benefits, which varied enormously from country to country. Many out-of-work people did not bother to register when they were no longer entitled to the subsidy or when the benefit was too small to bother collecting. Moreover, as we have seen, "unemployment" was a term applied mostly to industrial workers. Only a small minority of those underemployed in agriculture or in the traditional service sector were included in the official head count.

Table 7.1, taken from Eichengreen and Hatton (1988, 9), reflects the statistical problems involved in comparing rates of unemployment in the 1930s by showing two estimates made by sophisticated historical statisticians. The first column (Galenson and Zellner) provides statistics for the industrial sectors, while the second column's figures (Maddison) are adjusted to the overall size of the labor force. However, the figures in the second column typically understate underemployment. By only taking into account industrial underemployment, one of us has shown that in the case of a relatively backward economy (Italy), official statistics underestimated unemployment possibly by more than half (Toniolo and Piva, 1988).

Even when all this is taken into account, table 7.1 suggests a huge variation of unemployment rates across countries. This variation is caused by a number of variables, the most important of which is the level of economic activity. Table 7.1 also shows the huge proportion of unemployed workers relative to the total registered work force.

Table 7.1 Average unemployment rates, 1930–1938

Country	Galenson and Zellner	Maddison
Australia	17.4	n.a.
Belgium	14.0	8.7
Canada	18.5	13.3
Denmark	21.9	6.6
France	10.2	n.a.
Germany	21.8	8.8
Netherlands	24.3	8.7
Norway	26.6	n.a.
Sweden	16.8	5.6
UK	15.4	9.8
USA	18.2	26.6

Source: Eichengreen and Hatton (1988), 9.

The increasing amount of labor and unemployment statistics that appeared after the First World War, difficult to compile and compare as they are, is in itself an indicator of the policy makers' interest in labor issues, a fact shown also by the creation in 1919 of the International Labour Organization (ILO), based in Geneva. Besides promoting international conferences and conventions, the ILO was a major source of statistical and economic research on labor issues, among which unemployment figured prominently. In most countries, the theoretical and empirical study of unemployment attracted an increasing amount of intellectual energies both academic and governmental. Pioneering inquiries such as those described in the next section stem from the growing interest in the social consequences of unemployment, as stimulated by the swelling dimension of the phenomenon.

One of the most innovative and complete surveys of unemployment was compiled in the United Kingdom by a group of high-profile international scholars under the auspices of the Royal Institute of International Affairs. As a rough estimate, the study put total unemployment worldwide to be about three times higher at the end of 1932 than it had been in 1929. The study also argued that while traditionally full unemployment depended either on workers' "displacement" (e.g., by technical change or relocation of production) or on "temporary business fluctuations," a new form of unemployment had emerged in the 1930s called "depression unemployment" that had "been a matter of vital concern to Government in the last four years" (Royal Institute of International Affairs, 1935, 28). The Great Depression, it was argued, produced "hard core unemployment" consisting of persons who "have been out of work for long periods and are unlikely to obtain work unless the total demand for labour relative to available supply is very much increased" (Royal Institute of International Affairs, 1935, 30).

Outside of Europe and North America, unemployment during the 1930s largely took the form of increased underemployment, for which no statistics are available. It is possible to speculate that within individual countries and areas, three factors affected the rise in underemployment: the composition of output, the severity of the depression, and the tariff and monetary policies followed by the government. In India, falling grain and rice prices resulted in widespread social unrest in the countryside during 1930–1931, indicating that peasant conditions had deteriorated almost to the breaking point and, most likely, that underemployment was on the rise. The subsequent imposition of a tariff on wheat import provided only limited and temporary relief to the peasantry. China was peculiar in that the onset of the depression and increased underemployment was somewhat delayed until 1933, probably due to an unintended but beneficial early devaluation of the silver-based currency. In Japan, unemployment in the 1930s was contained by the early devaluation of the currency, war with China, and the spree of military-related government spending. In Latin America, particularly in Argentina and Brazil, the fall in price of the main export staples resulted in large increases in underemployment in the countryside.

7.3 The Personal Experience of Unemployment

Aggregate statistics tell something about the overall extent and pattern of hardship experienced by those who experienced loss of work during the Great Depression, but averages do not tell enough about who suffered most and how. Aggregate statistics have the virtue of generality, but they miss the detail of individual lives. As already mentioned, the magnitude of the relatively "new" phenomenon of unemployment attracted a wave of scholarly interest, not only by economists and statisticians but by sociologists as well.

Unemployment in Marienthal: A One-Factory Village

One of the most fascinating studies of the impact of unemployment on individual lives was conducted by a group of sociologists who studied an industrial village in Austria during the winter of 1931–1932 (Jahoda, Lazarsfeld, and Zeisel, 1971). First published in 1933, the results of their research provide a close look at the intimate lives of those living in an industrial village in which the factory had closed.

Marienthal could be reached from Vienna by a half-hour train ride to a neighboring village and then another half-hour walk over the flat countryside. Its population numbered about five hundred families in 1931. A cotton mill had furnished the chief opportunity for employment in the village since its founding almost a century before. The mill had progressed from cotton to rayon after the First World War. Despite industrial strife and a slowdown in demand in the mid-1920s, employment was at its peak in early 1929. By February 1930, however, production had ceased in the mill. The mill owners must not have expected business to pick up again, for they started to demolish the mill almost immediately. In the early 1930s, workers in Marienthal looked out over the rubble of their former place of employment.

Unemployment relief was governed by a 1920 law. Workers were entitled to relief if they had worked at least twenty weeks in the previous year and had no other income. Aliens were not eligible. The amount of relief varied with the worker's work history, wage, and family situation, and relief lasted for twenty to thirty weeks. A worker's claim to relief was voided if any work at all was undertaken. Workers lost their benefits for activities as limited as cutting down trees in return for firewood, delivering milk in return for some of the milk, and playing the harmonica in return for a little money. The result was idleness supplemented by minimal illegal activity, such as stealing coal from the railroad or potatoes from farmers.

Emergency assistance was available after unemployment relief ended. This aid was only slightly less generous and lasted for an additional twenty to fifty weeks. After that, assistance ceased. By the winter of 1931–1932, therefore, most families were still on some kind of relief, but they were approaching the end of it. Fewer than one hundred families in the village had income from work in Marienthal, neighbouring villages, or Vienna. The other four hundred families subsisted on relief of some sort, with the exception of nine families with no relief or assistance and eighteen with railroad pensions.

Four-fifths of the families had allotments in the common land owned by the village and the factory. Each allotment consisted of five plots of about two by six meters each. The plots were used to grow vegetables, varying with the season. Many families grew flowers as well, choosing cheerfulness over sustenance. About thirty families also bred rabbits. Despite the homegrown vegetables, diets were very monotonous. Meat was eaten only once a week by half the families, on Sunday. Very few families had meat more than twice a week, and what they had was usually horsemeat. In the language of economists, horsemeat in Marienthal was an "inferior good"; its consumption rose as income fell. Starches were the basis of most diets, and the flour used had changed from wheat to the cheaper rye. Sugar was replaced by cheaper saccharine. The evening meal typically was either coffee and bread or leftovers from the noon meal.

This poor diet consumed almost all the incomes of the families in the village. Families with children also bought milk, and most families bought coal for heat. But there was little money left over for clothes and other expenses. Shoes in particular were a problem. Families typically could not afford to replace shoes that had worn out, so they were patched and patched again. Some families even restricted the activities of their children to save the wear and tear on their shoes. Almost nothing was left over for recreation or capital expenses.

While spending collapsed back into food, and food into bread and coffee, movement collapsed back into the village. Trips to Vienna had been frequent during the 1920s, to go to the theater, do Christmas shopping, or attend school. With unemployment, the money to undertake these journeys vanished. The train fare was no longer affordable, and people relied more heavily on their bicycles. The isolation of rural villages that had been reduced by the railroad and by prosperity after the First World War reappeared in the depression.

The isolation was deepened by a decline in newspaper subscriptions. Subscriptions to the Social Democratic paper, which contained intellectual discussions as well as news, dropped by 60 percent from 1927 to 1930. This was not entirely a matter of money, because the paper had a cheaper subscription rate for unemployed workers; subscriptions to another paper with more entertainment value fell only by 30 percent. Detachment was hardly complete, however. Political organizations continued, albeit with reduced passion. Votes in the 1932 elections were almost identical to those in the 1930 election, and the National Socialists started organizing in the village.

Politics, like other leisure activities, should have benefited from the increased availability of time. But this advantage was heavily outweighed by an increase of apathy that reduced all forms of recreational activity. Library usage also declined; both the number of borrowers and the books checked out by each borrower fell. Card playing became a popular way to pass the time. One striking aspect of this lethargy was the fate of a park that formerly belonged to the village manor and had become a focal point for village life. In more prosperous times, villagers sat on its benches and walked on its paths on Sundays, and the grass and shrubs were neatly tended. In the depression, despite the increase in leisure time, the park fell rapidly into disuse and disrepair. The paths became overgrown; the lawns deteriorated; the park became a wilderness.

Villagers became suspicious of each other as they reduced their activities. There always had been denunciations of people seen or suspected of doing illegal activities, such as working while receiving relief. The number of denunciations rose dramatically in 1930 and 1931, but the number that stood up under investigation did not.

The observing sociologists classified most families as resigned to their condition. The families were hanging on, preserving as much of their life as they could on their meager budgets. All their activity was dedicated to getting by; little thought was given to the future. Some families still planned as before, but others collapsed entirely in mental and physical neglect and conflict.

The unemployed men passed their time doing essentially nothing. They sat around the house, went for walks—walking slowly—or played cards and chess at the Workmen's Club. They could not even recall much of any activity during the day when asked. In a compilation of time cards, more than half of the men's time was idle or unaccounted for. Another quarter was occupied in minor household tasks like shopping and getting water. Less than a quarter of the time was used in major household work, looking after children, or handicrafts.

Women were far more active. Although no longer working, they had the responsibility of keeping the household running and caring for the children. They spent time cooking, mending clothes to make them last longer, and managing their budgets. The men contributed less to the running of the household than before—sometimes not even turning up on time for meals—and the women had the full responsibility. Even though the women often had had a hard time completing their housework after working, they uniformly would have preferred being back at work.

One revealing key to the meaning of time for unemployed workers was their bedtime. While working, people generally went to bed around 11:00. They came home from work, ate, put the children to bed, went to a political meeting or had some other activity, talked a bit, and then went to bed. In the early 1930s, the women still went to bed late in the evening, taking the time to complete their household tasks, but the men went to bed before 9:00. There simply was no reason to stay awake; sleep expanded to take up the extra time.

The Life of the Unemployed Worker in London and Wigan

Another classic survey conducted a few months earlier, in the summer and fall of 1931, examined the experience of unemployed workers in Greenwich, a suburb of London (Bakke, 1934). In this study, a lone investigator lived among the workers, recording his observations and conversations. The results are less systematic than those from Marienthal, but they are similar in spirit.

The experience of a 28-year-old mechanic and lorry driver was reported in this Greenwich study. Three days after being out of work, the mechanic was very optimistic about finding another job. After all, he had never been out of work for much more than a week before. Three weeks later, he was not so sure. He had answered all the ads in the newspaper, but he was getting discouraged. "You feel like you're no good, if you get what I mean," he said.

After eight weeks, he was reduced to walking to seek jobs to save the bus fare, even though he was living with his parents to avoid paying rent. He had begun to lie about how long he had been without a job, to avoid being lumped in with the long-term unemployed. After eleven weeks, he was still actively searching, but now only randomly; answering ads did not seem promising any more. His comment at this point: "There's one of two things, either I'm no good, or there is something wrong with business around here."

By the seventeenth week, the mechanic was thoroughly discouraged and depressed. He was described as "sullen and despondent." Although not as depressed or idle as the workers in Marienthal, because there was evidence of work nearby that might be found, this English worker nonetheless saw his experience as similarly hopeless: "It isn't the hard work of tramping about so much, although that is bad enough. It's the hopelessness of every step you take when you go in search of a job you know isn't there" (Bakke, 1934, 64–67).

As in Austria, unemployed workers were eligible for unemployment assistance in Britain. Assistance was set up with the same restrictions: any work disqualified the recipient from further aid. The rules were policed by competing workers who reported real and suspected infractions.

Unlike Marienthal, productive activity in the whole city had not closed down in Greenwich. Workers consequently continued to search for work. The observer formed an early judgement on the effect of unemployment assistance on the willingness to search for work. He asserted that there was no effect at all; the benefit did not retard or reduce efforts to find jobs. Instead: "It has removed the cutting edge of the desperation which otherwise might attend that search" (Bakke, 1934, 143).

Our third report was made by the famous writer George Orwell. Orwell was commissioned by the Left Book Club to report on the condition of workers in northern England in the mid-1930s and went to a small town called Wigan, near Manchester (Orwell, 1958). He reported that there was little evidence of extreme poverty in the industrial north. Everything, he said, was poorer and shabbier than in London, but there were fewer beggars and derelicts than in the metropolis. The communal nature of life in the smaller communities enabled unemployed workers to pool their resources and scrape by.

Orwell did, however, comment on the dreadful condition of single unemployed men. They lived in depressing furnished rooms in which they could not stay all day. Outside, their main concern in the winter was to keep warm. The cinema, the library, even a lecture offered refuge from the cold. Orwell said he was taken to hear the "silliest and worst-delivered lecture I have ever heard or ever expect to hear," but while Orwell fled in the middle, the hall remained full of unemployed men.

The diet of unemployed families was based on white bread, margarine, corned beef, sugared tea, and potatoes. Orwell commented (1958, 95): "The peculiar evil is this, that the less money you have, the less inclined you feel to spend it on wholesome food. . . . There is always some cheaply pleasant thing to tempt you. . . . Unemployment is an endless misery that has got to be constantly palliated, and especially with tea, the Englishman's opium."

More recent authors have amplified these observations and provided details of unemployment in other countries. The general patterns are similar to those described here. Unskilled workers suffered more than skilled workers, idleness and discouragement abounded, and unemployment relief often provided the margin between some semblance of the previous life and disruptive poverty.

7.4 The Social and Demographic Pattern
of Unemployment

Unemployment was not evenly spread among all classes of workers when considered by age, sex, and occupation. Unfortunately, not much is known about this important problem for most countries. One exception is Britain, where more studies have been conducted than elsewhere.

In relation to age, Thomas (1988) found that the risk of becoming unemployed was very much the same for all adult age groups, but that after about age 45 it was increasingly difficult to find a new job after losing the old one. In the words of a pioneering investigator (Beveridge, 1937, 13): "The older man has less power of recovery industrially, from loss of unemployment, as he has less power physically, from sickness or accident." The results were higher unemployment and higher long-term unemployment among older workers.

On the other hand, there is evidence that it was young workers who were most liable to be without a job. According to a group of contemporary observers, "The difficulty in retaining or securing employment appears to arise at the point when the change-over takes place between the juvenile and the adult wage" (Royal Institute of International Affairs, 1935, 62). If they did find work, trade-union customs and their lack of experience generally made them the most vulnerable when employers needed to dismiss workers.

Women accounted for only a small proportion of all those who were out of work, less than 14 percent in 1933. This was largely a reflection of the fact that they were a smaller proportion of the labor force, but it was also the case that women were less likely than men to lose their jobs. Surveys also found that women were more easily discouraged than men after losing their jobs and therefore were more likely to leave the register than to continue to search for employment.

As far as occupation was concerned, unemployment was heavily concentrated in semiprofessionals and manual workers, the unskilled workers being the harder hit. As Thomas put it (1988, 123), "In general terms, the risk of unemployment fell as social class rose. Unskilled males were the most vulnerable, female higher professionals the least."

The authors of the 1932 Royal Institute for International Affairs report also demonstrated that the increase in unemployment in the 1930s was not the result of increased job leaving. Rather, it was that workers were not being reemployed as rapidly as before. Some were not rehired at all, or at least not for a long time. The proportion of the unemployed in Britain who were out of work for more than a year rose from about five percent in 1929 to more than twenty percent during the 1930s. The result was a bifurcated labor market: one group went in and out of work with some frequency, while the other remained unemployed.

The workers who were unemployed for long periods or permanently and those who suffered the highest rates of unemployment were predominantly located in the areas dominated by Britain's traditional activities: coal mining, iron and steel, shipbuilding, and textiles. The problems of these industries were considered in section 4.2. Here we note that declining production in particular industries as well as in nations as a whole meant declining employment. While it is true that greater aggregate demand would have reduced British unemployment (as it did after 1939), it also is true that even with higher demand, many workers in traditional industries would have had to move to jobs in newer industries.

For various reasons, such workers may well have been the last to be hired in those industries. Their skills may not have been transferable across industry lines. Also, employers may have wished to recruit younger workers or those without a previous history of employment in the declining industries with their specific trade-union traditions and work practices. Workers also may have been reluctant or unable to move to newer industrial locations. The result of these structural factors was that unemployment in Britain between the wars was particularly concentrated in certain areas. For instance, the male unemployment rate in 1932 was 36.5 percent in Wales, compared to 13.5 in London, and the gap tended to widen as the recovery got under way (Thomas, 1988, 124).

In France, unemployment was neither as high nor as concentrated in specific locations and industries as it was in Britain. This was in large measure a reflection of the different pattern of economic activity in France. The proportion of the labor force occupied in agriculture was much larger in France (see section 4.1), and although peasant farmers suffered in other ways during the depression, they were not deprived of all sources of income and were not forced into the ranks of the unemployed workers dependent on state assistance or charity for their survival. Within industry and trade, the structure of employment was also different, with a much larger proportion of small shopkeepers, outworkers, part-timers, and self-employed workers in small establishments. Many of these workers were also able to retain some sources of income during the downturn.

Two other factors contributed to France's more favorable position. First, compulsory conscription eased the problem of youth unemployment, but much more important was the fact that a substantial part of the burden was shifted onto foreign workers by controlling the influx of immigrant labour. Admission from abroad fell from 221,000 in 1930 to 60,000 in 1933 (Royal Institute of International Affairs, 1935, 74). Thus, when asking who the French unemployed were, it is possible to reply: the Algerians, the Italians, the Polish, the Portuguese, and the Spanish.

As for the United States, a survey taken at the end of the depression (March 1940) showed that 11.1 percent of male heads of household in the labor force were still unemployed (Margo, 1988, 329). "Unemployed experienced workers were often middle-aged or older (over age-45), foreign born, single, urban, less geographically mobile, and living in the north-east or west rather than in the north central states or the south. The unemployed had 1.2 fewer years of schooling than the employed, and far less wealth, as measured by the value of owner-occupied housing" (Margo, 1988, 330–31). Overall, unskilled laborers in such industries as construction faced a higher probability of becoming unemployed and a lower probability of finding a new job once unemployed. On the other hand, individuals who possessed higher-than-average human capital (as measured by years of schooling) and who were geographically mobile were more likely to be reemployed (Margo, 1988, 343). Women were more likely to work if their husbands were unemployed. The strength of household bonds proved in many cases crucial in mitigating the effects of unemployment.

7.5 The Cross-Country Pattern of Unemployment

As already mentioned, data on unemployment in this period are imperfect, but a rough indication of the pattern of industrial unemployment for countries for which acceptable statistics are available is shown in table 7.2, which shows unemployment rates in the 1920s and 1930s.

The countries in Table 7.2 fall into two groups. The first group, consisting of the United Kingdom, Belgium, and the Scandinavian countries had high unemployment throughout the interwar years. The contrast between the 1920s and 1930s was not very pronounced; the later decade was only slightly

Table 7.2. Unemployment rates, 1920s and 1930s

	1921–1929	1930–1938
Group I		
Denmark	18.7	21.9
Norway	16.8	26.8
Sweden	14.2	16.8
United Kingdom	12.0	15.4
Group II		
Australia	8.1	17.8
Belgium	2.4	14.8
Canada	5.1	18.5
France	3.8	10.2
Germany	9.2	21.8
Netherlands	8.3	24.3
United States	7.7	26.1

Source: Galenson and Zellner (1957).

worse than the 1920s had been. Japan may be seen as belonging to this group, with the qualification discussed below. The second group consists of France, the Netherlands, the United States, and Australia. Germany and Italy (not included in the table) also belong to this group, but they staged a more rapid reduction of unemployment in the second part of the 1930s. The countries in this second group had much higher unemployment in the 1930s than in the preceding decade.

Aggregate unemployment roughly reflects aggregate growth in the two decades, which in its turn depended to a considerable extent on monetary and exchange-rate policies. In fact, the two groups of countries in table 7.2 roughly correspond to the groups of nations to be identified in Chapter 8 as belonging to different trading areas. The sterling area—that is, the countries that followed Britain off gold in 1931—was afflicted by relatively high aggregate unemployment, partly due to the high rate of exchange at which the gold standard was reintroduced after the First World War (this applies both to the UK and to Scandinavia). On the other hand, countries in Group I devalued early in the depression and had the least severe increase in unemployment in the 1930s. Japan, for which no comparable statistics exist, can be seen as fitting within this group. In Japan, however, the deflationary targets of successive governments aimed at reintroducing the gold standard in the 1920s had to be repeatedly put on hold to deal with exogenous circumstances, such as banking crises and earthquakes, that required the creation of additional liquidity (Faini and Toniolo, 1992). Japan remained on the gold standard only for a handful of months and was quick to abandon it when the sterling area did.

Group II countries did not undertake violent deflationary policies in the 1920s (Belgium, with the lowest unemployment of all, actually pursued a competitive devaluation of the currency). In the 1930s, however, they remained on longer on the gold standard longer than any other country. These countries, therefore, suffered high and protracted unemployment in the 1930s after being able to contain it in the 1920s. Germany and Italy also fall within this group, but after 1934, they pursued much more aggressive expansionary policies (largely but not entirely related to rearmament) than the other countries in the group, with notable positive effects on employment. Toward the end of the 1930s, the German labor market was quite close to full employment.

The United States is peculiar within this group in that, unlike most European countries, they did not have to face the trade-off between deflation and currency stabilization, having effortlessly gone back to gold convertibility in 1919. The 1920s were among the fastest-growing periods in the history of the country and unemployment, while not negligible, was contained within acceptable boundaries. In the 1930s, on the other hand, the United States and Germany were the large countries with the highest levels of unemployment. However, unemployment remained exceptionally high much longer across the Atlantic than across the Rhine.

7.6 Unemployment, Benefits, and Real Wages

Earlier in this chapter we reported the unemployed Greenwich worker's comments on the effects of unemployment assistance on his willingness to search for a new job. In a highly controversial article, Benjamin and Kochin (1979) argued that the increase in British unemployment in the 1930s was essentially due to the increase in the level of these benefits. In other words, workers remained unemployed because they had little incentive to find a new job. Benjamin and Kochin attempted to demonstrate this proposition econometrically, by estimating an equation that explained the unemployment rate by the ratio of the unemployment benefit to the wage and the deviation of national income from its trend. Although a number of authors have shown that the evidence adduced by Benjamin and Kochin in support of their thesis is deficient, their hypothesis has not been completely demolished, and it is now generally accepted that some weight should be given to the role of higher unemployment benefits in increasing unemployment (Crafts, 1987; Eichengreen, 1987).

A further issue closely related to the question of unemployment is the behavior of real wages. Keynesian explanations of the depression start from the observation that workers bargain over nominal wages. When prices fall in a depression, real wages rise. The resultant profit squeeze intensifies the depression. This mechanism was evident during the Great Depression. As documented by Eichengreen and Sachs (1985), higher real wages in the mid-1930s were associated with higher unemployment.

This finding has created a problem for macroeconomists who conceptualize the wage bargain as the result of negotiations between highly sophisticated agents. These agents, particularly those acting for the workers, should have seen the demand for labor fading away and should have thus accepted lower nominal wages. The question for macroeconomists is, "Why did nominal wages not adjust to the rise in unemployment?" (Bernanke, 1993).

One answer that has been proposed in the context of discussions of European unemployment in the 1980s is that the labor market does not work in the atomistic fashion of other markets. In the market for apples, for example, the trader who has apples left over at the end of the day will lower their price to clear his stand. But the unemployed worker in this story does not have the ability to force down wages. Instead, the worker has become an "outsider" to the wage-setting process. Wages are determined by agreement between the employers and the unions, which represent employed workers—the "insiders." If the workers' agents care only about insiders, then in the bargaining process, they tend to settle for a combination of high wages and high unemployment, rather than the opposite. This could explain why increasing unemployment in the Great Depression failed to force nominal wages down faster than prices.

The exceptions to this story are Germany, and possibly Italy, where the fascist government repeatedly intervened to curb monetary wages. In Germany, alone among European countries, wages fell faster than prices. In Italy, real wages declined from 1934 onward. Except for Germany, real wages in 1933 were higher than in 1929 in every country for which data have been collected. For the many countries with rising real wages, the range in 1933 (1929 = 100) was between 104 and 119. For Germany, by contrast, real hourly earnings in manufacturing, mining, and transport in 1933 were 5 percent below their 1929 level (Eichengreen, 1994).

This quantitative evidence has intriguing implications for the Borchardt debate, referred to in section 4.2. If wages were too high in Weimar Germany (though this has not yet been firmly established), the problem was erased in the contraction. The conditions that allowed German wages to rise rapidly in the Weimar Republic evaporated with the onset of the depression.

Some writers have suggested an alternative explanation for the rise in real wages. In their view, it was not the result of an independent fall in prices without a corresponding adjustment in money wages, but of an autonomous increase in nominal wages. In either case, the rise in real wages would lead to higher unemployment, but there would be two quite different interpretations of why this had occurred. In the first case, it would be necessary to explain why there was a fall in prices; in the second case, it would be necessary to explain how workers were able to obtain the higher nominal wages. It is thus important for an analysis of the causes of increased unemployment to establish which of these two versions was correct.

Dimsdale et al. (1989) attempted to do this by means of an elaborate econometric study of the British experience. They concluded that both the recession and the recovery in the 1930s were consistent with the consequences of a large exogenous demand shock (such as we have described in our account of the depression) accompanied by a large fall in the real price of imported goods. This led to higher unemployment because wages and prices were sticky, so that real wages rose when import prices fell, making it unprofitable to employ workers at that level of remuneration. Autonomous changes in wages were not an important factor.

Our search for an explanation of the mass unemployment of the depression thus leads back to the causes of the large demand shock, which we have attempted to analyze in the preceding chapters. It cannot be said that workers were themselves responsible for their own plight because they had initiated the process by exerting pressure for higher wages.

The fact that high real wages could be one of the causes of high unemployment did not escape policy makers. In order to solve the problem, countries that had devalued their currencies in 1931 implicitly counted on inflation, assuming some kind of upward rigidity of money wages. The governments of gold-bloc countries, particularly Italy and France, tried to impose nominal wage cuts. Mussolini's Italy had adopted this policy as early as 1927 at the time of the stabilization of the lira at a revalued parity, and they introduced it again in the first part of the 1930s. In the same vein, Lavalle attempted to make French workers take a cut in their nominal wages. Such attempts, however, met with strong opposition from the organized labor movements and proved to be difficult to implement on a sufficiently large scale, even for dictatorial or authoritarian governments.

7.7 Work-Relief Policies

It was recognized at the time, as it is today, that much of the reason why unemployment and underemployment remained stubbornly high for so many years was that the depression lasted so long. As long as demand remained depressed—for the host of reasons we have discussed in previous chapters—so did output and employment. By and large, only macroeconomic policies capable of ending the slump would cure unemployment.

Policy makers, however, saw unemployment as a major social and political problem, and some of them sought means to alleviate it in the short term by means of ad hoc policies and particular public-work programs intended to create new jobs. As early as January 1931, the Committee for Unemployment of the International Labour Organization spoke in favor of "a concentrated implementation of large-scale international projects" (Schneider, 1986, 166). International pressure for governments to act on public works programs remained high, and these were eventually undertaken in several countries.

At the micro level, steps were also taken to reorganize the labor market. In some cases, these included attempts at improving employment-exchange offices in order to ease the possible mismatch between demand and supply of labor and to organize seasonal and casual labour more effectively. In the same policy category fall efforts to provide better vocational guidance to new entrants in the labor markets, and retraining for those who had lost their jobs.

Government intervention in these areas was variably active in many countries, but seldom was it really able to make much of a difference. Nevertheless, in this as in many other areas, the interventions signaled a new interventionist stance shared by most governments worldwide, albeit with different intensities, a stance that was to take root and develop on a much wider scale during and after the end of the Second World War. The 1930s created a widespread belief in the electorates of most countries that the Great Depression had highlighted a gigantic market failure, that unmitigated laissez-faire economics could not cure mass unemployment, and that only appropriate state policies could deliver full employment. Post-World War II reconstruction and much policy making in the 1950s and 1960s was based on these assumptions.

Keynes and the Campaign in Britain

The attempt to persuade the government to adopt a large-scale public works program funded by borrowing was conducted most vigorously in the United

Kingdom. It is worth spending more than a few lines on the British case, not only because England was Keynes's own country but also because many of the arguments advanced in London against unemployment-relief programs were shared in many other capitals.

The issue first emerged in the 1920s, when unemployment soared after the collapse of the postwar boom, and it gathered strength in the trade-union and labor movements, with support from the Liberal Party. By the time of the general election of 1929, unemployment had become the dominant issue dividing the parties, and the election was notable for the active participation of Keynes. He penned a brilliant pamphlet in support of the Liberal leader's proposals for a vast public-works program, *Can Lloyd George Do It?*, originally written with Hubert Henderson in 1929 and collected with his other *Essays in Persuasion* two years later. In spite of Keynes's sparkling prose and his brilliant critique of the Conservative Party's opposition to such expenditure, neither the electorate nor the government were at the time persuaded.

The issue remained at the center of political and intellectual debate as the depression deepened. In 1931, Keynes gave a detailed elaboration of his ideas in evidence to a Royal Commission but was once again unable to overcome the resistance of those whose views were still rooted in orthodox economic thinking. The theoretical breakthrough was not to come until he had completed his great work, *The General Theory of Employment, Interest and Money*, published in 1936; and even then the process of conversion was slow and partial, particularly in Whitehall and in the City (respectively, England's governmental and financial centers).

The government ministers and their advisors in the Treasury had a number of different reasons for their steadfast rejection of all proposals for state public-work spending aimed specifically at reducing unemployment. Some of their objections were practical and administrative: it took time to draw up plans for road-building, land had to be acquired, it was the responsibility of local authorities and not of central government, and so on. These were convenient debating points to make in political campaigns, but they could not be sustained when unemployment persisted for so long.

A second line of attack was that the causes were structural and long term—the problems of the declining industries discussed in section 4.2—and would not be alleviated by short-term measures. There is more merit in this argument, but inability to solve a problem completely is not sufficient justification for not doing what can be done. With unemployment rising to about three million by 1932, even the removal of a few hundred thousand workers from the dole queues would surely have been worthwhile.

This was not done because within the Treasury and in the financial and business community, there were deeper levels to the opposition to deficit government spending, which, it was believed, would undermine the reputation and reliability of London as a financial center. Still more fundamental, though probably too technical to be appreciated by more than a minority, was the argument that a program of government expenditure would not actually be an effective cure for unemployment. This proposition rested on a concept that has since come to be known as "crowding-out": any spending by the government would simply displace a corresponding amount of spending by the private sector, even if the increased government spending was not matched by an equivalent increase in taxation but instead was funded by borrowing. There would thus be no net gain in output or employment. At a time of mass unemployment and idle factories, this negative prospect could scarcely be attributed to shortages of labor or other physical resources. Rather, the argument was psychological and financial.

The source of the psychological crowding-out was the private sector's belief that budget deficits were a sign of financial profligacy and irresponsibility. If the government committed such sins, financiers and industrialists would lose confidence in the future stability and prosperity of the economy. Businessmen would refuse to invest in their enterprises, and bankers at home and abroad would refuse to buy the securities the government must sell if it was to cover its deficit. Such views might have been irrational given the prevailing conditions, but they were deep-rooted and powerful.

Financial crowding-out was a more abstract proposition and was the most fundamental determinant of the view held by the Treasury and their supporters among academic economists. According to these theorists, displacement of spending would occur because there was a limited supply of savings. If more of this finite fund were drawn on for public investment, less would be available for private investment. A possible escape from the logic of this doctrine might be available if there was a compensating reduction in investment overseas. That aside, public spending could only be effective in increasing total spending if it was associated with a relaxation of bank credit and lower interest rates. However, if the authorities wanted to take that route, it was not necessary for them to accompany it by public works. In the words of the original and most influential proponent of this doctrine (Hawtrey, 1925, 48), "The original contention that the public works themselves give additional employment is radically fallacious."

But, as we have seen, the Treasury and the Bank of England did not want to relax credit in the 1920s. On the contrary, it was an imperative requirement of the restoration and preservation of the gold standard that interest rates should be kept high. It was not until the country finally abandoned the gold standard in 1931 that they could begin to think in terms of a different strategy. From mid-1932, the fact that it was no longer necessary to defend sterling made cheap money a possibility for the first time since the war.

Before we leave this topic, we should note that recent research indicates that even if the program of public works advocated in 1929 had been adopted, the impact on employment and output would have been somewhat less than

Keynes and his colleagues had anticipated. We now know that the value of the multiplier—the expansion of expenditure as a result of the initial increase in spending—was not as great as they had thought. The benefits in increased activity at home would have been rapidly curtailed by higher imports, and an outlay of the magnitude proposed by Lloyd George would probably have created jobs for only about 300,000 of the more than one million who were out of work in 1929 (Thomas, 1981; Hatton, 1987). Those who would have found work if the program had been adopted would no doubt have welcomed even this modest increase.

At the onset of the depression, in 1931, the attitude of the Swedish government was similar to that in the United Kingdom, and they were not willing to adopt measures that required deliberate budget deficits. In 1933, however, a new government was elected, based on a coalition of the Social Democrats with the Farmers' Party. They were more responsive to proposals from a group of distinguished Swedish economists, notably Myrdal, Lindahl, and Ohlin, for a deliberate countercyclical fiscal policy, with deficits to be financed through government borrowing. A policy of this nature was implemented from 1933 to 1935, but only on a modest scale, and its effects were relatively limited. In 1933, however, unemployment had already began to decrease due to the more expansionary monetary policy inaugurated a year earlier.

The German Case

The system of welfare provision for those without a livelihood created in Germany during the war was developed in 1918–1919 into a form of social insurance for the unemployed. In 1927, the fortieth German Welfare Conference adopted the slogan "work not welfare," advocating the transition from financial support to support through labor (Homburg, 1987, 93). Therefore, there existed at the onset of the Great Depression a political and social context that favored public works as a means for unemployment relief. As we have seen, however, the Brüning government inherited three main problems: budget deficits, heavy reparations, and rising unemployment. The government focused on the first two problems, assuming that once those problems were solved, unemployment would be taken care of. For the time being, even unemployment benefits had to be partly sacrificed as tax revenues declined.

The conflicts within German policy can be seen in the discussions that took place in early 1932. The depression was at its worst, and unemployment was extremely high. The General German Trade Union Federation (ADGB) sponsored the WTB plan of job creation, as described in section 6.5. Vladimir Woytinsky was the chief source of the ideas in the plan. The ADGB requested a meeting with Chancellor Brüning to present this plan, but the government was only willing to undertake a work-creation program if the budget was balanced. Brüning insisted that expenditures for unemployment relief, welfare, and job creation had to be cut rather than increased as tax revenues declined. Brüning actually linked job creation to the effects of his deflationary policy on wages.

The labor minister nevertheless proposed a plan for work creation in several areas, chiefly government enterprises and agriculture. The Reichsbank vetoed this plan, on the grounds that it required undesirable credit expansion. The plan was leaked to the press, which did not help its progress in the Cabinet, but it provided a fig leaf for the labor minister when he appeared at an emergency ADGB congress on unemployment in April 1932. The only initiative taken by the Brüning government for work creation was a program approved by the Cabinet in May 1932, under the pressure of increasing public-opinion approval for work-relief programs. It allocated a relatively limited amount of government funds to road works, waterworks, and job creation.

Brüning was replaced by Papen in May 1932, and a month later the new government issued an emergency decree that contained "alongside measures for social contraction, which generally corresponded with the ideas of representatives of industry, public works projects in the area of transport and water as well as schemes for agricultural improvement" (Schneider, 1986, 173). The decree was issued at the time when the Lausanne Conference was deliberating the final and official status of reparations (see section 8.1). Only in September, after the conference had ended reparations for good, was an expanded program introduced. It emphasized incentives for private employers to hire workers and de-emphasized direct government employment. Among these incentives were lower wages for new employees, which the trade unions saw as being against rather than for the workers' interests. Although this program was relatively modest and had no discernible immediate effects, it was the model for succeeding plans.

Schleicher followed Papen in December and built on the existing plan. A Reich Commission for Work Creation was established. This policy was seen as a move to the left and a departure from the principle of a free-market liberal ideology. Schleicher's plan entailed the extension of loans on very favourable terms to those undertaking projects for work creation. Government agencies were to issue and supervise the loans, provided by advances from the Reichsbank on security from the Reich. This turned out to be the blueprint for the larger work-creation program introduced under Hitler.

Hitler was not bound by either reparations or foreign-exchange constraints, eased by tight controls. In contrast to the short-lived Schleicher cabinet, after a brief period of diffidence, Hitler enjoyed the support of big business and large landowners. The work-creation program initiated in 1932 entered full operation in 1933. A new, more extended plan, the Reinhardt Program, was approved in June. Soon afterward, the Law for the Creation of Motorways was passed. In September, additional funds were made available to prevent a seasonal slump, including provisions for grants and further tax cuts. Signs of economic recovery clearly appeared in 1933, as the number of jobless decreased. But the real breakthrough in the fight against mass unemployment did not occur until increases in military spending provided a major stimulus to aggregate demand.

The same can be said of Italy, if on a much smaller scale. In the summer of 1931, Mussolini launched a public-works program to enhance existing schemes aimed at creating jobs for seasonally unemployed agricultural workers. Such schemes were based more on social philosophies that inspired similar nineteenth-century programs (i.e., idleness is morally evil and socially dangerous) than on the ideas that Keynes was beginning to disseminate at around the same time. At its peak in 1933, the program created some 200,000 new jobs (Toniolo and Piva, 1988, 237). As in the case of Germany, however, it was only the large spree of military spending for the Abyssinian adventure that led to a substantial increase in industrial output and employment (Toniolo, 1980).

The New Deal

The American New Deal was probably the most comprehensive and (at least in principle) organic "plan" enacted in any market economy to lift a country out of the Great Depression. At the macro level, it focused on monetary, exchange-rate, fiscal, and financial policies, while at the same time seeking to modify the incentive structure at the micro level. It went through at least two major phases, the second one being modified in light of the experiences (and the mistakes) of the first, which had been enacted in haste during the spring of 1933. Scholars still disagree about the impact of New Deal policies on levels of activity and unemployment. Currently, however, the prevailing view is that the New Deal's overall impact was relatively modest. It is likely that a number of measures might actually have been counterproductive. For instance, Roosevelt's high-wage policy is seen as restricting the creation of new jobs (e.g., Temin and Wigmore, 1990; Temin, 1990). Most of the New Deal measures fall in the broad category of reflationary policies and are not discussed in this chapter, which is only concerned with actions directly aimed at immediate unemployment relief.

The Hoover administration had intervened, on a rather small scale, to support "poor relief" at the state level. But by 1933, even this modest form of support was in a state of collapse. Intervention on a larger scale was envisaged with the creation in 1933 of the Federal Emergency Relief Administration (FERA), which immediately made $500 million available to states in the form of grants rather than loans. Roosevelt, however, was opposed to dole payments, as he felt they lowered the morale of the recipient and led to an erosion of work skills (a socially more modern view than the one underlying Mussolini's distaste for the dole). FERA, therefore, directed states to set up useful public-work schemes to provide employment rather than dole payments as far as possible (Fearon, 1987, 236). A scheme for fair pay was developed based on estimates of the weekly needs of households. However, the federal government was unhappy with the seemingly disappointing progress of the FERA schemes, and as a further unemployment crisis was looming in November 1933, a new agency was created—the Civil Works Administration (CWA)—for the immediate creation of four million jobs, leaving FERA to care only for unemployable people. A third agency, the Civilian Conservation Corps (CCC), was also created to set up work camps for young people and war veterans.

By January 1934, the CWA had been able to create the targeted four million new jobs in road creation and repair, public-building construction, and park construction. It was the largest and perhaps the most successful work-relief program in the depression. However, it was relatively expensive, and it created political difficulties with those unable to get the CWA's relatively well-paid jobs, so the program was terminated in the spring of 1934.

FERA took over again, and in 1935 the agency developed five new emergency-relief programs, two of which focused on educational content, one was directed to the so-called "interstate" transient who did not qualify for relief support in any state, and the remaining two focused on rural America.

As work-relief programs made little impact on the roots of unemployment, they may perhaps be better seen as steps in the development of the American welfare state. According to Fearon, "in February 1934, FERA, CWA, and CCC together gave aid to eight million households or some 22 per cent of the population" (1987, 243). But this form of emergency relief was not an appropriate permanent arrangement. In 1935, Congress passed the Social Security Act, one of the most important and long-lasting New Deal reform laws. The act provided for old-age pensions and unemployment compensation. These provisions were not to be seen as relief to destitute people but as a general insurance scheme paid for by taxes on both employers and employees.

Chapter 8

The Fragmented World
of the 1930s

The two central themes in this chapter are the disintegration of the international economy that followed the onset of the depression and the more or less successful path to recovery in the main areas of the world. We look first at the extent of the disharmony and rivalry displayed by European nations and the United States at the World Economic Conference of 1933. Cooperation was desperately needed to mitigate the effects of the slump, but it was not forthcoming. Each country had its own agenda, its own economic and political priorities, and its own preferred solutions. The next sections examine the operation of the different trading areas that emerged in this decade, the economic policies followed by the main participants in each area, and their growth and employment outcomes.

Table 8.1 summarizes in a nutshell (with a good dose of oversimplification) the relation between exchange rate and domestic policies on the one hand and economic performance on the other, as measured by GDP per person. (This relation is discussed in more detail in the second part of the chapter.) By and large, recovery from the depression was faster and more robust in countries that, by an early dismissal of convertibility, were free to put in place fiscal and monetary polices apt to stimulate domestic aggregate demand.

England and the sterling area are the textbook case in point. By ending gold convertibility of the pound in September 1931, England was able to lower interest rates, thereby stimulating investment, particularly in the construction sector. The depreciation of the exchange rate stimulated both exports and the substitution of domestic products for foreign products. A somewhat muddled and inefficient way of getting rid of gold-standard constraints on domestic demand management without formally suspending convertibility (a move that some governments saw as a political suicide) was to introduce administrative controls on capital movements. For all practical purposes, this amounted to a devaluation of the currency. This policy was followed by Germany and later by Italy.

Table 8.1 Exchange-rate policies and paths to economic recovery in the 1930s (GDP per person; 1929 = 100)

	1929	1932	1935	1938
Early devaluation and domestic expansion				
United Kingdom	100.0	93.5	105.0	113.9
Sweden	100.0	94.8	109.4	122.1
Japan	100.0	96.8	104.6	120.8
Early devaluation, protection, and import substitution				
Brazil	100.0	89.5	101.1	112.2
Colombia	100.0	100.4	111.4	122.5
Controls on capital movements and domestic expansion				
Germany	100.0	83.0	101.7	123.3
Italy	100.0	95.3	101.8	107.2
Central planning and autarky				
Soviet Union	100.0	103.8	136.3	155.1
Late devaluation				
United States	100.0	71.1	77.5	87.0
Gold bloc (continuous deflation)				
France	100.0	84.0	86.8	94.8
Belgium	100.0	91.1	96.8	95.6
Switzerland	100.0	90.2	93.3	100.9
Overvalued peg to pound and deflation				
India	100.0	97.4	93.4	91.8

Source: GDP per person Maddison (2001, passim)

As shown in table 8.1 and discussed below, many variations of this pattern to recovery were possible, as illustrated for instance by the cases of Brazil and Japan. Recovery proved weak where devaluation came late, as in the case of the gold-bloc countries. As it turned out, each trading area or country followed its own policy as a second-best alternative to coordinated reflation. We begin therefore by reviewing the failed attempts at international cooperation that characterized the early 1930s.

8.1 Attempts at International Cooperation

U.S. President Herbert Hoover imposed a one-year moratorium on payments of reparations in July 1931, too late to avert the German crisis. In August, an international committee chaired by American banker Albert Wiggin could only urge world leaders to reestablish political confidence before the expiration of the moratorium, as the only condition for new international lending to Germany. In December 1931, a "Special Advisory Committee" at the Bank for International Settlements issued a report that recommended "the adjustment of all intergovernmental debts as the only lasting step to re-establish confidence," given the "unprecedented gravity of the crisis," which much exceeded "the relatively short depression envisaged in the Young Plan" (Toniolo, 2005, 129–30).

While the British government was leading an effort to convene a conference to discuss the recommendations of the Special Advisory Committee, German Chancellor Brüning stated in January 1932 that Germany would seek the complete cancellation of reparations. The French vehemently responded that they would not cede their right to reparations. The British and the Italians supported the Germans, leaving the French nearly isolated. The United States remained uninterested in reparations but adamantly opposed war-debt repudiation, thus forfeiting an opportunity to exercise leadership. Politics stood in the way of economic cooperation. As one observer put it: "If none of the governments could get its own way, at least they were able to block each other's path" (Bennett, 1962, 249).

Brüning's January 1932 statement and its repercussions in other capitals delayed the conference. Impending elections in France and Germany also contributed to the delay, as neither government would be in a position to make concessions prior to elections. The delay in convening the meeting contributed to the collapse of Chancellor Brüning's government.

The Lausanne Conference on Reparations

The Lausanne Conference finally opened in June 1932, with the French opposing substantial concessions, and the Italians, British, and Germans favoring a clean slate. The proceedings at Lausanne were complicated by a disarmament conference concurrently meeting in Geneva, where the United States informed England and France that it would not allow European default on war debts while funds sufficient to cover the payments were being used for armament spending. The British and the French favored a clause linking reparations with an American war debt settlement. Germany objected to the American argument, asserting that there was no link between the two obligations and that an agreement had to be definite and independent of America.

Eventually, a Lausanne Convention was signed that put an official end to reparations. As a face-saving measure for the French, Germany was required to deposit bonds worth 3 billion marks (£125 million) with the Bank for International Settlements. The bonds were to be floated by the bank after three years, if Germany was judged to be capable of paying. As it turned out, the bonds, never issued, were burned in 1948. Germany was thus permanently relieved of reparations obligations.

The 1933 World Economic Conference

An annex of the Lausanne Convention called for a world economic conference to address the major remaining international economic issues. The British Treasury had favored such a conference since late 1930. France had blocked England's attempts to coordinate an international conference in 1931, fearing pressures to join in an artificial international redistribution of gold and German manipulation of the conference to obtain a reparations reprieve. After the sterling devaluation of September 1931 removed British pressure for gold redistribution, and after the Lausanne Conference of June 1932 ended German reparations, both these obstacles to cooperation had been eliminated.

The Lausanne Conference had also spelled the end of wartime inter-Allied debts, but the issue formally remained open. The French and British asked President Hoover to postpone the December 1932 war-debt payment, but he refused. France and several other European nations simply did not pay their 1932 and 1933 installments. Great Britain paid by earmarking gold in the Bank of England, angering American public opinion and increasing President-elect Roosevelt's determination to keep war debts off the agenda for the World Economic Conference. As for reparations, war debts remained an internationally divisive issue, even when it had long become obvious that they would not be honored in the future. Too late, the United States officially recognized the situation by passing legislation in 1934 that put officially an end to wartime inter-Allied debts. Again, lack of effective leadership made cooperation impossible on the eve of the 1933 economic conference.

As the London conference approached, prospects for success grew ever dimmer. As the value of the dollar fell during May 1933, Roosevelt—freshly inaugurated as President—became less interested in exchange-rate stabilization, reversing the cooperative policies he had advocated. Meanwhile, the French government conveyed to the United States and British governments its belief that exchange stabilization (by which they meant a reintroduction of gold convertibility) was a prerequisite for success in London.

Central bank representatives from Britain, France, and the United States decided in June 1933 that exchange stabilization was possible. Each agreed to buy and sell gold to keep their currencies within prescribed limits of 3 percent either way. The provisions of the stabilization were to be kept secret, and the agreement was to be null if the details were made public. Declarations were prepared stating that the three governments intended to limit fluctuations of the dollar and sterling for the length of the conference, that stabilization on gold was the ultimate objective, and that they would avoid measures that might interfere with monetary stability.

Unfortunately, the news of dollar stabilization leaked to the press, and American markets responded quickly. The dollar strengthened, and commodity and stock prices fell as investors anticipated a return to deflation. Roosevelt telegraphed his negotiators in London to reject the agreement, insisting that he did not wish to restrict his domestic-policy options and that he was not certain at what level the dollar belonged. After attempts to sway the President failed, Roosevelt's rejection was announced at the conference, causing turmoil and intensifying speculation against the Dutch florin and the Swiss franc, but restoring the recovery of American markets.

After the collapse of this agreement, the French concentrated pressure on the British to stabilize and join the gold-standard countries, warning of impending monetary anarchy in Europe. In response, the British asked for a currency declaration, which was quickly drafted and approved by the gold countries. To the consternation of the French, however, the British invited American participation in the agreement. The United States representative revised the document until the only remaining points were a call for monetary stability, recognition that an eventual return to the gold standard was desirable, and a statement that individual nations would take action to avoid speculation. He advised Roosevelt to accept the document, fearing that the United States would be held responsible for the collapse of the conference.

Roosevelt nonetheless sent a message to London on July 1 rejecting the declaration. His infamous bombshell exploded in the faces of the conference and the public two days later. The message, loaded with inflammatory rhetoric, accused the stabilization discussion of interfering with the real issues that the conference should address. In Roosevelt's words (Roosevelt, 1969, 269): "The world will not long be lulled by the specious fallacy of achieving a temporary and probably an artificial stability in foreign exchange on the part of a few large countries only . . . . The sound internal economic situation of a nation is a greater factor in its well-being than the price of its currency."

Roosevelt later admitted that the message was too heavy in rhetoric, but several economists agreed with his general argument; Keynes even said that Roosevelt was "magnificently right" (Feis, 1966, 238). Nonetheless, parts of the logic and rhetoric of Roosevelt's message were contorted. His concerns about a United States gold drain were offset by the fact that the country possessed one-third of the world's gold reserves. His qualms about only two or three nations stabilizing were contradicted by the fact that several countries were ready to stabilize in terms of the dollar, franc, and pound. The distinction he stressed between governments and central banks was essentially irrelevant in considering a stabilization agreement. His central message, however, was that he wanted to give priority to domestic reflation; given the circumstances, this was the only correct option he had.

The failure and collapse of the World Economic Conference is traditionally attributed to Roosevelt's message. But the conditions for international

economic cooperation were not present in mid-1933. By this time, each of
the major countries was entrenched in the defense of its own economic and
political interests, as perceived by domestic constituencies. Instead of seeking
the necessary compromises to initiate international cooperation, each of the
major industrial and financial powers would become the center of a currency
and trading bloc of its own. Countries left out of such blocs, as many Latin
American countries were, had to try to find domestic solutions, usually by
retrenching into protectionism.

8.2 The Sterling Area

Britain's devaluation, however badly executed, allowed Britain to reduce interest rates and expand the economy. Devaluation improved the trade balance
and, more important, freed macroeconomic policy from the "golden fetters"
of the gold standard. Many of Britain's trading partners followed Albion's
example. They too benefited from the relaxation of constraints on expansionary policy. While none of these countries reached full capacity in the 1930s,
they grew faster and absorbed more unemployment than the countries that
clung to the gold standard.

The pressure to give up the gold standard was especially great among
relatively small countries with export-based economies for which the United
Kingdom was the primary market. Denmark, Sweden, Norway, and Finland
followed Britain off gold, but they did not immediately peg to sterling. By
January 1932, Japan, Venezuela, and Bolivia were adopting policies that
increasingly resembled basing on sterling. The countries that pegged to
sterling between 1931 and 1933 formed the sterling area, composed of the
colonial empire and India, semi-independent nations including Iraq and
Egypt, the dominions excluding Canada, and other countries, particularly in
Scandinavia.

The reasons for choosing to link with sterling varied among these groups.
India and the colonial empire were compelled to do so by Britain; this was not
unusual, as a sterling peg had previously been used to stabilize these currencies. Australia and New Zealand had already suffered exchange depreciation,
and they needed to be tied to sterling to retain competitiveness in the British
market. South Africa, after initially trying to maintain its gold parity, was
forced to devalue and peg to sterling for similar reasons.

Many smaller European and Latin American countries chose to link to
sterling because Britain was a primary export market, and because most of
their reserves were denominated in sterling. The Brussels Conference of 1920
and the Genoa Conference of 1922 had encouraged holding foreign currency
instead of gold, and unless these countries devalued and repegged to gold, they
would suffer large capital losses on their sterling reserves.

Just as there were multiple reasons for pegging to sterling, there were multiple mechanisms for maintaining this new parity. The currency-board system implemented for the colonial empire, Egypt, and Iraq provided an automatic relationship with sterling. A system of semi-independence, in which the exchange rate was rigidly fixed and maintained through large sterling reserves, was maintained in India, Australia, New Zealand, South Africa, and Portugal. The third policy, an autonomous system of maintaining a target sterling parity without holding large sterling reserves, was attempted in Scandinavia.

The British government studiously avoided encouraging countries outside the colonial empire and India to devalue or to peg to sterling, but it supported nations that voluntarily committed to the sterling area. In December 1931, the Bank of England provided a credit of £500,000 to the Bank of Finland, which was trying to maintain sterling parity through exchange controls. In the same month, a credit of £250,000 was granted to Denmark. Throughout the 1930s, Australia received sizable standby credits that, while never used, demonstrated British willingness to stabilize exchange rates within the sterling area.

Soon after the devaluation of sterling in September 1931, British Treasury officials began to consider a monetary policy for the empire. Treasury officials shared the political leaders' opinion that prices were too low, but they feared that the empire countries might promote inflationary programs of deficit monetization, public works, and deliberate credit expansion that could potentially destabilize sterling. In early 1932, the discussion of empire monetary policy developed into preparations for a British Commonwealth conference to be held in Ottawa.

Trade and the 1932 Commonwealth Conference in Ottawa

At the 1932 Ottawa meeting, monetary policy issues were confined to a committee through which the British advanced their policies, reassuring the dominions and India that monetary policy would be directed toward higher prices and recovery, but avoiding discussion of stabilization. The principal discussions at Ottawa were devoted to trade agreements. In February 1932, the United Kingdom had finally deserted its long-standing commitment to free trade. The government introduced the Import Duties Act, providing for an immediate 10 percent import duty on all goods except basic foodstuffs, raw materials, and goods already subject to duty. It also established an Import Duties Advisory Committee with power to recommend higher duties for specific goods, and the nominal tariff on most manufactures was quickly raised to 20 percent.

The United Kingdom delegates had hoped to obtain improved entry for British manufactures in the Commonwealth markets, but Australia, Canada, and the other dominions were unwilling to take any measures that would harm their emerging manufacturing industries. However, it was agreed that the dominions would give preferential access to British producers by raising higher tariffs against imports of manufactures from non-Commonwealth countries, and Britain would in turn grant Commonwealth producers preferential access to the British market for food and raw materials.

The policies adopted at the Ottawa Conference helped to bring about a considerable shift in the pattern of United Kingdom trade, with a marked increase in the importance of purchases from and sales to the dominions. The broad picture can be seen in table 8.2. The share of United Kingdom imports purchased from the four dominions increased dramatically from 13 percent in 1929 to 23 percent in 1938, and there was also a rise in the proportion acquired from India and from Britain's colonies in Africa. In Europe, only the Scandinavian countries and Portugal were able to maintain their share of the United Kingdom market.

Table 8.2 Changes in the direction of United Kingdom trade, 1929 and 1938 (percentages)

	UK Imports		UK Exports	
	1929	1938	1929	1938
British Commonwealth and sterling area				
Dominions[a]	13.0	23.1	19.6	25.4
Ireland	4.0	2.5	4.9	4.3
India, Burma, and Ceylon	5.5	7.4	11.5	8.5
Other British Commonwealth	6.4	9.3	10.0	14.1
Total Commonwealth	28.9	42.3	46.0	52.3
Scandinavian countries and Portugal	10.1	10.5	5.3	9.4
Total	39.0	52.8	51.3	61.7
Rest of the world				
Gold bloc[b]	14.1	9.6	11.5	9.5
Exchange-control group[c]	8.2	5.4	8.1	6.5
Other Europe	4.2	3.3	3.2	3.2
	26.5	18.3	22.8	19.2
United States	16.6	12.8	6.2	4.4
Argentina	7.2	4.2	4.0	4.1
Other Latin America	3.6	4.8	4.5	2.5
Other countries	7.1	7.1	11.2	8.1
Total	61.0	47.2	48.7	38.3
Total	100.0	100.0	100.0	100.0

[a] Australia, Canada, New Zealand, and South Africa.
[b] Belgium, France, Netherlands, Poland, and Switzerland.
[c] Austria, Czechoslovakia, Germany, Hungary, and Italy.

Source: League of Nations (1939), 285, 307.

The rest of the world, including the United States, the gold-bloc countries, the exchange-control group associated with Germany, and Argentina all lost ground. The share in British trade of the countries outside the empire and sterling area fell from 61 percent in 1929 to 47 percent in 1938. Since the actual value of United Kingdom imports in the later year was still well below the 1929 level, this meant a large absolute fall in the amounts sold to Britain by these countries.

On the export side, there was a very similar story. The share of the much-reduced United Kingdom exports sold to the four dominions rose from 20 percent to 25 percent, and the proportion taken by the colonies and by the Scandinavian countries also increased. The striking exception to this general trend within the Commonwealth and sterling area was the fall in British sales to India, where competition from both Japan and domestic producers continued to hit British textile exports. Despite this, the share of United Kingdom exports to the Commonwealth and sterling area countries increased from 51 percent in 1929 to 62 percent in 1938.

Cheap Money and the Sterling Area

When the World Economic Conference ground to a halt following Roosevelt's attack on attempts to stabilize currencies, the formation of the gold bloc led by France, with its intent to deflate world prices, caused alarm among the primary producing nations of the sterling area; they feared that the British might join the gold bloc. The Chancellor of the Exchequer's response was to reaffirm his commitment to cheap money and higher prices, but also to express concern that Europe, which eventually must abandon gold, should not fall apart in chaos during the conference. The British Commonwealth Declaration was signed on July 27, 1933, resolving to raise prices, ease credit and money except for monetizing government deficits, and keep exchange rates stable within the sterling area. It also added a perfunctory commitment to eventually restore the gold standard. The declaration succeeded in quieting talk of further depreciation in the empire, distracting attention from the general failure of the World Economic Conference, and reaffirming the usefulness of the Ottawa agreements.

As the dollar became more unstable and the United States did little to encourage pegging to the dollar, this declaration formalizing the sterling area made it a more attractive option for countries seeking to stabilize their exchange rates. Denmark, Sweden, and Argentina formalized their sterling pegs soon after the British Commonwealth Declaration. Norway had officially pegged to sterling in May 1933, having devalued 9.5 percent from the sterling gold parity rate.

From late in 1933 to 1938, the sterling-to-dollar exchange rate was reasonably stable, meaning that a large part of the world enjoyed five years of exchange-rate stability. Following devaluation of the franc in September 1936, France tried to maintain a fixed sterling rate, much as the Scandinavian countries had done from 1931 through 1933. Greece and Turkey also devalued slightly and linked to sterling, and Latvia moved from a franc peg to a sterling peg, with a substantial devaluation.

The cheap-credit policies of Britain allowed the sterling system to accommodate the cheap-money policies of Scandinavia, Australia, South Africa, and other devaluing nations. London facilitated the operation of the system by supplying sterling-area nations with the sterling reserves they needed. The stability of the pound throughout the decade encouraged a willingness to hold sterling balances, and the combination of increased production in South Africa and dis-hoarding in India supplied gold to the sterling area, ensuring convertibility.

While British policy could not create the international cooperation necessary to initiate worldwide recovery, most nations in the sterling area performed better in the 1930s than members of other trading and currency arrangements. Adherence to the gold standard had spread the depression; relaxing the harsh discipline of this rigid system was the first step to recovery. In fact, Great Britain and most of the countries that devalued in 1931 enjoyed a fairly rapid economic recovery and were able to absorb a good part of the depression unemployment. Once freed from the gold-standard commitment, the British government could lower interest rates to revive domestic demand, particularly in the construction industry, while the devaluation of the currency both stimulated exports and provided some protection from foreign competition. After 1932, such a protection, and the attendant import substitution in manufacturing, was granted by the tariff; at the same time, a slight revaluation of the pound and its subsequent stabilization allowed for competitive import of raw material.

India within the Sterling Area

India was an important exception to the relatively rapid sterling-area recovery from the Great Depression. The Indian position within the payment system of the British Empire had always been a peculiar one, as it entailed pegging the traditionally silver-based rupee to the gold-based pound sterling. In 1893, the silver standard had been replaced by a gold-exchange standard, but silver coins continued to make up the bulk of circulation (Rothermund, 1996, 88–90). At the beginning of the century, the rupee was pegged to the pound at an exchange rate of 1s 4d (15 rupees per pound). After the war, the Indian government maintained such a deflationary policy that in 1927 legislation was passed to fix the exchange rate to the pound at 1s 6d (a 12 percent appreciation over the already overvalued British currency). This parity was defended in 1927–1931 by way of deflationary monetary policies. These were carried out by melting down silver coins without proportionally increasing paper circulation (Mukherji, 2005, 369).

When the pound was taken off gold, the government of India hoped to be able to seize the opportunity for an adjustment of the pound-rupee exchange rate. George Schuster, the finance minister in the Viceroy's government, proposed to unlink the rupee from the pound and let it float so it could find its own market price. But London thought otherwise, and even Montague Norman, the Governor of the Bank of England and a patron of Schuster, found the proposal unpalatable. The rupee remained pegged to the pound at the 1927 rate of 1s 4d.

With the devaluation of the pound sterling, the price of gold in terms of pounds (and of the pegged rupee) increased. "A large part of the hoarded gold in India, including household possessions of gold in rural India, started to flow out of the country, a process that came to be known as 'distress sale' of gold," Mukherji notes (2005, 369). Together with the continuation of monetary deflation, the outflow of gold facilitated the maintenance of the exchange rate of the rupee, in spite of the large interest payments India had to make on its considerable foreign debt (almost entirely owed to London). The rupee often traded above its statutory (pegged) value.

A tight monetary policy (the bank rate was 7 percent until July 1932 and 4 percent thereafter) was coupled with cuts in government expenditure. In particular, little was done to reduce unemployment by way of public works, while expenditure on public health, education, and irrigation was curtailed.

With its overvalued currency, India did not benefit from the Ottawa agreements and the British recovery as did other Commonwealth countries that were allowed to devalue with the pound. If imperial preferences somewhat lessened the competition from non-Empire countries, the latter acquired an edge on the Indian market. Moreover, Indian traders complained about the way the country had been treated in setting up the Imperial preference scheme. These complaints, however justified, highlight a rising discontent among the Indian trading middle class. Such discontent, compounded with the general distress and the hardship in the countryside, had a lasting political impact, so that a number of historians see the "decolonization process" as beginning with the Great Depression.

India's per capita GDP stagnated throughout the 1930s, falling by 6 percent between 1929 and 1939 (Maddison, 2001). The value of India's exports per capita fell by about 40 percent between 1929 and 1950, as compared to a 13 percent decline in total world exports. India, therefore, turns out to be a peculiar case within the sterling trading area, which elsewhere managed to lessen the impact of the depression and hasten recovery by an early currency devaluation accompanied by easy money and domestic-market protection within the system of imperial preferences. The Indian case once more stands out as a confirmation of one of the main tenets of this book: misguided macroeconomic demand management stood in the way of economic prosperity.

Latin America: Almost in the Sterling Area

After an initial orthodox deflationary response to the shock of 1929–1930, Latin American countries discovered in 1931 that "it was possible to abandon gold standard rules and did so with alacrity" (Thorpe, 1998, 111). Defaults on foreign debt rapidly followed, as currency depreciations made payments on both principal and interest unbearable at a time of falling export revenues. With few exceptions, Argentina being the most noticeable one, by 1934 most Latin American countries had defaulted. Devaluation and default (which markets took surprisingly lightly) allowed room for expansionary fiscal policies. Recovery came in many cases quite rapidly when these hitherto open economies took a more inward-looking policy stance. Import quotas and tariffs were introduced in Brazil and Chile, while some countries began to support the export sector (the Brazilian government, for instance, brought large quantities of coffee to sustain its price, going as far as burning coffee instead of coal in train locomotives). Argentina, traditionally linked to the British financial and product markets, remained relatively open to the sterling area, under the Roca Runciman Treaty of 1933, which gave the United Kingdom important tariff concessions. Recovery from the depression turned out to be slow.

After the initial moment of respite and recovery, several governments increasingly stepped up their intervention in the economy, mainly to promote import substitution and supply diversification. The government of Getulio Vargas in Brazil was particularly active in promoting a large spectrum of growth-enhancing and inward-looking policies. Other Latin American governments (e.g., Colombia's) engaged in expansionary fiscal policies, but in most countries, circumstances dictated more radical reforms: increased wage flexibility, land reform, price regulation, public works, and improved financial structures (Heim, 1998, 45). It has therefore been argued that the increasing isolation of the subcontinent turned out to be a blessing in disguise. Declining export revenue (due both to falling prices and the emergence of a protectionist "center") and the drying up of foreign lending forced policy makers to experiment with new economic policies to promote industrialization (Diaz Alejandro, 1984; Heim, 1998).

The results of these policies were quite remarkable. By 1932, Brazil and Colombia had already recovered their 1929 GDP level, even before exports had begun to recover (Thorpe, 1998, 113–14). With export recovery under way from 1933, Argentina and Mexico also sped up growth, recovering pre-depression income levels by 1934 and 1935 respectively. In every case, manufacturing output grew faster than GDP, as import substitution and diminished dependence on a small number of export staples stimulated domestic supply.

Manufacturing growth rates ranged from 3 percent per annum in Argentina to more than 8 percent in Colombia.

8.3 The Gold Bloc

Continental Europe (excluding Scandinavia) stayed with gold, although they did so in two very different ways. The gold bloc led by France stayed on the gold standard, preserving open currency exchanges at pre-Depression currency values. The Nazi area, led by Germany, elaborated the currency controls it had instituted in 1931, formally preserving the value of the mark while abandoning any of the theoretical benefits of the gold standard and enjoying freedom in monetary and fiscal policy.

The gold bloc of the 1930s included most countries of the Latin Monetary Union of 1865, which—under French leadership—created an area of free currency circulation comprising France, Italy, Belgium, French, and Switzerland (with other countries joining later). Before 1914, the currencies of all these countries traded at equal parities, all being modelled on Napoleon's *franc germinal*. After 1914, parities could not be maintained, and in the 1920s, each currency stabilized, and gold convertibility was reintroduced at different parities.

In response to Roosevelt's message to the World Economic Conference and the turmoil that emerged in its aftermath, the representatives of France, Belgium, Holland, Switzerland, Italy, and Poland released a joint declaration stating that their governments would strive to maintain the gold standard and the stability of their currencies at their current parities, both to create a stable gold platform for the recovery of international exchange-market stability and to promote social progress at home. Representatives of their central banks met in Paris, and on July 8 they pledged to support each other's currencies, settling each other's claims in gold-convertible currencies or gold.

While the gold bloc was to develop a reputation for possessing little cohesion and no organization, its initial declaration successfully ended the speculation against the Dutch florin and the Swiss franc that had persisted during the proceedings of the World Economic Conference. Despite this strong beginning, however, the gold bloc remained a symbolic organization. No progress was made in developing the connections among the central banks or the government policies of the gold bloc nations after the July 8 meeting.

Of all the trading blocs that emerged in the aftermath of the London Economic Conference, the gold bloc was the only one still constrained to follow the stringent deflationary policies demanded by the gold standard. The continuing efforts in these countries to hold their economies to this harsh course made recovery from the depression of the early 1930s particularly slow. Unemployment stayed relatively high, as described in section 7.2.

This misguided ideological purity was one of the factors that stood in the way of international cooperation.

Within the constraints of the existing gold parities, countries had only two options to protect their trade balances: exchange controls and deflation. Among the central European nations, including the emerging trading bloc around Germany, tariffs were supplemented by exchange controls, nominally leaving the countries on the gold standard but effectively rendering the system meaningless. In contrast, most countries in the gold bloc regarded exchange controls as incompatible with the workings of the gold standard and against the spirit of the system. Continued deflation was the only available policy, therefore, and the core gold-bloc countries sustained this policy for as long as they could.

The French had been successful in the early years of the decade in keeping their current-account deficit small through trade barriers, but by 1933 the situation was steadily growing worse. The decline in economic activity was accompanied by lower government revenues, resulting in budgetary deficits that caused great alarm among the French populace, who still bore the memory of the inflationary cycles of the mid-1920s. The political effects of expenditure cuts and new taxes created a situation of turmoil in which there were four governments in 1932, three in 1933, and four in 1934. Even though the decline in prices left the real wages of pensioners, veterans, and government employees higher than their original levels, attempts to reduce fiscal expenditures by reducing payments to these groups were highly unpopular.

Within the gold bloc, the high prices resulting from the overvalued gold-standard parities of the currencies discouraged trading among the bloc's members. French trade with Belgium decreased 13 percent between 1933 and 1934, and French trade with Switzerland decreased by 40 percent. To encourage trade among themselves, the gold-bloc nations met in Geneva in September 1934 and signified their agreement to increase trade and tourism within the bloc and to arrange another conference to meet in Brussels in October to discuss trade policy. Poland was not allowed to participate in either the Geneva or the Brussels conferences, ostensibly because its economy was structured differently from those of the other members of the gold bloc, but more likely because the other members were reluctant to include a nation whose economy was in as desperate need of assistance as Poland's was in 1934.

The conference opened with the Italian and Dutch delegations expressing reluctance to reaffirm their countries' commitment to maintain the gold standard and their currency parities. Under French guidance, the conference was brought to a close with an agreement for gold-bloc countries to continue bilateral negotiations to allow for a ten percent increase in gold-bloc trade by June 30, 1935. The conference therefore was successful to the extent that the gold bloc survived intact. But the results of the proposed negotiations were not the least bit encouraging for gold-bloc unity. The French agreed in principle to increase Belgian trade, but the proposed 10 percent increase was unattainable.

Belgium had been severely hurt by its loss of competitiveness in British markets with the sterling devaluation in 1931. In September 1934, the Belgian government asked for more French assistance, but neither loan arrangements nor proposals to lower French quotas on Belgian goods were enacted. In March 1935 the British government limited steel imports, worsening Belgium's plight. In desperation, the Belgian government reopened talks with France to seek economic assistance. Again, the French could not offer more than token assistance. Returning from Paris essentially empty-handed, the Belgian government was forced to impose exchange controls. A new government devalued the Belgian franc on March 30, repegging it 28 percent lower, at a level calculated to restore the prices of Belgian goods to the levels of British and American prices.

When the gold bloc was officially declared in the aftermath of the World Economic Conference, French opinion was firmly opposed to devaluation of the franc as an alternative to deflation. Memories of the inflation and currency crises of the early 1920s were still an extremely powerful force. However, as the disparity between the recovery of countries with depreciated currencies and the stagnation of gold-bloc countries became apparent, individuals within French political and journalistic circles began to support devaluation, although public opinion remained strongly opposed. The primary danger to the franc was perceived to be the budget deficits that threatened to resurrect the debt monetization and the resulting inflationary cycles that had caused the economic chaos of the 1920s. Fearing these consequences, successive French governments struggled with programs to reduce expenditure and augment decreasing revenues, but economic contraction and budget deficits persisted.

The Popular Front, a coalition of the Radical, Communist and Socialist parties led by Léon Blum, took office in June 1936 with a plan to restore economic growth with a French New Deal. Blum renounced deflationary policies, but he did not devalue. France consequently suffered serious depletion of its gold reserves. The Popular Front introduced a shortened work week of forty hours without a reduction in wages, and the government raised wages to stimulate consumption and ignite the economy. The Matignon Accords, which forced employers to sign a package of wage increases, were the Popular Front's solution to widespread labor unrest.

By mid-1936, there was widespread support for devaluation among politicians, publicists, and banking and financial experts, but still not among the general populace. The government's opposition to devaluation during 1934 and 1935 had so effectively convinced the French public that devaluation would cause a return of inflation that this opinion persisted among the populace through 1936, initially precluding a unilateral devaluation. Ultimately, however, it proved impossible to withstand the pressure against the franc; this final episode in the disintegration of the interwar gold standard is taken up in section 9.4.

Clinging to the gold standard, France and the other remaining members of the gold bloc were helpless to alleviate the depression in their countries. The professed cure for disequilibrium was the persistent source of the disease. When they could no longer maintain this stance, they had to choose between currency controls like the Germans or devaluation like the UK and United States. Abhorring the former, they chose the latter.

8.4 The Nazi Trading Area

Germany's Currency Controls

After the banking and currency crises of July 1931, the German government allowed banks to reopen only after freezing foreign deposits and limiting foreign-exchange transactions to the Reichsbank. In the summer of 1931, therefore, Germany abandoned the gold standard for all practical purposes by imposing controls on foreign-exchange transactions, but did not devalue the mark. The initial exchange controls were strengthened in September, following the sterling devaluation, by more efficient measures. These required owners of gold and foreign assets to sell them to the Reichsbank, restricted the amount of foreign exchange available to importers, and compelled exporters to surrender their foreign-exchange proceeds to the Reichsbank. Behind the shelter of controls on capital movements, an expansionary monetary policy was introduced in the summer of 1932 and was beginning to have a positive impact on output and employment by January 1933, when Adolf Hitler and the Nazi party came to power.

As described in section 6.5, the Nazi government inherited from the Weimar Republic a set of policies including exchange control, work-creation projects, government intervention in banking, and the program for agriculture. The Nazis also continued to formally maintain the gold value of the mark, under the protection of administrative controls on conversion. Germany had always had a high degree of government involvement in the economy and in foreign-trade policy. The Nazis added terror to the government's toolkit for enforcing compliance with economic controls, including exchange and trade controls.

The deterioration of world trade in the 1930s was magnified in Germany by the devaluations of sterling and the dollar, relative to gold and the mark, by the rise of protectionism, and by capital flight resulting from Jews fleeing persecution and from domestic and foreign responses to Nazi policies (see section 9.1). In the short term, the government's responses in 1934 were increased foreign-exchange restrictions and a moratorium on interest payments on debt to foreigners. A long-term strategy was contained in the "New Plan" of Hjalmar Schacht, the president of the Reichsbank and the minister of finance, which encouraged autarky by restricting imports and provided commodity boards to create greater administrative control of trade. In 1935, a scheme was initiated to extend subsidies to German exports that were not competitive on world markets because of the overvalued mark. These inward-looking policies proved to be quite effective in promoting the expansion of domestic output. Between 1932 and 1938, Germany's real GDP per person grew at a most respectable rate of 6.6 percent per year.

The trade policies of the Nazis, moving toward autarky, initially were directed to increase consumption and reduce unemployment, but later policies focused on rearmament and preparing for a war economy after a shortage of foreign exchange convinced the Nazis they could not afford both guns and butter. German goals included military preparedness and administrative control over the domestic population, with politics taking precedence over economics. The price paid for this was fewer available import goods and increased labor intensiveness.

The Nazis initiated bilateral trade agreements that took several forms during the decade. One of the first systems was the private-compensation procedure, which created agencies that attempted to balance imports and exports by matching private exporters and importers to ensure offsetting trade. One characteristic of this system was the use of blocked marks, frozen funds held by foreigners and used at a discount to buy German exports. Through the use of blocked marks, German exporters could obtain higher prices in terms of marks for their products, and foreign importers purchasing these marks at a discount could purchase German exports at a lower price in terms of the foreign currency. Because this system was highly profitable for German exporters, its use was limited to additional exports, those goods that were not competitive in foreign markets due to the overvalued mark.

A second, more flexible method was the bilateral-exchange clearing system, which attempted to balance credits and debits on a national level. The mechanism of this system was conducted through clearing accounts in the Reichsbank. German importers paid marks to the Reichsbank account of the trading partner, where the funds were held until they could be used to pay German exporters for goods sold to the other country. If the accounts held insufficient funds, the exporters had to wait for imports to increase, and if there were excess funds, importers had to wait for increased exports. The central bank of the trading partner held similar clearing accounts for its exporters and importers. After the initial agreement with Hungary, Germany made arrangements of this type with Estonia, Latvia, Bulgaria, Greece, Yugoslavia, Romania, Czechoslovakia, and Turkey. While the details of each arrangement were different, all of these clearing agreements shared the common goal of opening trade controls to help export industries.

Germany's trade with Western Europe, traditionally an area of export surpluses, was limited by the decline in international trade and the rise of exchange controls. Germany negotiated Sondermark Agreements with France, Belgium, the Netherlands, Switzerland, Italy, the Scandinavian countries, Spain, and Portugal to preserve these valuable export markets. These Sondermark Agreements involved partial rather than full clearing systems, with the establishment of clearing accounts for additional trade. Normal levels of trade were conducted according to foreign-exchange quotas, and the special accounts for additional trade, the trade that developed beyond normal levels, operated in the same manner as the bilateral-exchange clearing agreements between Germany and southeast Europe.

In 1934, the Auslander Sonderkonten fur Inlandszahlung (ASKI) procedure was introduced, replacing the private-compensation procedure, which had been less restrictive and had been used to avoid strict exchange controls. The ASKI procedure established accounts at German banks where foreign exporters' proceeds were held. Foreign exporters needed to secure permission from German exchange-control authorities to trade with Germany, with German imports limited to only those deemed necessary by the commodity-control boards. ASKI balances could be used to purchase certain nonessential German goods, but the goods had to be shipped to the country of the account holder. Two types of ASKI accounts developed: accounts for individual foreign exporters, and accounts for foreign commercial banks that represented a group of foreign traders.

The New Plan also created a system of payment agreements with Great Britain, Belgium-Luxembourg, Canada, France, and New Zealand. These agreements provided for the release of free foreign exchange to pay for imports and to transfer payment on old German debts. In addition, Germany agreed to import goods equal to a specified fraction of its exports to each country. The effect of the New Plan was to extend and develop the exchange controls of the early 1930s, replacing the ineffective ones with more stringent controls.

The exchange-control system in place after the New Plan consisted of three different arrangements: the stringent ASKI agreements, the more moderate clearing agreements, and the more lax payments agreements. Germany's free trade was limited to only a small group of countries, including the United States, because the overvalued mark doomed Germany to a trade deficit where trading agreements were not in effect.

The Reorientation of Germany's Trade

Germany's bilateral trading agreements accounted for 50 percent of Germany's trade by 1938. German trade with southeast Europe often is overemphasized, as the Balkans bought only seven percent of Germany's exports in 1935 and 11 percent by 1938. While these parts of Europe were regarded as prime areas for German economic and trade expansion, there was significant resistance to any kind of limiting relationships with Germany. Germany incurred trade deficits with most of her Balkan neighbours during the 1930s, and the largest German trade was conducted with western Europe, Latin America, and the Middle East.

Kitson (1992) concludes that Germany sacrificed terms-of-trade advantages that could have been won from its position as monopolist in export markets and monopsonist in import markets. Other objectives replaced improvements in the terms of trade, as isolation from the world market, reduced dependence on imports, and reorientation of trade to safe, adjacent countries took precedence. According to Neal (1979, 392) it was relatively costless, and often politically rewarding, for Germany to forgo the advantages of monopoly exploitation.

While England, France, the Netherlands, Belgium, Japan, and Italy increased trade within their empires—not always with satisfactory impacts on their domestic economies—Germany, which had no empire, was forced to develop a currency bloc, altering its pattern of trade. The pattern of changes between 1929 and 1938 is shown in table 8.3.

German trade was reoriented in favour of southern and eastern Europe, the countries with which it conducted the stricter policies of ASKI and clearing agreements. As trade between Germany and southeastern Europe increased, these nations became more dependent on exports to Germany's market for basic foodstuffs and raw materials. These countries were isolated in the post-Depression trade world, and Germany, paying prices 20 percent to 40 percent

Table 8.3 Changes in the direction of Germany's trade, 1929 and 1938 (percentages)

	German Imports		German Exports	
	1929	1938	1929	1938
Europe				
Southern and eastern Europe[a]	9.8	18.7	11.2	20.8
Scandinavian countries	7.4	11.3	10.2	12.9
Austria[b]	1.5	—	3.3	—
Gold bloc and Czechoslovakia	23.6	16.1	35.2	26.0
United Kingdom	6.4	5.2	9.7	6.7
	48.7	51.3	69.6	66.4
Rest of the world				
British dominions and colonies	12.5	10.3	4.3	6.1
United States	13.3	7.4	7.4	2.8
Latin America	12.1	16.8	7.8	12.1
Other countries	13.4	14.2	10.9	12.6
Total	100.0	100.0	100.0	100.0

[a] Bulgaria, Greece, Hungary, Italy, Romania, Spain, Turkey, and Yugoslavia.
[b] Not shown separately after unification with Germany in 1938.
Source: League of Nations (1939), 278, 300.

above the world level for agricultural commodities, was the most attractive market. A trading bloc was effectively established, providing Germany with a dependable source of necessary commodities.

Between 1929 and 1938, Germany's exports to southeastern Europe, Spain, and Italy rose sharply from 11 percent to 21 percent of total exports, and the proportion of Germany's imports from this region increased from 10 percent to 19 percent. There was also an increase in the share of German trade with the Scandinavian countries, especially Sweden, and with Latin America. By contrast, Germany's trade with the gold-bloc countries, Czechoslovakia, and the United Kingdom became relatively less important as these countries turned to other sources and markets, especially within their own empires.

Although successful in reorienting German trade, the Nazi policies never made southeastern Europe one of Germany's major trading partners, and some of the increase that did occur was simply the reestablishment of older trading patterns that had been disrupted by the inflations and upheavals of the 1920s (for details, see Aldcroft, 2006).

Italy between Germany and the Gold Bloc

The Italian case is somewhat peculiar in that, while a member of the gold bloc, it followed a trade pattern and a path to economic recovery that increasingly resembled that of Germany.

With the floating of the pound in 1931, the lira—having previously stabilized at a high rate—turned out to be overvalued with respect not only to sterling but to the other gold-bloc currencies as well. Mussolini tried once again, as in 1927, to curb wages and salaries by decree, in order to compensate for the revaluation of the currency. This time, however, the policy was less successful: real wages remained stable between 1929 and 1932 and rose thereafter. Controls on capital movements (foreign-exchange controls, in the language of the 1930s) were therefore introduced, at first surreptitiously then in a most open fashion, in order to stem the outflow of gold reserves. Italy needed its gold reserves if it wanted to stay in the gold bloc, an important objective for Mussolini, who placed pride in the stability and strength of the lira. In July 1935, to stem speculation during the African campaign, the Italian government prohibited gold exports. Together with controls on capital movements came clearing agreements. After a moment of political tension with Germany in 1934–1935, Italy reoriented its trade toward its northern neighbour, happy to enter into clearing deals. Trade with the colonies, never of major importance, was carried out within the currency area of the lira. Argentina, a traditional trading partner, signed clearing agreements with Italy, as did several European countries, including Great Britain. The lira, like the mark, remained on gold only formally, thank to a panoply of exchange controls, tariffs, quotas, and clearings.

Economic recovery came in early 1935 with Mussolini's decision to invade Abyssinia. Deficit spending on armaments produced a sharp increase both in total employment and in the number of hours worked in manufacturing. Sanctions imposed by the League of Nations (which incidentally drew many opposition members on Mussolini's side) prompted the launch of an autarky (import substitution) program that brought Italy closer to the trading area of Germany.

Japan as a Different Mixed Case

Japan—the third member of the future Axis—also created its own trading area, which expanded with the Japanese military expansion. Externally, Japanese economic policies were like those of the sterling area, based on devaluing the currency and gaining the possibility of expansive domestic policies. Internally, Japan was more like Germany and Italy in emphasizing military expenditures and expansion.

In the 1920s, successive Japanese governments committed to a return to gold at a relatively high parity. But easy money and government spending were called for in the wake of the Kanto earthquake of 1923 and after a major spree of bank failures in 1927. Deflation was postponed to allow for whatever monetary expansion was needed to provide lending of last resort (Faini and Toniolo, 1992). From a macroeconomic viewpoint, the tragedies of the 1920s were a blessing in disguise, as the administration of the bitter medicine of deflation was repeatedly postponed, to the advantage of output and employment growth. It was only in 1929 that the Hamaguchi cabinet produced an austerity fiscal budget leading to the reintroduction of the gold standard, at the prewar parity, in January 1930 (Metzler, 2006) .

If this was not the appropriate moment for a return to convertibility, Japan was quite swift in redressing the policy mistake. One of the first moves of a new cabinet that took power in December 1931, with Takahashi as minister of finance, was to again suspend gold convertibility, in January 1932. Only two years after its ill-timed reinstatement, the Japanese gold standard was buried for good. Left to float, the yen depreciated by 60 percent in 1932.

As in the case of Germany and Italy, recovery came from military expenditure. The Japanese depression turned out to be mild and short-lived. By September 1931, the armed forces had acquired a prominent political role in Japan, and the country began military operations in Manchuria. By early 1932, the region was entirely occupied by Japanese forces. This acquisition of new territory enlarged the overseas Japanese Empire, which already included Korea and Taiwan. The empire's boundaries coincided with the inner circle of the yen trade area, where international commerce was organized along the lines of similar areas (such as the British and German areas), which featured a manufacturing center and a less developed primary-producing periphery.

Japan succeeded in riding out the world depression remarkably well. The devaluation of the yen stimulated exports, while domestic demand for military purposes resulted in an impressive industrial growth. That growth, however, increased the dual character of the economy, composed of rapidly expanding heavy industry and mining concerns (the Zaibatsu) on the one hand, and low-wage consumer industry and agriculture on the other. The 1930s were not free from social tensions, and militarism became ever more pervasive and aggressive. In 1937, a new military campaign in China brought large parts of that country under Japanese control.

8.5 The United States and Russia as Polar Opposites

America and the Soviet Union, future allies in the Second World War, pursued diametrically opposite policies in the 1930s. They both achieved economic growth, if at very different speeds, but the United States did it by opening up the economy, while Russia closed its economy even more than Germany did. The Soviet Union did not experience a depression, and its GDP per person grew by 6.6 percent per annum between 1932 and 1938. Over the same period of time, the growth rate in the USA was 3.5 percent, and output in 1938 was still below the 1929 level. Russia and the United States were at very different stages of economic growth as the depression began, and some differences may have come from the enormous potential for catch-up existing in the backward Soviet economy. Much more of the discrepancy came from ideology.

President Roosevelt took office at the beginning of March 1933, about a month after Hitler became chancellor of Germany. To some, the two new leaders looked indistinguishable: "new men" who would rescue the world from the grip of the Great Depression. The two men were very different, of course, and it is a historical curiosity that it took some people several years to figure this out. Roosevelt set out to preserve democracy in the United States, while Hitler moved quickly to destroy it in Germany. Germany ended up fighting both the United States and Russia in the Second World War, and one of the reasons Germany and its cobelligerents lost was the robust economic growth of the United States and Russia in the 1930s (Overy, 1996). They achieved their growth by implementing very different policies, to which we now turn.

The New Deal in the United States

As Roosevelt took office at the start of March 1933, he was greeted by a massive run on American banks that was produced in part by his reluctance to proclaim his adherence to the gold standard during the long gap between his election in November 1932 and his inauguration. He responded to the bank runs by proclaiming a "bank holiday" and closing *all* banks in the United States. This holiday represented the final collapse of the American financial system. The new president gathered a diverse group of advisers around him, and he seems to have adopted all their suggestions as he tried to put the economy back together again. In a flurry of activity he proposed myriad bills to Congress in the next three months that are known collectively as the New Deal.

The first strand was macroeconomic in modern terms. Roosevelt abandoned the gold standard in April 1933 in the context of agricultural reform. He appointed a new head of the Federal Reserve System who would allow the money stock to expand as gold flowed into the United States. He supported banking reform, from the clean-up required to end the bank holiday to the separation of commercial and investment banking in the Glass-Steagall Act. This act also mandated the formation of the Federal Deposit Insurance Corporation, which was designed to avoid future bank runs by insuring the bank deposits of ordinary people. It took effect only after recovery had begun and bank runs were no longer an issue, but it has prevented the recurrence of bank runs in postwar recessions.

A second strand was agricultural reform. The Agriculture Adjustment Act (AAA) allowed the government to control the production of agricultural commodities. By restricting production, policy makers hoped to increase agricultural prices. Devaluation also increased prices, most notably in wheat, which was traded on an international market. The dollar price of wheat jumped 30 percent when the dollar was devalued (Temin and Wigmore, 1990). The program's overall goal was to raise agricultural prices to a level that would provide the same purchasing power in 1933 that they had provided before the war, in 1914. The prewar conditions were adopted as "parity," against which all current arrangements were judged.

Industrial reform followed the model of agricultural reform. The National Industrial Recovery Act (NIRA) provided incentives for employers and employees to negotiate agreements on hours of work, wages, and other working conditions. If these agreements were in accord with codes drawn up by the government, they were exempt from antitrust laws. In fact, the government did not challenge any agreements; it delegated authority to industry groups. The resultant contracts shortened working hours in an attempt to spread the work over more people. At the same time, in an unprecedented act in the middle of a depression, the agreements raised wages. Employers agreed to this increase in their costs if they in turn were allowed to raise prices.

As with agriculture, the intent of the NIRA was to raise prices in order to restore confidence in the economy and implement Roosevelt's famous dictum: "The only thing we have to fear is fear itself." The NIRA succeeded in these aims, and both prices and production rose rapidly in the later 1930s. A sharp recession in 1937 interrupted this progress, and unemployment remained high, as described in Chapter 7, throughout the decade.

The Reciprocal Trade Agreements Act of 1934 also reformed United States tariff policy. Gone was the previous pattern of omnibus trade bills with abundant scope for logrolling and high rates. In its place was a plan to negotiate foreign trade agreements that would not require direct congressional approval. Although the original bill was passed amid fierce partisan dissent, the change in trade policy turned out to be permanent (Irwin and Kroszner, 1999).

There are many explanations for why the recovery in the United States was not rapid enough or continuous enough to eliminate its massive unemployment. One explanation is that the many reforms sometimes got in the way of each other. The increase in prices engineered by the AAA and the NIRA served to absorb much of the increase in the money stock that resulted from capital inflows. Another explanation is that high wages continued even after the NIRA was declared unconstitutional in 1935, discouraging employment of more workers. Yet another reason may be that the unemployment at the nadir of the depression was so large that even a rapid increase in production was not enough to eliminate it quickly.

Collectivization in the Soviet Union

Once the Soviet revolution had finally succeeded in the civil war against the "white" armies, the Soviet Union set about developing its economy in almost extreme isolation from the rest of the world. One of the features of the post-1914 "globalization backlash" was the subtraction from world trade of the enormous wealth in agriculture and natural resources contained in the former Russian Empire. Counting precisely on that wealth, Stalin set out to overcome Russia's economic and technical backwardness by building "socialism in one country." The concept was a powerful one. "Bolshevism was combined with nationalism, and the destiny of the revolution was left in the hands of Russia" (Berend, 2006, 146).

The state took upon itself the task of modernizing and developing the economy. Once firmly in power, in 1927–1928 Stalin started a major industrialization drive. After long preparation, in 1929 the first Five-Year Plan was launched, which set the overambitious goal of more than doubling industrial output by 1932. Ever since the reign of Peter the Great, Russia had been accustomed to major development drives, often followed by depression brought about by economic and social exhaustion. But even in Russia, nothing had ever been attempted on such a gigantic scale and with such brutal, ruthless use of the state's monopoly on violence. Stalin's "second revolution" spread terror throughout the country. Economic growth became the only idol, to which everything else had to be sacrificed.

Peasants made particularly good fodder for the economic god. When the Bolsheviks found that they could not get grain from Russian farmers in the late 1920s, chiefly because the farmers had nothing to buy with their earnings, the

Bolsheviks collectivized Russian agriculture. Farmers were extremely unhappy about this change, particularly the "kulaks," prosperous farmers whose lives were at risk as the grain shortages were blamed on them. Farmers responded to government coercion by slaughtering and eating their farm animals, which meant there were no animals to work the land in the early 1930s. Massive famine was the result, in which as many as five million people may have died. The famine obviously did not accelerate economic growth; instead it facilitated government control over the peasants (Allen, 2003).

Forced transfer of labor and capital from agriculture to manufacturing and from consumer-goods production to investment-goods production, accomplished through carefully executed (if wasteful) central planning, tremendously accelerated the transformation of the Soviet Union from an agrarian economy to an industrial economy. The statistical debate over measurement of Russia's GDP growth in the 1930s is still unresolved, but recent studies (e.g., Allen, 2005) leave little doubt of its astonishing speed. While in 1929–1939 the whole world was more or less successfully struggling to find ways out of the depression, the product per person of the Soviet Union increased by about 61 percent, experiencing only a very minor setback in 1932.

Surprisingly, foreign trade also increased considerably, again against the prevailing world trend. If, between 1914 and 1929, Russia's exports declined by almost 5 percent per annum, in 1929–1959 they experienced a handsome annual growth rate of more than 3 percent, compared to a virtual stagnation of total world trade and the negative growth rate that characterized western European export trade. In fact, the Soviet Union increased both its output and its exports faster than any of the other trading areas.

The Third International could thus tout the astonishing success of socialism against the visible failure of capitalism to deliver recovery, let alone growth and full employment. Few outside the Soviet Union knew of the purges, concentration camps, and police brutality within its borders, which explains why "the world admired what happened there" (Berend, 2006, 150).

Chapter 9

Industrial Progress
and Recovery

The failure of aggregate demand in the 1930s meant that employment and output in industrial economies declined. But the capabilities of these economies did not disappear with jobs. Idle capital reduced the need for net investment, but replacements still offered the opportunity for improvement, and new products and new methods continued to be introduced, even in the worst of times. This chapter shows that the abundant capital flows from rich countries to poor countries of the 1920s vanished completely in the depression. It goes on to record the progress of individual economies and industries in this more hostile economic environment, and it reviews the policies adopted to promote recovery in some major economies. It records the astonishing improvement in productivity that provides a positive counterpoint to the doleful economic conditions that dominated contemporary discussions. It closes with the final attempt at international cooperation before the Second World War, the Tripartite Agreement of 1936.

9.1 Capital Outflows from Europe

From 1931, the nature and direction of the movements in international capital changed dramatically. The overall dimensions of the process were about the same as they had been in the previous phase, but the content and dynamics of the flows were completely different. In the 1920s, the net movement of capital was predominantly from the rich creditor countries to the less-developed debtors in Europe and elsewhere. This pattern of international capital movement thus conformed very broadly to that of pre-1914 foreign lending, even though it was supplemented to an unprecedented degree by short-term investments. In the 1930s, this traditional pattern was sharply reversed. Vast sums now flowed from the less-developed nations to their former creditors, from countries with deficits on their balance of payments to countries in surplus,

160

from capital markets where interest rates were high to those where they were lower.

The flood of bonds and shares that had poured out of the capital markets in New York, London, Paris and other financial centers now dwindled to a thin and irregular trickle. Potential lenders retreated in the face of the rapid deterioration in economic conditions and prospects, damaging financial crises, and numerous defaults by debtors unable to cope with the collapse of primary-product prices and of their foreign earnings. The occasional new issues of long-term capital that were made in the 1930s were outweighed by the amortization of former loans by those debtors who maintained their repayments. The migration of capital characteristic of the new phase consisted predominantly of short-term funds, moving swiftly and on a vast scale, and determined almost entirely by speculative forces and the threat of war.

The currency crises of 1930 and 1931, the loss of confidence in the stability of various economies, and the loss of value of their currencies played the major roles in stimulating the seemingly perverse flows of "hot money" from the debtors to the creditor countries. Enormous sums were withdrawn by asset holders, who simply wished to preserve their investments in the face of currency depreciation and the domestic inflation associated with it. These movements were swelled by a very high level of activity by speculators—some trying to avoid losses when they expected depreciation of their own currencies, others looking for capital gains from the short-term purchase of a foreign currency that was expected to appreciate.

To protect their limited reserves of gold and foreign exchange against these mounting pressures, more countries were compelled to impose exchange controls. This provoked further withdrawals before the available loopholes were closed. Repatriation of German and other securities was made increasingly profitable by the widening disparity between the prices quoted for these securities on domestic exchanges and the lower levels at which they were valued abroad. The strong recovery of security prices on Wall Street from the spring of 1933 provided a further inducement to move capital to the United States.

One important effect of the decline in long-term lending and the growth of exchange controls was the separation of national financial markets. Before the war, interest rates in much of the world followed similar patterns. The existence of this international capital enabled less-developed countries to tap the savings of more-developed countries to build the infrastructure they needed for economic growth. The integration of an international capital market vanished in the 1930s. Interest rates diverged, and these useful capital flows dried up. It would take many years to recover the international integration of capital markets that preceded the Great Depression (Obstfeld and Taylor, 2004).

From the middle of the decade these economic factors were powerfully supplemented by political concerns. A succession of developments, including the Italian invasion of Ethiopia, the German reoccupation of the Rhineland,

and the Spanish Civil War, raised the alarming prospect of world war, with its attendant dangers to wealth from seizure or destruction by the enemy and from the imposition of increased taxes, capital levies, and exchange restrictions. As the panic spread, Great Britain and the United States came to be seen increasingly as the only safe and reliable havens for capital.

The results of these tendencies were a transfer of capital to the United States of almost $5.5 billion from 1934 to 1937, and further large movements across the Atlantic in 1938 and 1939. The flow toward the United Kingdom began a little earlier, and over 1931–1937 the net import of funds amounted to roughly $4 billion. In the same period there was also a small net movement of about $600 million to Switzerland, Sweden, and the Netherlands (Feinstein and Watson, 1995). The countries responsible for sending these vast sums cannot be identified reliably from the available data, but it seems likely that the great bulk of this capital, perhaps $6–7 billion, was an outflow from continental Europe, with France, Germany, and Belgium leading the exodus. Switzerland and the Netherlands also remitted large sums to the United States, though much of this may have come initially from other sources.

As the economic climate darkened, both foreigners and nationals became increasingly anxious to transfer their funds to stronger and safer currencies, and the resulting withdrawal of short-term capital put the central monetary authorities under enormous pressure. In Germany, Austria, Hungary, Poland, Italy, and many other countries, the inevitable step was the imposition of progressively more stringent and comprehensive exchange controls. This measure further intensified the eagerness of asset holders to escape from such currencies, and the extent to which they succeeded in doing this will not be reflected in the records of the debtor nations but can be seen in the massive accumulation of gold by the recipients, notably the United Kingdom and, after the stabilization of the dollar, the United States.

The gold inflow to the United States helped the recovery there to progress rapidly. Roosevelt was not yet ready to adopt Keynesian-style expansive fiscal policies, but he appointed a Fed chairman who would not sterilize gold inflows. The investors' rush to safety in the 1930s therefore allowed the American money supply to expand rapidly, allowing interest rates to remain low and industry to expand. But while the rate of expansion was high, unemployment also remained high, as described in Chapter 7 (Romer, 1992).

The decline in France's international financial position reveals the costs of staying on gold. In the late 1920s, the undervaluation of the franc and the weakness of sterling enabled France to make massive additions to its reserves of gold and foreign exchange, and also to lend abroad, albeit on a modest scale, French investors having lost much of their enthusiasm for foreign investment after their experiences in 1917. From 1931, when Britain left the gold standard and devalued the pound, the franc lost its strength, and capital ebbed away as investors became progressively more pessimistic about future economic and political conditions in France. The outflow in 1931–1937 was more than $2 billion and may have been considerably larger.

The German accounts show a net outward movement in this period of more than $1 billion. For the most part, this was not the result of speculative flows but a deliberate program for the reduction of foreign indebtedness. The transformation of exchange controls from "an emergency measure to a totalitarian institution" (Ellis, 1941, 158) gave the regime tight control over all current-account and capital-account payments and provided the context in which securities could be repurchased and debts repaid.

9.2 An Overview of a Limp Recovery

The poor economic conditions of the Great Depression dragged on throughout the 1930s. High unemployment continued in industry, and low prices continued in agriculture. Most countries in the 1930s earned the bulk of their income in agriculture, and they suffered from the low prices dogging that sector. There was no way to restrict the production of farm outputs, and the prices of farm products fell further and stayed lower than the prices of industrial goods. Less-developed countries, already starved of foreign capital flows, suffered additionally from adverse terms of trade. The imposition of exchange controls, multiple exchange rates, bilateral trade agreements, quantitative restrictions, and other barriers to normal international commerce only made the problems worse. Persistent stagnation in the incomes of millions of farmers and raw-material producers, and the stubborn continuation of deflationary policies in the gold-bloc countries, were the result.

All these tendencies clearly were highly detrimental to the revival of international trade from the catastrophically low levels to which it had collapsed in the early 1930s (see section 6.1). Relief from the contraction would thus have to come primarily from the expansion of domestic demand. Lower prices, and thus higher real incomes, would contribute to this for those who had jobs, but this alone would not be a sufficient stimulus. Before we examine the policies adopted to promote recovery in some of the leading countries, it will be helpful to set the scene with a brief review of the overall picture.

The sustained weakness of world trade can be seen in table 9.1. There was some recovery in the volume of world exports (row 2), but it was not sufficient to regain the 1929 level. Export prices (row 3) continued their downward course until 1935 and then managed only a very weak recovery. By 1937, the best year in the 1930s, the value of international trade was still only a miserable 45 percent of its value in 1929.

The trends in output of industrial and primary products are traced in the first three panels of table 9.2. The recovery in industrial production (row 1) was slightly better in Europe than in the United States and Canada. Even there,

Table 9.1 Indices of world trade, 1932–1937 (1929 = 100)

	1932	1933	1934	1935	1936	1937
1. Value at current prices[a]	39	35	34	35	38	45
2. Export volume	74	75	78	82	86	96
3. Export price	52	47	44	43	44	47

[a] Index of the value of exports by seventy-five countries measured in pre-devaluation U.S. gold dollars.

Source: League of Nations (1939a), 8.

Table 9.2 World production and prices, 1933–1937 (1929 = 100)

	1932	1933	1934	1935	1936	1937
1. Industrial production						
a. World[a]	64	72	78	86	96	103
b. Europe[a]	72	77	86	93	101	110
c. North America	54	64	67	76	89	93
2. Primary production—food						
a. World	100	102	101	101	103	106
b. Europe[a]	104	106	107	107	107	109
c. North America	100	100	98	91	96	97
3. Primary production—raw materials						
a. World	75	81	87	95	106	119
b. Europe[a]	73	77	85	91	98	109
c. North America	64	69	71	78	91	108
4. World prices						
a. Food	50	46	42	40	42	46
b. Raw materials	44	40	40	39	41	47
c. Manufactures	63	56	50	48	48	51

[a] Excluding the Soviet Union.

Sources: Rows 1–3: League of Nations (1939b), 423–24. Row 4: League of Nations (1939a), 61.

however, the revival had only enough strength to carry the volume of output in 1937 some 10 percent above the 1929 level, a growth rate for this important sector of the real economy of only 1.2 percent per annum over a period of eight years. Production in north America was unable to achieve even this much, and the level in 1937 was still 7 percent below the previous peak.

Production of food continued to be broadly stable (row 2), but with food prices stagnant at around 40 percent of their 1929 level, farm incomes remained very depressed. Producers of industrial raw materials fared rather better in terms of the recovery in output between 1932 and 1937 (row 3), responding to the revival in production in the industrial economies, but this was not sufficient to lift prices (row 4b), so that their incomes—and thus their capacity to import manufactures—languished well below the level of the more prosperous 1920s.

Industrial Production Recovers in Some Countries

Industrial recovery came from the interaction of government policies and the expansion of demand. We survey some of the experiences, treating countries roughly in the order of their government domination of economic activity. The Soviet Union, largely isolated from the trading and financial booms of the 1920s, still experienced something like a depression in the 1930s. Both Germany and Russia experienced hyperinflations in the early 1920s, followed by successful price stabilizations. But while prices were afterward free to vary in Germany, the Russians controlled their prices. Monetary expansion in the Soviet Union therefore showed up in inflationary pressure and shortages, not higher prices. Shortages affected the supply of urban food. The Bolsheviks, not understanding the underlying reality of suppressed inflation, commandeered the needed food. This led to less food being offered the following year and then to forced collectivization of Soviet farming (Johnson and Temin, 1993).

Soviet peasants responded by consuming their capital, that is, by killing and eating their animals, leading to even less food in following years. The result was a massive famine that may have killed five million people. It was not part of the world depression, but the suffering was among the worst in the world during the 1930s. The Bolsheviks nonetheless carried on with their ambitious plans for industrialization. In a series of five-year plans, the Soviet Union allocated increasing resources to industry, with dramatic results. The resulting rapid growth in steel production can be seen in table 9.3. This rapid growth was not the result of the famine, but rather of the "soft

Table 9.3 Crude steel production, 1928–1938 (millions of tons)

Year	USSR	Germany	UK	US
1928	4.3	14.4	8.5	56.6
1929	4.9	16.1	9.6	61.7
1930	5.9	11.4	7.3	44.6
1931	5.6	8.2	5.2	28.6
1932	5.9	5.7	5.3	15.1
1933	6.9	7.5	7.0	25.7
1934	9.7	11.7	8.9	29.2
1935	12.6	16.2	10.0	38.2
1936	16.4	18.8	11.8	53.5
1937	17.7	19.2	13.0	56.6
1938	18.1	21.9	10.4	31.8

Sources: Temin (1991), 586; Mitchell (1962), 137; U.S. Department of Commerce (1975), 693.

budget constraint" that allowed industrial plants to grow, even if they were not profitable (Allen, 2003).

Nazi Germany did not abolish private property, but it controlled production by a mixture of carrots and sticks to managers. The Nazi four-year plans were similar to the Soviet five-year plans, and they both substituted administrative control of resources for a market allocation. Prices were not allowed to fluctuate in either country after the Nazis controlled prices in 1936. Neither country was very good at central planning in the 1930s, however, and the resulting industrial growth was accomplished with much waste. Consumers in both countries suffered as resources were clumsily directed toward heavy industry. German steel production stayed above Soviet levels throughout the 1930s, as shown in table 9.3, although much of the German growth was recovery from the Great Depression, not new growth (Temin, 1991).

A word needs to be said about the experience of IG Farben under the Nazis. As a major German firm, it was intimately connected with the Nazi government; as a producer of chemicals, it was part of the Nazi military buildup. The question has been raised of IG Farben's culpability in Nazi savageries. The picture is mixed. On the one hand, executives of IG Farben were not immune to the terror of the Nazis. No company, however large, could withstand the totalitarian state. On the other hand, IG Farben employed slave labor from Auschwitz during the war. There was no compulsion to do so; it was a decision to get cheap labour. Even though IG Farben was not a totally free agent, it participated far more than it had to in the Nazis' persecution of Jews and other disfavored groups (Hayes, 1987).

Neither the United Kingdom nor the United States controlled industry like the Nazis and Bolsheviks did, although industry was constrained. British policy continued to cope with the consequences of slow economic growth. The depression was not as severe in Britain as in other industrial countries, and recovery was thus not as spectacular. Steel production grew slowly. It was about the same as German and Russian production in the depths of the depression, but only about half as large at the end of the 1930s. Industry in the United States was affected by the National Industrial Recovery Act, part of Roosevelt's New Deal, which first allowed industry to set prices and wages in 1933–1934. The high levels of U.S. steel production show how big the U.S. economy was relative to those of other countries, including the major industrial countries. These other countries were catching up in the 1930s, but they still were behind the United States at the end of the decade.

Industrial production in Japan rose more rapidly than in any of the major western countries. This was partly the result of leaving gold so quickly in December 1931, but Japanese industry grew far more rapidly than British industry. The rapid recovery was due to expansionary fiscal policy that used deficit finances to support industry. Japanese policy makers were not disciples of Keynes, but they also were not slaves to classical economic doctrines.

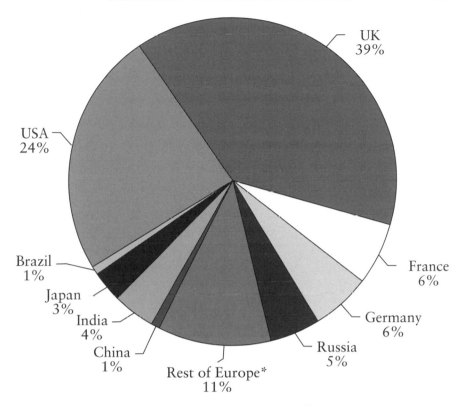

Figure 9.1. World cotton output in 1920. Source: Mitchell, 2003.

Instead, the military demand for ever more resources provided the stimulus for the expansion of demand (Cha, 2003).

A sense of the spread of industry to more countries can be seen in the differences between figure 9.1 and figure 9.2, which show the world share of cotton production in 1920 and 1939. The UK share of world cotton production fell from 39 percent to 24 percent in the interwar years. The shares of other European countries held their own, while the United States also lost some market share. The large gainers were newly industrializing economies, like Japan, India, and Brazil.

9.3 Technical Progress in Agriculture and Industry in the 1930s

Productivity continued to improve through the 1930s, despite the unfavorable conditions in many countries. For Europe as a whole, the rate of growth

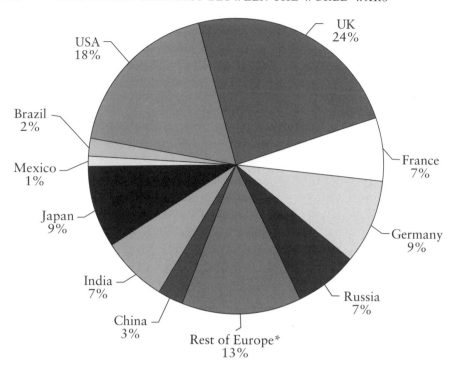

Figure 9.2. World cotton output in 1939. Source: Mitchell, 2003.

of GDP per hour worked was approximately 1.5 percent per annum from 1929 to 1950, compared to 2.2 percent per annum from 1913 to 1929 (Maddison, 1991, 274–75). In contrast, the growth rate of GDP per hour rose in the United States from 1.4 percent to 1.9 percent, due mostly to progress in the 1930s (Gordon, 2000; Field, 2003). The impressive rate of productivity growth in the 1930s stands in sharp contrast to the continuation of mass unemployment. Productivity growth made it harder for the industrial expansion to employ all willing workers. In addition to the underlying process of technical progress and the possibility of benefiting from earlier advances in the leading countries, performance in individual countries was affected by movements in employment and in hours worked. Developments in some of the individual sectors and countries are noted in the following paragraphs.

Agriculture was the classic victim of increasing supply and decreasing demand. The long-run trend in the demand for agricultural products was to decline relative to the demand for other products as incomes rose. The demand for grains fell absolutely as diets improved with income and people ate more meat. In addition, the demand for European products fell in the interwar years due to the influx of agricultural imports from the Americas and the fall in demand during the depression.

Despite the sustained agricultural depression of the interwar period, technical change continued. The use of fertilizers increased output per acre; the use of tractors increased output per worker. Svennilson (1954) commented that the tractor was to agriculture what the steam engine was to industry; yet the progress of tractors was slow in the interwar years. Tractors had become profitable for many American farmers in the 1920s, but the burden of high debt and low prices retarded tractor purchases. The depression accentuated both of these trends, and tractor purchases collapsed. One of the New Deal's aims was to revive American agriculture; the Agricultural Adjustment Act helped to raise prices by restricting production, and the Farm Credit Administration refinanced farmers' debts. The result was rapid diffusion of tractors in the American Midwest during the later 1930s (Clarke, 1991). The diffusion of the tractor was slower in Europe than in North America. Europe started off the 1930s with only one-sixth as many tractors per hectare as North America. The number of European tractors doubled in the 1930s, but the North American tractor density was still more than four times as high at the end of the decade.

The clash of increasing productivity and reduced demand meant lower prices and fewer agricultural jobs. The share of the labor force engaged in agriculture continued its long-run decline in industrial countries, but the depopulation of the countryside was resisted. Many farmers, instead of looking for alternative work when farming no longer was profitable, sought government aid to preserve their incomes as farmers. Each country has its own myth of its agrarian past, and each country has a slightly different way of embedding this legacy in the distribution of political power; but the uniform outcome has been government support of agriculture.

Coal mining followed a similar path after the First World War. Coal was the industrial fuel par excellence in the nineteenth century; it was coal-using activities that were replacing agriculture. But the consumption of coal reached its peak during the boom years of the late 1920s. As with agriculture, there was a short-run fall in demand during the depression that accentuated a long-run shift of demand away from coal. The combination reduced miners' income and pushed them into other activities.

Britain had gained from being the workshop of the world in the nineteenth century, and most of the new activities used coal. Textiles were manufactured in Lancashire because coal was mined there, not because cotton grew there. Railroads used coal; steamships did too. Just as Britain was first to produce these products, it was the first to engage in large-scale coal mining. The consequence of this early start was that British coal mines were the oldest in the world when the demand for coal stopped growing after the First World War. They had the deepest shafts and the highest costs. British miners therefore felt the decline in demand most keenly. The social unrest that was such a prominent part of interwar British history was the result.

Problems in the coal mines led to the general strike of 1926 and an act to allow coal mines to amalgamate voluntarily. When that did not achieve the desired effect, another act of 1930 set up a compulsory coal cartel. It set prices and restricted production, but fiercely individualistic owners resisted modernization and the closing of older and less efficient mines.

Germany had newer coal mines, but it was still subject to the general fall in the rate of growth of demand. The Ruhr coalfield was successfully cartelized and "rationalized"; that is, smaller, less efficient mines were closed, and machines were introduced. The results were that productivity and profits rose, in sharp contrast to British mines. But the mining labor force fell in Germany as it did in Britain. The increased mechanization substituted for the age of British mines in reducing the demand for labor.

Coal production in the United States peaked in the early 1920s. The subsequent decline in coal production brought poverty to many workers and towns in the Appalachian Mountains. The United Mine Workers, under the charismatic leadership of John L. Lewis, attempted to alleviate the miners' distress and to link their fortunes to those of industrial workers elsewhere. The National Industrial Recovery Act of 1933 promoted union organization and collective bargaining. After the act was declared unconstitutional, the Wagner Act of 1935 resurrected the rights of workers established by the NIRA. Lewis joined with other labor leaders to form the Congress of Industrial Unions in 1935. The growth of American unions in the 1930s was helped both by the changes in workers' rights and by the impact of the depression on employment (Freeman, 1998).

Other traditional industries—especially textiles, steel, and shipbuilding—had similar problems. Their growth slowed markedly in the interwar period due to a mixture of short-term and long-term influences. British industries suffered more during the 1920s than those in other countries. They all suffered in the 1930s, and traditional industries in developed countries were particularly hard-hit (see figure 9.2).

The Growth of the New Industries

Not all industries had such cheerless experiences. The growth of new industries gave rise to what Gordon called "One Big Wave" of increasing productivity in America. This wave started in the 1920s and continued after World War II, but it had its peak in the 1930s. Gordon attributed this big wave to progress in four groups of new inventions. The first invention was electric power, introduced into industrial plants in the 1920s (see Chapter 4) and becoming widespread in the following decade. Electric motors also were behind the growth of consumer durables like washing machines and refrigerators. The second important invention was the internal-combustion engine. Trucks, tractors, and automobiles spread across America. Airplanes made their appearance in the 1930s but were not yet widespread. The third group of inventions was in petrochemicals. These inventions promoted the use of internal-combustion engines and also began to reduce illness. The final group of inventions was the complex of entertainment and communication changes that made radio ubiquitous and TV a reality (Gordon, 2000).

Computing also had its roots in the interwar years. There were many developments of control systems in the United States that operated along analog lines to extend the abilities of the systems' operators. Digital computers were in their infancy, but analog devices of all sorts developed rapidly. The analog systems were important for the development of computers, because even digital computers do not work by themselves; they are operated by people who still engage the world along analog lines. Many of these guidance and control systems were developed by American industry under military contracts, and they laid the foundation for American military success in the Second World War (Mindell, 2002).

The problems of the traditional industries in Europe were partly offset by the promise of these new industries, though their special contribution to the growth in productivity and real income during the 1930s should not be overstated. For example, Aldcroft and Richardson state: "It is obvious that without the new industries—motor-cars, rayon, household appliances, radio and electrical engineering, for example—the increase in productivity and real income [in Great Britain] would have been very small compared with what was actually achieved in the interwar period" (1969, 270). Von Tunzelman (1982) subjected this assertion to a test utilizing admittedly imprecise input-output data. He found that if these new industries had grown only at the average rate for all industries, gross output in 1935 would have been reduced by less than four percent.

The chemical industry was not a new industry in the interwar years, but it did re-create itself. The industry began early in the nineteenth century with the production of inorganic chemicals, such as soda ash, sulfuric acid, and superphosphate. It transformed itself toward the end of the century with the production of organic chemicals, such as dyestuffs, pharmaceuticals, and photographic chemicals. It began a third generation during the First World War with the attempt to replace imported products with domestic production.

New methods of producing nitrogen led the way toward new methods of synthesizing organic chemicals. The yield from oil refineries was raised by new methods in the 1930s, leading to the beginning of plastics industries. The giant firms formed in the 1920s—ICI and IG Farben—dominated in various international agreements. Economies of scale in the production of chemicals by these new methods guaranteed that independent companies from other countries could not offer effective challenges to these cartels.

The automobile industry came of age in the interwar years. Mass production had been introduced by Henry Ford just before the First World War with the famous "Five-Dollar Day," but mass production only began to spread after the war. Unified production and marketing with periodic model changes was introduced by General Motors in the 1930s. GM planned in the 1920s to fill out its product line to present a car for every customer, and it implemented these plans in the 1930s with the introduction of the Pontiac and the Oldsmobile. These changes transformed the automobile industry from a specialty craft to a central modern industry.

The predominance of the automobile came later to Europe than to the United States. Incomes were lower in Europe, reducing the demand for cars, and public transportation was better (in part because distances were smaller), further reducing the demand. Automobile production in the four largest European producers—Great Britain, Germany, France, and Italy—together never reached half the American production in the interwar years.

Electric power generation in Britain originated in the activities of numerous separate power companies. Recognizing that the fragmented British electric supply was falling behind that of the Continent—only about six percent of British households had electricity at the end of the First World War—Parliament created a Central Electricity Board in 1926. The Board designed and constructed a national power grid into which the private generating companies fit. The bulk of the grid was constructed in 1929–1933, when it provided an inadvertent fiscal stimulus. Its main aim was to increase the efficiency of intraregional power flows, not yet to make a truly national power supply.

The use of electricity in Britain increased steadily during the interwar years. The construction of the national grid is not visible in a break in the series. Instead, the cumulative effect of better technology, national distribution, and lower rates brought an increasing electrification of society. Residential use grew the fastest, reaching two-thirds of households by 1938, but industrial and commercial establishments also converted to the new power source, as did urban transport systems and railroads.

As in America, electrification of homes increased the demand for consumer durables, the new products of the interwar years. Initially, electricity was used solely for illumination. Heat was the next use, in cookers, irons, and space and water heaters. Vacuum cleaners and radios followed rapidly during the 1930s. As with electricity itself, the wider distribution of these new appliances reduced the costs of producing them, further stimulating their use.

Developments on the Continent were similar, albeit at different rates. The French and Germans were more centralized from the start, avoiding the characteristic British fragmentation. The Italians started out well but failed to construct a national power grid during the 1930s. The hilly Italian terrain had made hydropower important, and each plant and locale generated its own electricity from local water wheels or turbines. The diversity of standards and organization made national unification even harder to achieve in Italy than in Britain.

With radios came a market for radio programs. Messages had been transported over cables since the middle of the nineteenth century. Wireless communication made its entry early in the twentieth century through Marconi's efforts to promote ship-to-shore communication. Broadcasting was a creation of the interwar years, supplementing the previous systems of point-to-point communication by telegraph and telephone.

The birth of broadcasting created immediate issues of public policy. Radio frequencies were licensed by the government to "deserving" individuals in the United States. Recognizing at least dimly the importance of this nascent communication channel, European governments wanted to keep control of it. They were opposed by technologically aggressive entrepreneurs who wanted to reap private gains from their new innovations. The struggle was a continuing one, resulting in uneasy compromises that differed between countries and shifted over time.

The structure of private industry in the new broadcasting sector quickly reduced to a stable oligopoly. The Marconi, CSF, and Telefunken companies in Europe vied with the American RCA for a worldwide market. The contest was only partly like a traditional oligopoly. The uneasy balance between public and private control was a characteristic of many countries, and companies had to compete for political favors as often as for technical advantages.

Point-to-point wireline communication also increased during the interwar years, with the extension of telephone service. Germany held an ambivalent position in the development of European telephone service in the 1920s. Politically isolated and in conflict with her neighbors, Germany nevertheless was a vital part of emerging European telecommunications. The Germans were invited to meetings on technical standards because they and the Americans were in the technological vanguard. Germany sat in the center of Europe, making connections for many other countries that wished to communicate through Germany by means of German telephone cables. As in broadcasting, telephonic communication was dominated by political concerns. And as with power generation, construction of a coordinated system was impeded by local technical conditions.

Other innovations of the 1930s are listed in table 9.4. Many of these new products would only become widespread after the war, but the low demand during the depression did not appear to inhibit the process of innovation nearly as much as it depressed sales of goods and services.

9.4 The Tripartite Agreement

French gold losses mounted in the spring of 1936, as noted in section 8.3. Blum's Popular Front government, whose appeal was largely based on its repudiation

Table 9.4 Innovations in the 1930s

USA	Europe	Other
3M Scotch tape[1]	Jet engine (UK)[15]	
Neoprene[2]	Electron microscope (Germany)[16]	
Analog computer[3]	Introduction of nuclear energy (UK)[17]	
Stop-action photography[4]	Discovery of the neutron (UK)[18]	
Electronic flash[5]	Road reflectors (UK)[19]	
Polaroid photography[6]	Magnetic recording (Germany)[20]	
Parking meter[7]	Radar (UK)[21]	
Radio telescope[8]	First artificial element, technetium	
FM radio[9]	(Italy)[22]	
Nylon[10]	Ballpoint pen (Hungary)[23]	
Voice recognition machine[11]	Freeze-dried coffee (Switzerland)[24]	
Photocopier[12]	Turboprop engine (Hungary)[25]	
Spam[13]		
Teflon[14]		
Helicopter		
More effective retail system (product assortment, marketing, etc)		

Sources:
1. "Inventor of the Week Archive: Richard Drew." The Lemelson-MIT Program. http://web.mit.edu/invent/iow/drew.html.
2. "Wallace Hume Carothers." Chemical Heritage Foundation. http://www.chemheritage.org/classroom/chemach/plastics/carothers.html.
3. "Vannevar Bush's Differential Analyzer." Encyclopedia Britannica. http://www.britannica.com/eb/article-216034.
4. The Edgerton Exploit Center. Available: http://www.edgerton.org/biography.html 5. The Edgerton Exploit Center. Available: http://www.edgerton.org/biography.html
6. "Edwin Herbert Land." National Inventors Hall of Fame. http://www.invent.org/hall_of_fame/91.html.
7. Conley, Christopher. "Parking Meters Get Smarter." *Wall Street Journal*, June 30, 2005. http://online.wsj.com/public/article/SB112008647932273412-lI8rQmFI3ciQB2GPDztP8N0jcfY_20060629.html?mod=TFFP1YAHOO.
8. "Radio Telescope Developed." National Aeronautics and Space Administration. http://edmall.gsfc.nasa.gov/aacps/news/Radio_Telescope.html.
9. Hinckley, David. "Celebrating FM's 70th Anniversary." New York Daily News, http://www.nydailynews.com/entertainment/ent_radio/story/317065p-271202c.html.
10. Nylon: 1935, DuPont, available: http://heritage.dupont.com/touchpoints/tp_1935–2/depth.shtml.
11. "History of Speech Recognition." *NetByTel Industry Newsletter.* http://www.netbytel.com/literature/e-gram/technical3.htm.
12. Arabe, Katrina. "Chester's Dream: The Genesis of the Modern Photocopier." Industrial Market Trends. http://news.thomasnet.com/IMT/archives/2001/04/chesters_dream.html.
13. "Spam Family of Products History." Hormel. http://media.hormel.com/templates/knowledge/knowledge.asp?catitemid=14&id=94.
14. "Roy J. Plunkett." Chemical Heritage Foundation. http://www.chemheritage.org/classroom/chemach/plastics/plunkett.html.
15. "Sir Frank Whittle," Obituaries, *Daily Telegraph*, August 10, 1996. http://www-g.eng.cam.ac.uk/125/achievements/whittle/telgraph.htm.
16. "History of the Microscope." About.com. http://inventors.about.com/library/inventors/blrazor.htm.
17. "Discovery of Fission." American Institute of Physics. http://www.aip.org/history/mod/fission/fission1/02.html.
18. Cambridge Physics. http://www.phy.cam.ac.uk/camphy/neutron/neutron_index.htm.
19. Griggs, Kim. "Where the Color Meets the Road." *Wired News.* http://www.wired.com/news/autotech/0,2554,59833,00.html.

of deflation, was forced to make emphatic declarations that it opposed devaluation. Even while Blum was defending the franc by publicly announcing his opposition to devaluation, his opinions were drifting toward devaluation, and he privately began to explore the possibilities of an international accord to prevent competitive devaluation of the dollar or the pound in the event of a French devaluation. To defend the French gold reserves, the government was faced with a choice between deflation, devaluation, and exchange control. Deflation was eliminated as an option by its failure to achieve recovery, or even stability, during its many incarnations during the first half of the decade.

Faced with the choice between exchange control and devaluation, the financial and banking communities favoured devaluation as the lesser of two evils. Imposition of exchange controls would lead to French autarky, isolating France from its allies, the western democracies. Exchange control was regarded as a fascist option, requiring extensive controls, far-reaching administration, and severe penalties to be effective. While many members of financial circles and the right-wing press favored devaluation, the French public remained resolutely opposed, as were the Communist party and many members of the Radicals and the Socialists.

The French government's problem was unprecedented in the need to negotiate internationally before devaluing. Unlike the devaluations of the dollar and sterling, which were relatively simple, largely domestic decisions, the franc devaluation was jeopardized by the prospect of competitive devaluations or increased trade barriers in the devalued nations. The floating pound and the dollar were likely to respond to a French devaluation.

The United States asked France in the summer of 1936 whether a joint American and British statement that the dollar and the pound would not depreciate in the event of a reasonable franc devaluation would ease the process of French devaluation. The French opposed this tripartite declaration as merely amounting to a unilateral devaluation, which the Blum government could not accept so readily after campaigning with the promise not to devalue. The British also did not want any commitment that would force them to support the franc and would link the pound to gold. They did not want France pegging to sterling; they wanted France to peg the franc on gold to allow continued

20. "S. Joseph Begun." National Inventors Hall of Fame. http://www.invent.org/hall_of_fame/10.html.
21. "British Man First to Patent Radar." UK Patent Office. http://www.patent.gov.uk/media/pressrelease/2001/1009.htm.
22. Bentor, Yinon. –"Periodic Table: Technetium." http://www.chemicalelements.com/elements/tc.html.
23. Whalley, Joyce Irene (1975). *Writing Implements and Accessories: From the Roman Stylus to the Typewriter*. Detroit: Gale Research.
24. "The Timeline of Instant Coffee." Nestle. http://www.nestle.co.uk/ProductNewsAndOffers/AboutOurBrands/Beverages/History+of+Instant+Coffee.htm.
25. "Jet Engine Types." http://inventors.about.com/library/inventors/bljetenginetypes.htm.

British operations in francs. The British did express their willingness to unofficially keep the pound as stable as possible, while retaining control of the sterling rate. In the spirit of cooperation they agreed to devise some formula for the rates, preferably a meaningless one.

France did not pursue negotiations immediately, expecting an improvement in the domestic situation, but the anticipated calm never developed. The government announced a 21 billion franc rearmament program in September 1936 and proceeded to experience a massive gold outflow. France then responded by presenting a draft prestabilization agreement to Britain and the United States. This called for nations to direct monetary policies toward maintenance of stability and consideration of the international effects of domestic policies.

Washington and London objected to the excessive references to cooperation and stability. They also disliked any reference to the gold standard. The United States objected to a reference to social classes, which would not be palatable to the American public, and to a formula for the French devaluation that would adjust the franc to world prices. The British were uneasy because the new French proposal did not clearly define the extent of the franc devaluation, which the Treasury feared might exceed one hundred francs to the pound.

A revised French draft offered a compromise suggesting that the French and British cooperate daily, allowing each to convert holdings of the other's currency into gold. This compromise was the basis of what became known as the 24-hour gold standard. The two exchange authorities subsequently agreed that each morning they would inform each other if they intended to engage in currency operations during the day. If they agreed on the operation and the rates that would be used, a gold price would be established at which currency could be redeemed for gold at the end of the day.

The United States rewrote the second French proposal and submitted it to Britain and France on September 19. The American version, which was to form the basis of the final agreement, retained flowery French allusions to peace and liberty while offering reasonable dollar stability, accepting the French devaluation, and promising cooperation with the French and British governments. But with an agreement appearing imminent, an American confusion emerged to jeopardize the negotiations. The American officials had misinterpreted the British position on stabilization of currencies.

Washington informed London that the United States was interested in a $5 pound, plus or minus ten cents. United States officials assumed that the British would consider it a reasonable level, as $5 had been the average rate for the past year, while the British Exchange Equalization Account managed the exchanges. In fact, the British disliked the $5 parity but had maintained that rate to avoid forcing devaluation of the franc and other gold-bloc currencies. The American message was immediately rejected by the British, who replied that no such agreement had ever been implied or arranged and that there would be no stabilization of the dollar-pound exchange. In order to salvage the

Tripartite Agreement, the Americans responded to the British objections by agreeing to disagree. The United States retained the view that a $5 pound was appropriate but was willing to concede the point to allow the announcement of the declarations.

The British, French, and American governments released the Tripartite Agreement on September 26, 1936. A large fraction of the declarations was devoted to French-favored avowals of belief in peace, prosperity, increased living standards, truth, beauty, and goodness. While the British were skeptical of this phraseology, the Americans took it seriously. Secretary of the Treasury Morgenthau believed that the declaration would be significant in restoring peaceful conditions to the world.

More significantly, the declaration included the references to relaxing quotas and exchange controls that the British wanted, although France was not specifically mentioned, and the French did very little to lower trade barriers after the release of the agreement. The British agreed not to retaliate against the French devaluation, but there were no promises about rates because the British refused to constrain their domestic policy. The agreement also included announcements calling for increased cooperation among the central banks and equalization funds of the Tripartite Powers.

The Tripartite Agreement marked the total failure of the gold standard to stabilize the international economy. The tangled negotiations needed to produce even this minimal agreement showed the tattered remains of international organization. Minimal and partial cooperation was possible with great strain, but more was unattainable. Germany and Italy were not interested in international forums and not welcome at them. The French and British were too weak to provide effective leadership. The United States under Roosevelt had turned inward, providing more of an obstacle than an opportunity for cooperation.

The agreement did avoid a round of competitive devaluation. Currency movements were generally mild in the few remaining years of peace. But it would have been far better for all of Europe if an agreement for a coordinated devaluation could have been concluded five years earlier, when Britain abandoned the gold standard.

The Netherlands and Switzerland followed France off the gold standard in September 1936, officially ending the gold bloc three years after its inception. Recovery was quick in these two nations, as it had been in Belgium. Export markets recovered, and expansionary policies were implemented. The Italian government used the occasion of the French devaluation as an excuse to devalue the lira and reduce exchange controls, and Czechoslovakia devalued the crown a second time. The Tripartite Agreement was received negatively in France, where it was commonly believed that the Blum government had reneged on its promises not to devalue, and where the international accord was seen as a sham hiding the French devaluation.

The benefits of devaluation were largely offset in France by the increase in French prices. In June 1937, under the pressure of gold losses and budget deficits, the Blum government resigned and was replaced by a government that allowed the franc to float. The French economy remained stagnant from 1936 to 1938, at which point a new government ended the forty-hour work week, imposed new taxes and budgetary economies, and attacked fiscal fraud. The French economy then rebounded rapidly, but it was too late; the Nazi menace was at the door.

Chapter 10

Epilogue: The Past
and the Present

The "Second Thirty Years War," as the period 1914–1945 has been referred to, was a defining moment in the history of humankind. It had a lasting impact on the following decades. Its geopolitical consequences are summarized by the end of a Eurocentric world, the rise of two superpowers, the demise of colonialism, and the emergence of new economic giants in the Pacific basin. In the economic and social sphere, wars and depression resulted in new economic policy making, permanently bigger states, and the rise of the welfare state. Whatever value judgments one may pass on these developments, it cannot be denied that their impact is lasting and pervasive.

The tragedies of the "Second Thirty Years War," some of which were only briefly referred to in this book (which is confined to the economic history of the period), also yielded some powerful lessons to those who took over government responsibilities in the decades following 1945. This book has argued that the shock of the First World War, a most unwise postwar settlement, and the policies adopted after the war led to the Great Depression, high unemployment, and "globalization backlash." The failure of institutions was exacerbated by failures of leadership and cooperation. Judging from the postwar years, it can be said that policy makers did learn, if painfully slowly, from the interwar mistakes. Other blunders were made after the Second World War, but, by and large (and with one exception), those of 1914–1945 were not repeated on a large scale. Among the main lessons brought home after 1945 were the need for a wise and generous postwar settlement, the assumption of international leadership by the United States (and, in its own area of influence, by the Soviet Union, albeit mostly by coercive methods), the dawning of the European Community (which was originally driven by the desire to avoid new conflicts), the efforts to re-create an open international economy, and a new international monetary system.

Before examining the longer-run impact of the "Second Thirty Years War," let's first review the second postwar settlement as a moment of western cooperation, under firm U.S. leadership, which laid the foundations for a period of sustained economic growth.

10.1 The Aftermaths of Two World Wars: Similarities and Differences

The process of creating peacetime institutional, political, and economic conditions after the end of the Second World War (referred to as "postwar settlement") considerably differed from the process described in Chapter 2 as characterizing the Versailles, St. Germain, and Trianon peace treaties. As the result, reconstruction was very rapid. Three to six years after the end of hostilities, even those countries whose economies were most damaged by the conflict had recovered their highest prewar GDP levels. Moreover, and more importantly, reconstruction was followed by a quarter of a century of exceptionally high rates of growth, more rapid than anything experienced before or since. This was particularly true of continental Europe and of Japan, but most of the world also grew faster than before.

Not only was economic growth extremely rapid after the Second World War, but fluctuations were very mild and unemployment particularly low. So exceptional and unexpected was this stream of events that the years 1950–1973 came to be known as the "golden age," and in countries like Germany and Italy, people talked of an "economic miracle." Why was the outcome of the "second postwar settlement" so distinctly different from that of thirty years earlier?

In a broad historical perspective, it is possible to see that the world had changed since 1919. The United States emerged from the Second World War as the undisputed leader of the western world and this time was ready to accept the responsibility. The lesson of Versailles had been absorbed: a sufficient degree of international coordination and cooperation had to be established if stability and prosperity were to be achieved. The United States could provide the relevant preconditions for a new international order based upon mutual trust and collaboration, but it could not impose this; Western Europe and Japan were encouraged and put in the positions to play their parts.

The blame for the unsatisfactory first postwar settlement cannot be laid solely at the door of incompetent politicians and central bankers; its outcome was deeply rooted in Europe's history and its social and political structures. The changes required in order for the post-1945 settlement to yield a better outcome were finally possible as a result of a long historical process inaugurated with the crisis of European liberal capitalism at the end of the nineteenth century. Maier (1987, 162) argued that reversing that crisis took half a century: "The cumulative achievement required the institutional flux that was left in the wake not of one but of two wartime upheavals."

The military, political, and social situation of 1945 was so much more favorable to the creation of preconditions for stability and consensus than that of 1919 precisely because it came at the end of this long and tragic historical process. There were two components of the midcentury settlement: international (the deeply felt need for peace and leadership) and domestic (the legitimation of the new democratic regimes in Europe and Japan), and they were mutually reinforcing. This created a virtuous circle, in sharp contrast to the previous occasion, when ill-designed peace treaties amplified the domestic fragility that afflicted European countries in the aftermath of the war.

The international part of the second postwar settlement rested on the determination of the United States and the United Kingdom to reverse the conditions that had prevailed in the interwar period. The bitter lessons of 1919 and the 1930s were well learned. The aim this time was to create a radically different framework of international economic relations, one that would enable countries to cooperate in trade and investment to their mutual advantage and so help to sustain high levels of domestic activity. The economic advantages of such cooperation were powerfully reinforced by the belief that this would also promote world peace. The promotion of Western cooperation received a powerful push by the division of Europe into two main camps and the onset of the Cold War.

As early as 1941, Roosevelt and Churchill recognized the need to avoid the problems that the enormous burden of war debts had created after 1918. The outcome was the generous scheme for Lend-Lease, under which supplies required by the United Kingdom for the war effort were in effect provided free of charge by the United States and Canada. In 1942, the two powers also reached a preliminary agreement to set international economic relations on a new footing. The 1944 Bretton Woods conference of the forty-four United Nations powers allied against the Axis, and which gave rise to the system of that name, was a deliberate attempt to avoid the deficiencies of the interwar gold standard. It is noteworthy that consensus on the broad lines of the whole project "derived from a shared interpretation of the interwar years, which owed much to the analysis of the League of Nations" (Foreman-Peck, 1995, 240).

Bretton Woods set the framework for a new international monetary system based on fixed exchange rates, with a gold-convertible dollar as anchor currency. It was accepted, however, that there might be special circumstances in which it might be necessary for a country to adjust the relative value of its currency, and procedures were created under which this could be done. Britain took advantage of these procedures in 1949 and 1967; France did the same in 1955 and 1957; and West Germany revalued the mark in 1969. Two international bodies were established: the International Monetary Fund was designed to allow the smooth adjustment of temporary balance-of-payment disequilibria, and the International Bank for Reconstruction and Development (normally known as the World Bank) was to take care of longer-term development needs. Commercial policy was dealt with under the auspices of The General Agreement on Trade and Tariffs, signed in Geneva in 1947. This initiated the lengthy process of reducing tariff barriers on manufactured goods.

In the immediate postwar years, the discipline of the Bretton Woods system could not yet be sustained by the still-prostrate western European economies. In particular, free currency convertibility, after decades of state-run foreign exchanges, seemed to be incompatible with balance-of-payments equilibrium, as shown by the short-lived 1947 experiment with a convertible pound. The United States encouraged the creation of the European Payments Union (1951–1958), a Europe-wide system of multilateral payments that paved the way to full convertibility.

In order to revive the transatlantic trade that would allow the reconstruction of Europe and the continuation of wartime full employment in the United States, the latter recognized its responsibility for providing the essential bridge to prosperity in the form of grants and loans to finance Europe's huge trade deficits. It was another farsighted departure from the attitudes that prevailed after Versailles. There were inevitably some frictions in the discussion of the terms on which aid and loans would be granted and initial uncertainty about how harshly Germany and Japan should be dealt with, but the contrast with the post-1918 wrangling over war debts and reparations was enormous.

Immediate relief aid (UNRRA) was provided to avoid major hardship in devastated Europe. A large loan was made to the United Kingdom. More than this was needed, however, if trade was to revive to the extent necessary. Europe's foreign-exchange reserves were virtually exhausted, and exports to the dollar area were still very low, making it impossible for Europe to import vital supplies and equipment from the United States and Canada. What was needed was a major injection of purchasing power into the international economy *in dollars*. A similar problem had arisen after 1919, and in that era it was left to private capital markets to handle it, with the destabilizing results that we have seen (sections 5.3 and 5.4). This time, the United States made available a total of more than $13 billion in grants and loans to Europe between 1948 and 1951 through the Marshall Plan (officially the European Recovery Program).

While scholarship has failed to uncover direct links between American aid and European investment, it seems clear that the Marshall Plan kept the nascent investment plans of the western European countries from being strangled by foreign-exchange scarcity. The Marshall Plan also eased the harshest postwar living conditions, fostering a relatively peaceful social context in which reconstruction could be more easily effected, and it contributed to the creation of a new climate of confidence and cooperation within and between the nations of Europe, which was a critical element in the domestic aspects of the new postwar settlement.

One other contrast between the two postwar settlements is also of great importance. The 1920s were dominated by disagreements between the former enemies, most conspicuously the bitter disputes between France and Germany over reparations and territory. The political leaders who came to power after the Second World War were determined to avoid such divisive and destructive policies and instead initiated the successive measures that led by 1956 to the formation of the European Common Market. At that point it included only six countries—with the United Kingdom, the Scandinavian countries, and others outside—but it provided economic unity at the heart of Europe.

All these constructive measures sharpened the distinction between the Atlantic economy and the centrally planned economies led by the USSR. Although invited to join in the Marshall Plan, the communist nations were not willing to allow the Americans to have the say in their affairs this would have involved. After initial hesitation, the Soviet Union and its allies also declined to participate in the arrangements established at Bretton Woods. The postwar international system of which we speak therefore refers to only a part of the world economy. Trade and finance among the communist nations was organized quite separately and was not part of the system of free multilateral trade and payments.

It would be claiming too much to say that the monetary flexibility that the Bretton Woods system provided in place of the rigidities of the interwar gold standard was the principal key to European prosperity after the Second World War. Numerous problems had to be overcome in order for this prosperity to be achieved. We have emphasized certain changes in policy and institutions, but numerous other factors also changed between 1919 and 1945. Because we are observing history, not conducting a controlled experiment, we cannot be certain which subset of these changes was responsible for enabling the world economy to escape a repetition of the disasters of the interwar period. We can say, however, that macroeconomic policies, monetary conditions, and international trade arrangements can help to solve problems, or they can make matters worse. We believe that they did the former after the Second World War, and the latter after the First.

10.2 A Lasting Legacy

When saying that 1914–1945 was the defining era of the twentieth century and beyond, we mean that some bitter lessons were learned, such as those that made the second postwar settlement outlined in the previous section so different from the first postwar settlement. We also mean something more structural and long-lasting than that: at least five major political and economic features of the second half of the twentieth century matured as the result of two world wars and the Great Depression. They are: the end of Europe's worldwide supremacy, the demise of formal colonial empires, the open evidence of an

"American century," the diffusion of the welfare state, and the enhanced role of the state in management of the economy.

The End of European Supremacy

At the end of the Second World War, Europe had already begun a process of relative economic decline vis-à-vis the United States. In fact, the U.S. growth rate had been higher than western Europe's ever since the end of the end of the U.S. Civil War, except in the 1930s. By 1950, Western Europe's GDP per capita was only half that of the United States (it had been about 70 percent in the 1870s), but until 1914, Europe's overall economic weight and international political clout assured its prominence in world affairs. The United States did not surpass Great Britain in terms of GDP per capita until the first decade of the twentieth century, and it was only when Europe was politically and economically weakened by the "Second Thirty Years War" that it was progressively marginalized.

It is perhaps a paradox that the process continued after the Second World War, when Europe grew faster than the United States, converging to the latter's productivity levels (see below). But worldwide influence (some would say "dominance") hinges on much more than economic variables. While the United States continued to be the world's productivity leader (even though the gap with other countries narrowed), it took upon itself a political leadership role as well, beginning in 1941–1945, which it had previously refused. Part of this leadership role derived from a military buildup on a scale never before seen in the history of mankind. In 1913, America had an army about the size of Belgium's. Its involvement in two long and costly world wars required the creation the largest armed forces in the world, which remained largely in place after 1945 due to the challenge posed by the Soviet Union.

The End of Colonial Empires

The second major legacy of depression and war was the end of colonialism. The phenomenon is partly related to the weakening of Europe: after the war, colonial powers found it increasingly difficult to foot the bill of empire. But decolonization had deep social and political roots and was destined to happen regardless of Europe's economic, political, and military strength. The movement for the independence of India gained strength in the interwar years, during which Gandhi turned India's Congress Party from an elite vanguard into a mass political movement. British policies in India during the Great Depression alienated segments of the business community, but it was the contribution made by the subcontinent to the victory in the Pacific theater that gave international and domestic legitimacy to India's request for independence.

More generally, military service overseas brought people from parts of the British Empire in contact with each other, raising their political consciousness.

The Allied Charter, agreed by Churchill and Roosevelt in August 1941, outlined for the first time principles that would rule the postwar world. They included the end of any territorial expansion at the expense of other countries, and they affirmed the old Wilsonian principle of the right of self-determination for all the peoples of the world. Sweeping Japanese victories in the Pacific theater undermined the trust of people in Malaysia, Burma, the Dutch Indies, and the Philippines in the ability of their colonial masters to prove effective defense (possibly the main argument advanced to legitimize colonialism). In these circumstances, Queen Wilhelmina of the Netherlands promised her colonies a more autonomous status after the war. In January 1943, Britain and the United States formally announced the renunciation of the semicolonial rights they had extracted from the weak Chinese Empire a century earlier.

Some colonial empires were erased by the war itself: the defeat of Germany, Japan and Italy resulted in the loss of their colonies, most of which were temporarily transferred under the jurisdiction of one of the victorious powers which, however, could not long hold to them.

In the immediate postwar environment, the independence of India from London in 1947 paved the way to a vast movement of decolonization. The old empires, however, lived on stubbornly. The Dutch fought a useless war before granting independence to Indonesia in 1949. British Malaysia did not become independent until 1957. France was particularly recalcitrant in holding to its Empire, starting a colonial war in Indochina in 1946 that would not be concluded until 1975, constituting a major crisis for the West for more than a quarter of a century.

In the Middle East, the United Kingdom gave up Palestine in 1948, while France's short-lived attempt to hold on to its post-World War I protectorates in Lebanon and Syria ended as early as 1946. Nevertheless, British colonies in sub-Saharan Africa continued to attract a steady flow of migrants from the "fatherland" until the early 1960s. It was the Cold War that hastened the process of decolonization, as the Soviet Union and the United States—which granted independence to the Philippines in 1946 but kept all its other colonial possessions in Puerto Rico, the Virgin Islands, the Panama Canal Zone (until 1999), American Samoa, and Guam—competed with each other to gain the favor of the various independence movements. This led to a number of "proxy wars," most of which are now relegated to footnotes in history textbooks; the one with the longest-lasting consequences was, as has already been mentioned, the Vietnam War. The other colonial empires were also gradually liquidated. The last one to fall was the Portuguese Empire, in the mid-1970s. On some occasions, colonial developments had a profound impact on political developments at home: the defeat in Algeria also ended the French Fourth Republic and brought De Gaulle to power for the second time, and the war in Mozambique brought the Caetano regime to an end in Portugal in 1975.

It must be added that, if the Great Depression and World War II hastened the end of the "formal" empires of the European powers (United Kingdom, France, the Netherlands, Belgium, Spain, and Portugal), created from the sixteenth to the nineteenth centuries, the division of the world devised at Yalta to avoid postwar clashes among allies resulted in areas of influence that many in the postwar world saw as new, "informal" empires. The Soviet Union, in particular, imposed its political system on Eastern Europe and allowed countries behind the "iron curtain" only a limited degree of independence in domestic affairs and none at all in international affairs (with the notable exception of Yugoslavia). The United States, for its part, not only created powerful alliances to contain the Soviet bloc but also made sure that communist parties in western Europe did not gain any relevant power. Moreover, the United States exercised a strong influence over most of Latin America, helping friendly governments to remain in office and trying, often successfully, to remove unfriendly ones. This led many observers to speak of "neocolonialism."

The American Century in Full Swing

The third lasting legacy of 1914–1945 was the emergence of the United States, the world's largest and most innovative economy, as the natural leader of the "free world." Once America, after the hesitations of the 1920s and 1930s, finally acknowledged its need to take policy leadership, it became apparent to all that the twentieth century was the American century. It was in full swing at midcentury.

The United States stood like a colossus astride the world economy, but it was challenged by the Soviet Union and the ideology of communism. The Soviet economy, which started from a much poorer basis and had enormously suffered in giving its decisive contribution to the defeat of the Axis, was no match for the American economy, either in providing consumption goods for its citizens or in providing exports that would sell on international markets. However, even allowing for enormous propaganda exaggerations, the Soviet economy grew rapidly in the 1950s and 1960s, providing an "alternative model" to capitalism that seemed attractive to a number of postcolonial governments. Nevertheless, the "American way of life" remained a powerful symbol for most of the world of the wonders that the free market and western democracy could deliver. The "American century" is as much about unprecedented American political and military might as it is about the irresistible glitter of a "consumer society" that revolutionized lifestyles worldwide, affecting almost every aspect of postwar culture.

The Emergence and Resilience of the Welfare State

The fourth lasting legacy of the interwar years was the emergence of the welfare state. Social public spending had started before the interwar years, but such spending had remained negligible as a share of GDP. In 1880, "aside from small pension subsidies in Norway and Denmark, no government paid nationwide subsidies for pensions, housing or even unemployment" (Lindert, 2005, 172). At the time, only a dozen countries paid small subsidies for traditional poor relief and health services, not reaching 1 percent of GDP. Public social transfers increased after 1880 in some countries, but in 1930 their amount was still below 3 percent of GDP, except in Germany, where it was close to 5 percent. According to Lindert, "the social transfer revolution came in the 1930s and 1940s. Throughout Europe, North America, Australasia and Japan, the Great Depression and the War taught people that their fortunes could sink and they needed collective insurance" (2005, 126). Roosevelt launched aid to the unemployed and Social Security for elders and the disabled. Upon seizing power in the 1930s, the Swedish Social Democrats launched a program for a comprehensive welfare state that set the country on the road to an egalitarian recovery. Together with "blood and tears," Churchill promised that the country would provide for all when the struggle was over. In that vein, the 1942 Beveridge Report outlined an ambitious plan of national insurance that many see as the manifesto for the modern welfare state.

Promises were kept after the war. The spread of democracy, in particular of universal female suffrage, provided an irresistible political push, while rapidly rising national incomes made generous social-transfer provisions possible. In the longer term, it turned out that they such policies were also compatible with fast income and productivity growth. By 1980, the welfare state was firmly consolidated into the social pact of the advanced countries and was spreading to the developing ones. At the end of the twentieth century, the amount of total public social transfers ranged from more than 30 percent of GDP in the Scandinavian countries to about a quarter in the largest European continental countries and to minimums of 14 and 12 percent of GDP in the United States and Japan respectively (Lindert, 2005, 177–78).

Macroeconomic Management

As we have argued throughout this book, macroeconomic policy mismanagement largely explains the depth and length of the Great Depression. We also discussed the changes that the depression's shock induced in the economics profession and in actual policy making. Even before the great intellectual breakthrough of the *General Theory* in 1936, a number of economists had taken a more critical attitude toward the prevailing laissez-faire orthodoxy. Governments, for their part, were compelled to find ways to mitigate the impact of unemployment (e.g., with public works programs) and to provide incentives to hire and produce. Regardless of the merit of such policies in individual cases, they signaled that governments in the 1930s were much more inclined to actively intervene in the process of resource allocation than they had been only a few years earlier.

This interventionist attitude was magnified by the war. Any wartime economy is typically characterized by a rapid shift of control over the allocation of productive factors from the private sector to the government sector. The sheer amount of resources poured into the military effort between 1939 and 1945 made it the case that governments exercised a higher degree of control over the production process than ever before. Patriotism and the struggle for survival (as in the case of Great Britain, particularly between 1940 and 1942) provided the necessary public support for the government's grip on the economy. But there was another reason why pervasive government intervention was accepted and even welcomed: in contrast to the 1930s, the wartime years were a period of full employment.

Toward the end of the war, political leaders and influential economists began to worry about the return to mass unemployment once the military effort was over. While Bretton Woods was intended to provide the international cooperative environment for a lively expansion of trade and for mitigating the transmission of deflationary pressures from country to country, it was domestic policy management that remained most deeply affected by the intellectual and factual impact of the 1930s and the war. After 1945, wartime controls and regulations were slowly lifted; the lesson of the first postwar settlement taught the wisdom of gradualism. While markets reestablished their roles in a peacetime economy, the practical lessons of the Keynesian revolution made their inroads in government circles almost everywhere. The *General Theory* had by then been translated into the most important languages, and economists were actively turning its complex theoretical novelty into practical policy advice. For at least two decades, the notion that the business cycle could be tamed and even "conquered" through demand management became the new orthodoxy.

10.3 Three Postwar Periods and Three Growth Episodes in the United States

The United States grew rapidly after the Second World War, and expectations were high. This had been true after the end of the First World War in the 1920s, and it also would be true after the end of the Cold War in the 1990s. The progress of the Dow Jones Industrial Average on the New York Stock Exchange in these three decades is shown in figure 10.1. The increases were all but indistinguishable in these three postwar decades. There have been many reasons given for the stock market to rise that way, but surely one is the end of a major war. This kind of climactic event is liable to give rise to a decade of euphoria, and it seems to have done so in each of these decades.

The euphoria of the 1920s is well known as an irony of history. President Calvin Coolidge bid adieu to Congress at the end of 1928 with the statement that "the requirements of existence have passed beyond the standard of necessity

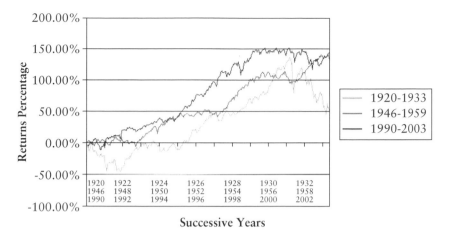

Figure 10.1. Stock market (DJIA) returns. Source: Temin, 2006.

into the region of luxury." Irving Fisher agreed in October 1929: "Stock prices have reached what looks like a permanently high plateau. I do not feel there will soon, if ever, be a fifty- or sixty-point break below present levels."

The postwar prosperity after the Second World War is remembered with more fondness. The end of both the Great Depression and the war seemed to provide for a new beginning. Dean Acheson, secretary of state throughout the 1940s, titled his memoirs *Present at the Creation*. President Truman said, "If we can put this tremendous machine of ours, which has made victory possible, to work for peace, we can look forward to the greatest age in the history of mankind." We do not regard these statements as hyperbole or the rise in stock prices shown in figure 10.1 as a boom, because prosperity and rapid economic growth continued well after the first postwar decade.

The 1990s also opened with a ringing announcement of the opportunity before us (Temin, 2006). The end of the Cold War may not have had the emotional appeal of the end of the War to End All Wars, but it echoed the sense of a new dawn. As in 1919 and 1945, the political map was redrawn. Leaders of old countries needed to formulate policies to deal with new and newly constituted countries. President George H. W. Bush stated in March 1991: "Twice before in this century, an entire world was convulsed by war. Twice this century, out of the horrors of war hope emerged for enduring peace. Twice before, those hopes proved to be a distant dream, beyond the grasp of man. . . . Now, we can see a new world coming into view. A world in which there is the very real prospect of a new world order."

The "new economy" of the 1990s had echoes of the "new economy" of the previous postwar decades and was labeled as the coming of a new economy by its participants. The defining innovation in the 1920s was a means of communication: the radio. More important for growth of the economy was the spread of electric motors. Electricity had been discovered long before the 1920s, but its effect on the economy took several decades. David (1991) argued that this delay was to be expected. If an electric motor simply replaced a steam engine, there would be only a small effect on productivity. If, however a factory was reorganized to take advantage of separate motors at each machine, replacing a central steam engine, then more gains were to be expected. But this reorganization could not take place as soon as electricity became available. There was an inevitable delay while people absorbed the implications of the innovation and then reorganized activities accordingly.

The decade following the Second World War may be thought of as adapting to the automobile. This is a consumer good rather than a producer good, but it transformed a system nonetheless. The analogue of new factory layout was the federal highway system, constructed after the war ended. It gave rise to new suburban locations, symbolized forever as Levittown. And it gave rise, in an exuberant response to the release from wartime shortages, to the great gas-guzzling finned cars of the 1950s (Offer, 1998).

The boom of the 1990s may have been due to similar causes. Personal computers became available in the 1970s, and there was lots of talk of the "paperless office," but the spread of computers was slow, and business practice was not altered in response to the initial availability of distributed computing power. Only after people began to understand what computers could and could not do did they reorganize their business activities. The explosion of the information technology sector and the dot-com boom of the 1990s may have been the result.

The lines in figure 10.1 continue beyond the end of the decade to indicate that the period of euphoria and rising expectations has not typically lasted more than a decade. In all three cases, the advances of the postwar decades were checked at the decade's end. In the continuing prosperity of the 1960s, the pause in the growth of the stock market was barely noticed, while in the depression of the 1930s, the fall in the stock market was not only noticed but was accused of causing the depression. In our time, a stock market crash and pause did occur, but they did not have a similar impact on output and employment.

10.4 The Post–Cold War Settlement in Perspective

The end of the Cold War has produced a shock that is in some respects comparable with that delivered by the end of the two world wars. The problems have arisen first from the reduction in military expenditure from the levels thought necessary on both sides during the Cold War, and second from the fundamental economic restructuring that was required in the former socialist countries. As it turned out, such a restructuring took much longer and was more painful than anticipated by most economists in the early 1990s. The "J curve" was extremely pronounced, with per capita incomes falling by as much as 50 percent in several of the former Soviet republics, causing notable impacts on such basic welfare statistics as life expectancy. In the Balkans, the "transition" was marked by a long conflict and even genocides: part of the region is still in a very fragile equilibrium and in need of foreign support to guarantee peace and a minimum of security.

One may see analogies with the problems caused after the First World War by the breakup of the Habsburg and tsarist empires. Was all this suffering necessary? We know from the preceding comparison of the experience following the First and Second World Wars that a major postwar shock does not mean there will necessarily be a long, deep economic or social crisis. What is critical is the form of the response and the economic and political settlement that the international economy is able to establish to deal with the new conditions. There are grounds for thinking that the international response to end of the Cold War has more parallels with the first postwar settlement than with the second one. In particular, a new Marshall Plan was not offered to the former Soviet economies to ease the welfare impact of the "transition," nor was a package of favourable trade or payments assembled. It seems, therefore, that the lessons learned so bitterly and well by the architects of the post-1945 settlement was lost on western leaders over the following thirty-odd years.

More generally, looking back over the almost eighty years that have now passed since the Great Depression, one may wonder how much of the need for international multilateral cooperation outlined by the disasters of the 1930s is still incorporated in the ideology and practice of the most powerful world leaders.

10.5 The Globalization Backlash and the "Second Globalization"

This book is largely about the economic aspects and consequences of the backlash that followed the "first globalization," which came to an abrupt end in August 1914. After the First World War, the attempts at re-creating an open and stable international economy were largely unsuccessful. As we have seen, unwise peace treaties, international rivalries, the emergence of new players in the domestic sociopolitical arena, and the intellectual inadequacies of certain leaders all created an unstable environment in the 1920s, which opened the way to the most disastrous depression in the history of mankind and to the retreat, in the 1930s, of each country into the supposed safety of autarky. The globalization backlash was in full swing.

From today's perspective, one may marvel at the slow progress made by international economic integration after the Second World War, particularly as far as cross-border capital movements were concerned. But both the legacies and the lessons of the 1930s and 1940s explain the slow reemergence of a global economy after 1945. The autarkic superstructures of many economies had produced a pattern of resource allocation as well as a set of vested interests that took time to fully remove. Trade was relatively rapidly liberalized within western Europe. It took longer for trade barriers between Europe and the United States to fall, but it was in the field of international capital movements that the second globalization was slow in matching the first one. It was only sometime in the mid-1980s that cross-border capital movements again reached their pre-World War I share of the world's GDP.

Prudence in this area stemmed from the lessons of the 1930s, when unrestricted, free short-term capital movements contributed to a rapid international transmission of the depression. Acutely aware of the problem, the architects of the Bretton Woods system allowed member countries to retain the freedom to impose restrictions on international short-term capital mobility. This resulted in a degree of financial repression, particularly in Europe and Japan, which did not seem to negatively impact the extraordinary productivity and output growth of the 1950s and 1960s. Only from the mid-1980s onward did unrestricted cross-border capital movements became the rule rather than the exception.

With the return of unfettered capital mobility came a higher degree of international financial instability, as witnessed by the Mexican crisis of the early 1980s and by the Russian and Asian crises of the late 1990s. Painful as these were, however, they retained a regional character rather than taking on the global reach of the Great Depression of the 1930s. Moreover, their impact on the real economy was less severe and more short-lived than in the interwar period. The same can be said of the 2000–2001 stock market crash. While comparable in magnitude to that of 1929–1930, it remained confined to the financial sector, with a relatively minor impact on employment and output. The second globalization seems so far to be more resistant to the same shocks that gave the final blows to the first one, at the end of the 1920s.

At the time of writing the final lines of this book, the second globalization is in full swing, and the growth of the world economy continues at a fast pace, second only to that of the postwar golden age, 1950–1971 (Rhode and Toniolo, 2006). The emergence of new economic giants in Asia is reshaping the geoeconomic map, with long-term consequences that we are only now beginning to imagine.

Yet, in spite of its apparent resilience and continuous progress, the second globalization is vulnerable to the same diseases that eventually brought the first one to its end. Today as yesterday, they are of two kinds: domestic and international. Domestically, the main threat to further international economic integration comes from the changes in income distribution that it inevitably brings about, together with technical progress, its main vehicle. The lesson from the pre-1914 years as well as from the 1920s is that rapid changes in income and wealth distribution are not only, as one would expect, strongly resisted by those negatively affected; in extreme cases, they may undermine the very fabric of the society, with momentous, far-reaching, and tragic consequences, as shown by the history of the 1920s and early 1930s. In order to live with and prosper from globalization, countries need strong, mature democracies capable of commanding consensus on compensations to be granted the losers of the internationalization process and able to compromise and keep an open dialogue with every relevant group in society. Most of the democratic regimes of the 1920s were not endowed with such a mature and sophisticated approach. Populism, when not outright dictatorship, was often the shortcut for coping with domestic changes induced by the attempts to reglobalize the economy, within the constraints of an ill-conceived peace.

As for the threats to international relations coming from the integration of the international economy, much that was said in the previous pages of this book is a reminder of what might lie ahead, and more important, of what should be done to avoid another backlash. As already mentioned, the second globalization has been characterized by the rapid growth of two giant economies for which there is no previous historical parallel: they surely dwarf the emergence of Germany on the world stage after 1860. Such huge changes in the relative economic sizes of nations affect international relations to a very large extent. The preexisting political world balance has been and will be enormously upset. The process must be governed by the international community if the inevitable tensions are to be contained within manageable limits. The opposite lessons of the 1920s and of the 1940s/1950s are there to warn us. Only the future will say whether multilateral cooperation will emerge strong enough, perhaps under a soft but farsighted leadership, after the uncertainties and mishaps of the first years of the twenty-first century.

Guide to Further Reading

There is a huge literature dealing with various features of the economic history of Europe in the interwar period and the related political disputes. The following survey is confined to published work in English and is intended as a brief guide to books and articles most relevant for further study of the topics discussed in this book.

Major Themes

General Works

Munting and Holderness (1991) is the most recent general introduction to the economic history of the period and is very concise and well-organized. Tipton and Aldric (1989) give more emphasis to social history. There is much useful information and an excellent analysis of the period from 1914 to 1945 in the series of four volumes on the First World War by Hardach (1977), the 1920s by Aldcroft (1977), the 1930s by Kindleberger (1973), and the Second World War by Milward (1977). Moggridge (1989) gives a very clear and thorough assessment of interwar financial and exchange rate policies, as does Kindleberger (1989) for commercial policy.

There is an illuminating analysis of the postwar political conflicts that played such an important role in subsequent economic developments in Maier (1975); other important studies of these issues are Schuker (1976), Silverman (1982), and Boyce (1987). The vexed topic of reparations continues to attract attention from scholars, and has been debated by Felix (1971), Marks (1978), Trachtenberg (1980), Silverman (1982), and Schuker (1988).

The Great Depression

The most important modern studies of the fundamental macroeconomic issues are Temin (1989) and Eichengreen (1990, 1992a). Fearon (1979) and Eichengreen (1992b) provide a clear and concise introduction to recent views on the causes of the great depression. Foreman-peck et al (19TK) make an ambitious attempt to construct a comprehensive econometric model to test a number of propositions about the depression and subsequent recovery. There are also important insights to be gained from earlier accounts, including the classic report written for the League of Nations by Ohlin (1931) and interpretations of the crisis by Robbins (1934), Hodson (1938), and Lewis (1944).

For readers who want more information about the closely related events in the United States, Fearon (1987) is a very good introduction to the economic history of the interwar period, and Bernstein (1987) provides a perceptive recent discussion of developments from 1929. A graphic account of the Wall Street stock-exchange collapse is given by Galbraith (1955).

The Recovery and the 1930s

The policies adopted to promote economic recovery in the 1930s are discussed in Temin (1989) and in Eichengreen and Sachs (1985). Significant contemporary studies include Hodson (1938), Arndt (1944), and Lewis (1944). Landes (1969) also has a useful chapter on this decade. The best modern accounts of the recovery in individual countries are Richardson (1967) on Britain and Overy (1994, 1996) on Germany.

For other aspects of economic policy in this decade, see Kaiser (1980) on international economic relations; Clarke (1977) and Drummond (1979) on the Tripartite Agreement between Britain, France, and the United States; Drummond (1972, 1981) on Commonwealth economic policy and on sterling and the sterling area; Ellis (1941) on the detailed operation of exchange controls; and Neal (1979) and Kitson (1992) on Nazi clearing agreements and trade policy.

Banking, Finance, and the Gold Standard

Drummond (1987) is a good explanation of the basic concepts of the gold standard, and an influential contemporary view of how it worked is given in Hawtrey (1939). Eichengreen (1990, 1992) examines many aspects of its operation in the interwar period, and interesting earlier research is reported in Jack (1927), Brown (1940), Nurkse (1944), and Bloomfield (1959).

The way in which the return to gold contributed to the exceptional international scope of the Great Depression, as well as to its severity and duration, is analyzed in Temin (1989) and Eichengreen (1992a). Bernanke and James (1991) is an important study of the relationship between the gold standard and the banking crises, but it assumes a more advanced knowledge of economics.

Feinstein (1995) has several comparative studies of exchange-rate policy, as well as detailed histories of interwar banking policies in each of the main countries. The role of the banks in individual countries is also examined in James, Lindgren, and Teichova (1991) and in a special supplement to the *Journal of European Economic History* (1984).

Trade, Production, and Unemployment

Svennilson (1954) is an exceptionally informative and comprehensive analysis of developments in industry and trade in interwar Europe, and of the related technological advances; the relevant chapters in Landes (1969) should also be consulted on these topics. Caron, Erker, and Fischer (1995) contains several stimulating studies of European innovation and technical change. Maizels (1965) is a superb analysis of the changes in the composition and direction of international trade, and the study undertaken by Hilgerdt for the League of Nations (1941) is still a useful source of information on European trade.

Tracy (1964) is a good starting point for an account of the developments in agriculture. The League of Nations (1931) and the Royal Institute of International Affairs (1932) are interesting as indications of how the problem was seen by contemporaries. Timoshenko (1953) and Malenbaum (1953) are both substantial investigations of this important sector.

The introduction to Eichengreen and Hatton (1988) is the best guide to the movements in unemployment, with information about individual countries in the other chapters. Other useful studies include Garside (1990) on the situation in Britain and Stachura (1986) on Germany.

The Period after the Second World War

Until recently it was left mainly to the applied economists to study postwar developments, but economic historians are beginning to enter the field and can bring to the task the advantage of a longer perspective. Crafts and Toniolo (1996) is an excellent example and a very good starting point for further reading on this period. Milward (1984, 1992) provides an authoritative study of postwar reconstruction and of the moves toward a common economic community. The best introductions to the process of convergence are Abramovitz (1990) and Maddison (1991, 1995). Dornbusch, Nolling, and Layard (1993) examine the theme of reconstruction after the Second World War and the lessons this might have for the transition in process in eastern Europe.

National Studies

The economic problems of interwar Germany have generated a large literature in English, but the material available on the other continental economies is relatively limited. However, there are good chapters on individual countries in Cipolla (1976) and in a number of the collective studies which report on recent research; for example, Cottrell and Teichova (1983), James et al. (1991), Garside (1993), Feinstein (1995), and Crafts and Toniolo (1996).

The series of reprinted studies recently published under the general title of *The Economic Development of Modern Europe Since 1870* also has many relevant articles and chapters on the interwar period, many of which are not easily accessible elsewhere. The series includes volumes on Austria (Matis, 1994), Belgium (van der Wee and Blomme, 1996), Denmark (Persson, 1993), France (Crouzet, 1993), Ireland (Ó Gráda, 1994), Italy (Federico, 1994), the Netherlands (van Zanden, 1995), Sweden (Jonung and Ohlsson, 1997), and Spain (Martin-Aceña and Simpson, 1996).

Britain

Pollard (1992) and Floud and McCloskey (1994, vol. 2) are the most complete and up-to-date general economic histories of modern Britain and will also serve as comprehensive guides to the huge literature that is available on interwar Britain, which cannot be fully reviewed in this brief survey. Aldcroft (1970) is a good survey and covers the period in considerable detail, but some parts have been superseded by later work. Matthews, Feinstein, and Odling-Smee (1982) explore many aspects of the overall economic growth of the economy, placing the interwar period in a longer historical perspective.

The outstanding account of the return to gold is Moggridge (1972), and a useful collection of representative articles on the subject is reprinted in Pollard (1970). There is a judicious account of financial policy in the history of the Bank of England by Sayers (1976). Although Nevin (1955) is now somewhat dated, it is still informative on the collapse of the gold standard and the introduction of cheap money. The 1931 devaluation is analyzed and set in context with later devaluations in Cairncross and Eichengreen (1983). Clarke (1988) is an illuminating history of the evolution of Keynes's theory of macroeconomic policy, and the slow evolution of actual policy in response to these advances in economic theory can be studied in Middleton (1985), Peden (1987), Booth (1989), and Tomlinson (1990).

Aldcroft and Richardson (1969) brings together articles by these two authors that stimulated much of the modern discussion of British policy and performance. The recovery is analyzed in more detail in Richardson (1957), and there are useful studies of individual industries in Buxton and Aldcroft (1979). A rather different perspective is given by the editors and other contributors to Elbaum and Lazonick (1986). Von Tunzelmann (1982) is an innovative study of the impact of technical progress on the structure of the economy. The contribution of the introduction of tariff protection to the recovery is examined in Kitson and Solomou (1990).

Two interesting but highly technical studies of the interwar labor market are Dimsdale, Nickell, and Horsewood (1989) and Beenstock and Warburton (1991). The latter gives more weight to supply-side factors in accounting for the rise in unemployment.

France, Belgium, Italy, and the Netherlands

The best modern economic history of Italy is Zamagni (1993). Comparable up-to-date accounts of other countries are lacking, though Kemp (1972) presents an interesting if rather critical view of developments in France. Mouré (1991) is the most valuable modern study of exchange-rate policy in France, and other aspects are discussed in Wolfe (1957), Eichengreen (1990), and Eichengreen and Wyplosz (1990). The revaluation of the Italian lira is examined in Cohen (1972), and there are comparative studies of France and Italy by Asselain and Plessis (1995) and of France and Belgium by Cassiers (1995). The economic policies of Italian fascism are analysed in Welk (1939), Toniolo (1980), and Cohen (1988). For the gold-bloc countries, some aspects of the experience of the Netherlands in the 1930s can be studied in Griffiths (1988) and of the French experience in Jackson (1985, 1988).

Germany

Hardach (1980) and Braun (1990) provide general economic histories of the period. The many studies of the early postwar years and their extraordinary hyperinflation include Bresciani-Turroni (1937), Laursen and Pederson (1964), Feldman et al. (1982), Holtfrerich (1986), Webb (1989), Feldman (1993), and Ferguson (1995). McNeil (1986) is a modern history of American capital flows to Weimar Germany.

James (1986) is the best introduction to subsequent macroeconomic policies and the descent into the depression, and he has also made a very full study of the policies of the Reichsbank and other financial aspects (James, 1985). There is also a very detailed treatment of these issues, based on extensive original research, in Balderston (1993, 1995). The diplomatic aspects of the crisis are covered by Bennett (1962).

Borchardt (1991) is a welcome English translation of several penetrating and original studies of German economic policy and performance, and von Kruedener (1990) contains a good summary of the debate stimulated by his view that high wages were a crucial cause of economic collapse. The most recent contribution to this topic is Voth (1995).

There are a number of excellent studies of the economic recovery in Germany and of the Nazi war economy. The first detailed analysis was made by Guillebaud (1939); subsequent studies include Klein (1959), Milward (1965), James (1986), and Temin (1991). Overy (1994, 1996) provides the latest and most comprehensive examinations of the issue.

Eastern and Central Europe

There are a few general economic histories, including Berend and Ranki (1974a) and Teichova (1989) on eastern and central Europe as a whole, Berend and

Ranki (1974b) on Hungary, Lampe and Jackson (1982) on the Balkan states, Teichova (1988) on Czechoslovakia, and Landau and Tomaszewski (1988) on Poland. The first two volumes of Kaser and Radice (1985, 1986) report the results of much original research on the countries in this region.

Specialist studies are harder to find. The Austrian crisis of the early 1920s is covered in Walré de Bordes (1924), and Schubert (1991) has recently published a full account of the famous crisis of the Credit-Anstalt bank, which many see as the trigger for the crisis of 1931. Teichova (1985) is a detailed examination of the extent and effect of foreign investment in interwar Czechoslovakia.

Other European Countries

For the Scandinavian and southern European countries, the material available in English is very limited. The few general economic histories include Hodne (1983) on Norway, Johansen (1987) on Denmark, and Harrison (1985) and Sanchez-Albornoz (1987) on Spain. Lester (1939) gives a very full account of the exchange-rate policies adopted by Denmark and Norway in the 1920s, and there is a study of the contrasting policies of Sweden and Finland in Haavisto and Jonung (1995).

Jonung (1981) examines the depression in Sweden, and there is an older study by Montgomery (1938). Dahmén (1970) covers many of the advances in Swedish industry. For Greece, Mazower (1991) is an important study of the Great Depression. There are also several excellent articles on the Scandinavian countries and on Spain, Greece, and Portugal in the various collective works mentioned earlier.

References

Abramovitz, Moses (1990). "The Catch-Up Factor in Post-war Economic Growth." *Economic Inquiry*, 38, 1–18.

Aldcroft, Derek H. (1970). *The Inter-War Economy: Britain 1919–1939*. London: Batsford.

Aldcroft, Derek H. (1977). *From Versailles to Wall Street*. London: Allan Lane.

Aldcroft, Derek H. (2006). *Europe's Third World: The European Periphery in the Interwar Years*. Aldershot: Ashgate.

Aldcroft, Derek H., and Richardson, Harry W. (1969). *The British Economy, 1870–1939*. London: Macmillan.

Allen, Robert C. (2003). *Farm to Factory: A Reinterpretation of the Soviet Industrial Revolution*. Princeton, N.J.: Princeton University Press.

Arndt, H. W. (1944). *The Economic Lessons of the Nineteen-Thirties*. London: Oxford University Press.

Asselain, Jean-Charles, and Plessis, Allain (1995). "Exchange-Rate Policy and Macro-Economic Performance: A Comparison of French and Italian Experience between the Wars," in Charles Feinstein (ed.), *Banking, Currency, and Finance in Europe between the Wars*. Oxford: Oxford University Press, 187–213.

Bagehot, Walter (1873). *Lombard Street: A Description of the Money Market*. New York: Scribner, Armstrong and Co.

Bairoch, Paul (1968). *The Working Population and Its Structure*. Brussels: Université Libre de Bruxelles.

Bakke, E. Wight (1933). *The Unemployed Man: A Social Study*. London: Nisbet.

Balderston, Theodore (1982). "The Origins of Economic Instability in Germany, 1924–1930: Market Forces versus Economic Policy." *Vierteljahrschrift für Sozial und Wirtschaftsgeschichte*, 69, 488–514.

Balderston, Theodore (1983). "The Beginning of the Depression in Germany, 1927–30: Investment and the Capital Market." *Economic History Review*, 36, 395–415.

Balderston, Theodore (1993). *The Origins and Course of the German Economic Crisis, 1923–1932*. Berlin: Haude and Spener.

Balderston, Theodore (1995). "German and British Monetary Policy, 1919–1932," in Charles Feinstein (ed.), *Banking, Currency, and Finance in Europe between the Wars*. Oxford: Oxford University Press, 151–86.

Beenstock, Michael, and Warburton, Peter (1991). "The Market for Labour in Interwar Britain." *Explorations in Economic History,* 28, 287–308.

Benjamin, D. K., and Kochin, L. A. (1979). "Searching for an Explanation for Unemployment in Interwar Britain." *Journal of Political Economy,* 87, 441–78.

Bennett, Edward W. (1962). *Germany and the Diplomacy of the Financial Crisis.* Cambridge, Mass.: Harvard University Press.

Berend, Ivan (2006). *An Economic History of Twentieth Century Europe.* Cambridge: Cambridge University Press.

Berend, Ivan T., and Ranki, Gyorgy (1974a). *Hungary: A Century of Economic Development.* Newton Abbot: David and Charles.

Berend, Ivan T., and Ranki, Gyorgy (1974b). *Economic Development of East-Central Europe in the 19th and 20th Centuries.* New York: Columbia University Press.

Bergson, Abram (1961). *The Real National Income of Soviet Russia since 1928.* Cambridge, Mass.: Harvard University Press.

Bernanke, Ben (1983). "Nonmonetary Effects of the Financial Crisis in the Propagation of the Great Depression." *American Economic Review* 73, 2577–76.

Bernanke, Ben (1995). "The Macroeconomics of the Great Depression: A Comparative Approach." *Journal of Money, Credit and Banking* 27, 12–18.

Bernanke, Ben, and James, Harold (1991). "The Gold Standard, Deflation and Financial Crisis in the Great Depression: An International Comparison," in R. Glen Hubbard (ed.), *Financial Markets and Financial Crises.* Chicago: Chicago University Press, 33–68.

Bernstein, Michael A. (1987). *The Great Depression: Delayed Recovery and Economic Change in America, 1929–1939.* Cambridge: Cambridge University Press.

Beveridge, Sir William (1937). "An Analysis of Unemployment, II." *Economica,* 4, 1–17.

Blanchard, Olivier Jean (1987). "Reaganomics." *Economic Policy* (October), 17–56.

Bloomfield, Arthur I. (1950). *Capital Imports and the American Balance of Payments.* Chicago: Chicago University Press.

Bloomfield, Arthur I. (1959). *Monetary Policy under the International Gold Standard, 1880–1914.* New York: Federal Reserve Bank of New York.

Booth, Alan (1989). *British Economic Policy, 1931–1949: Was There a Keynesian Revolution?* London: Harvester Wheatsheaf.

Borchardt, Knut (1979). "Constraints and Room for Manoeuvre in the Great Depression of the Early Thirties: Towards a Revision of the Received Historical Picture," in Knut Borchardt, *Perspectives on Modern German Economic History and Policy.* Cambridge: Cambridge University Press, 1431–60.

Borchardt, Knut (1984). "Could and Should Germany Have Followed Great Britain in Leaving the Gold Standard?" *Journal of European Economic History,* 13, 471–98.

Borchardt, Knut (1990). "A Decade of Debate about Brüning's Economic Policy," in Jurgen Baron von Kruedener (ed.), *Economic Crisis and Political Collapse: The Weimar Republic 1924–1933.* New York: Berg, 991–51.

Borchardt, Knut (1991). *Perspectives on Modern German Economic History and Policy.* Cambridge: Cambridge University Press.

Bowden, Sue, and Offer, Avner (1994). "Household Appliances and the Use of Time: The United States and Britain since the 1920s." *Economic History Review*, 47, 725–48.

Boyce, Robert W. D. (1987). *British Capitalism at the Crossroads, 1919–1932.* Cambridge: Cambridge University Press.

Bresciani-Turroni, C. (1937). *The Economics of Inflation.* London: Allen and Unwin.

Braun, Hans-Joachim (1990). *The German Economy in the Twentieth Century: The German Reich and the Federal Republic.* London: Routledge.

Broadberry, Stephen N. (1993). "Manufacturing and the Convergence Hypothesis: What the Long-Run Data Show." *Journal of Economic History*, 53, 772–95.

Broadberry, Stephen, and Harrison, Mark (2005). *The Economics of World War I.* Cambridge: Cambridge University Press.

Brown, William Adams (1940). *The International Gold Standard Reinterpreted, 1914–1934.* New York: National Bureau of Economic Research.

Buxton, Neil K., and Aldcroft, Derek H. (1979). *British Industry between the Wars: Instability and Industrial Development.* London: Scolar Press.

Cairncross, Alec, and Eichengreen, Barry (1983). *Sterling in Decline: The Devaluations of 1931, 1949 and 1967.* Oxford: Blackwell.

Calomiris, Charles W., and Mason, Joseph R. (2003). "Fundamentals, Panics, and Bank Distress During the Depression." *American Economic Review*, 93, 1615–47.

Carbonnelle, C. (1959). "Recherches sur l'évolution de la production en Belgique de 1900 á 1957." *Cahiers Économiques de Bruxelles*, 1, 3533–77.

Caron, François, Erker, Paul, and Fischer, Wolfram (1995). *Innovations in the European Economy between the Wars.* Berlin: Walter de Gruyter.

Carr, Edward H. (1937). *International Relations Between the Two World Wars, 1919–39.* London: Macmillan.

Cassiers, Isabelle (1995). "Managing the Franc in Belgium and France: The Economic Consequences of Exchange-Rate Policies, 1925–1936," in Charles Feinstein (ed.), *Banking, Currency, and Finance in Europe between the Wars.* Oxford: Oxford University Press, 214–36.

Cha, Myung Soo (2003). "Did Takahashi Korekiyo Rescue Japan from the Great Depression?" *Journal of Economic History*, 63, 127–44.

Chandler, Alfred D., Jr. (1977). *The Visible Hand: The Managerial Revolution in American Business.* Cambridge, Mass.: Harvard University Press.

Chandler, Alfred D., Jr. (1990). *Scale and Scope: The Dynamics of Industrial Capitalism.* Cambridge, Mass.: Harvard University Press.

Childers, Thomas (1983). *The Nazi Voter: The Social Foundations of Fascism in Germany, 1919–1933.* Chapel Hill: University of North Carolina Press.

Choudhri, Ehsan U., and Kochin, Levis A. (1980). "The Exchange Rate and the International Transmission of Business Cycle Disturbances." *Journal of Money, Credit and Banking*, 12, 565–74.

Cipolla, Carlo M. (1976). *The Fontana Economic History of Europe*, vol. 5. London: Fontana.

Clarke, Peter (1988). *The Keynesian Revolution in the Making.* Oxford: Oxford University Press.

Clarke, Sally (1991). "New Deal Regulation and the Revolution in American Farm Production: A Case Study of the Diffusion of the Tractor in the Corn Belt, 1920–1940." *Journal of Economic History*, 51, 101–23.

Clarke, Stephen V. O. (1967). *Central Bank Cooperation, 1924–31.* New York: Federal Reserve Bank of New York.

Clarke, Stephen V. O. (1977). *Exchange-Rate Stabilization in the Mid-1930s: Negotiating the Tripartite Agreement.* Princeton Studies in International Finance, No. 41. Princeton, N.J.

Cohen, Jon S. (1972). "The 1927 Revaluation of the Lira: A Study in Political Economy." *Economic History Review*, 25, 642–54.

Cohen, Jon S. (1988). "Was Italian Fascism a Developmental Dictatorship? Some Evidence to the Contrary." *Economic History Review*, 41, 95–113.

Cottrell, Philip L., and Teichova, Alice (1983). *International Business and Central Europe, 1918–1939.* Leicester: Leicester University Press.

Crafts, Nicholas F. R. (1987). "Long-Term Unemployment in Britain in the 1930s." *Economic History Review*, 40, 418–32.

Crafts, Nicholas, and Toniolo, Gianni (1995). "Post-war Growth: An Overview," in N. Crafts and G. Toniolo (eds.), *Europe's Economic Performance 1945–1993.* Cambridge: Cambridge University Press, 13–17.

Crouzet, François (ed.) (1993). *The Economic Development of Modern France since 1870.* Aldershot: Edward Elgar.

Dahmén, Erik (1970). *Entrepreneurial Activity and the Development of Swedish Industry.* Homewood, Ill.: Irwin.

David, Paul A. (1991). "Computer and Dynamo: The Modern Productivity Paradox in a Not-Too-Distant Mirror," in *Technology and Productivity: The Challenge for Economic Policy.* Paris: OECD, 315–48.

Della Paolera, Gerardo, and Taylor, Alan M. (2001). *Straining at the Anchor: The Argentine Currency Board and the Search for Macroeconomic Stability, 1880–1935.* Chicago: University of Chicago Press.

Diaz Alejandro, Carlos (1984). "Latin America in the 1930s," in Margaret Thorpe (ed.), *Latin America in the 1930s: The Role of the Periphery in World Crisis.* New York: St. Martin's Press.

Dimsdale, Nicholas H., Horsewood, Nicholas, and Van Riel, Arthur (2006). "Unemployment in Interwar Germany: An Analysis of the Labor Market, 1927–1936." *Journal of Economic History*, 66, 778–808.

Dimsdale, Nicholas H., Nickell, S. J., and Horsewood, N. (1989). "Real Wages and Unemployment in Britain during the 1930s." *Economic Journal*, 99, 271–92.

Dornbusch, Rudiger, Nolling, Wilhelm, and Layard, Richard (eds.) (1993). *Post-war Reconstruction and Lessons for the East Today.* Cambridge, Mass.: MIT Press.

Drummond, Ian M. (1972). *British Economic Policy and the Empire, 1919–1939.* London: Allen and Unwin.

Drummond, Ian M. (1979). *London, Washington, and the Management of the Franc, 1936–39.* Princeton Studies in International Finance, No. 45. Princeton, N.J.

Drummond, Ian M. (1981). *The Floating Pound and the Sterling Area, 1931–1939.* Cambridge: Cambridge University Press.

Drummond, Ian M. (1987). *The Gold Standard and the International Monetary System, 1900–1939*. London: Macmillan.

Eckstein, Alexander (1955). "National Income and Capital Formation in Hungary, 1900–1950," in S. Kuznets (ed.), *Income and Wealth*, vol. 5. London: Bowes and Bowes, 152–223.

Eichengreen, Barry (1985). "International Policy Coordination in Historical Perspective: A View from the Inter-war Years," in Willem Buiter and Richard Marston (eds.), *International Economic Policy Coordination*. Cambridge: Cambridge University Press, 139–78.

Eichengreen, Barry (1987). "Unemployment in Interwar Britain: Dole or Doldrums?" *Oxford Economic Papers*, 39, 597–623.

Eichengreen, Barry (1986). "The Bank of France and the Sterilization of Gold, 1926–32." *Explorations in Economic History*, 23, 56–84.

Eichengreen, Barry (1990). *Elusive Stability: Essays in the History of International Finance, 1919–1939*. Cambridge: Cambridge University Press.

Eichengreen, Barry (1992a). *Golden Fetters: The Gold Standard and the Great Depression, 1919–1939*. Oxford: Oxford University Press.

Eichengreen, Barry (1992b). "The Origins and Nature of the Great Slump Revisited." *Economic History Review*, 45, 213–39.

Eichengreen, Barry (1994). "Wages and the Gold Standard: Perspectives on the Borchardt Debate," in Christoph Buchheim, Michael Hutter, and Harold James (eds.), *Zerrissene Zwischenkriegszeit*. Baden-Baden: Nomos, 1772–803.

Eichengreen, Barry, and Hatton, Timothy J. (1988). "Inter-war Unemployment in International Perspective: An Overview," in Barry Eichengreen and Timothy J. Hatton (eds.), *Interwar Unemployment in International Perspective*. Dordrecht: Kluwer Academic Publishers, 15–19.

Eichengreen, Barry, and Sachs, Jeffrey (1985). "Exchange Rates and Economic Recovery in the 1930s." *Journal of Economic History*, 45, 925–46.

Eichengreen, Barry, and Wyplosz, Charles (1990). "The Economic Consequences of the Franc Poincaré," in Barry Eichengreen, *Elusive Stability*. Cambridge: Cambridge University Press, 153–79.

Elbaum, Bernard, and Lazonick, William (1986). *The Decline of the British Economy*. Oxford: Oxford University Press.

Ellis, Howard S. (1941). *Exchange Control in Central Europe*. Cambridge, Mass.: Harvard University Press.

Faini, Riccardo, and Toniolo, Gianni (1990). "Deflation Reconsidered: Japan in the 1920s." *European Economic Review*, 34, 616–23.

Faini, Riccardo, and Toniolo, Gianni (1992). "Reconsidering Japanese Deflation during the 1920s." *Explorations in Economic History*, 29, 121–143.

Falkus, Malcolm E. (1975). "The German Business Cycle in the 1920s." *Economic History Review*, 28, 451–65.

Falter, Jurgen (1986). "Unemployment and the Radicalisation of the German Electorate 1928–1933: An Aggregate Data Analysis with Special Emphasis on the Rise of National Socialism," in Peter D. Stachura (ed.), *Unemployment and the Great Depression in Weimar Germany*. New York: St. Martin's Press.

Fearon, Peter (1979). *The Origins and Nature of the Great Slump, 1929–1932*. London: Macmillan.

Fearon, Peter (1987). *War, Prosperity and Depression: The U.S. Economy, 1917–1945*. Deddington: Philip Allan.

Federico, Giovanni (ed.) (1994). *The Economic Development of Modern Italy since 1870*. Aldershot: Edward Elgar.

Feinstein, Charles H. (1972). *National Income, Expenditure and Output of the United Kingdom*. Cambridge: Cambridge University Press.

Feinstein, Charles H. (ed.) (1995). *Banking, Currency, and Finance in Europe between the Wars*. Oxford: Oxford University Press.

Feinstein, Charles H. (2005). *An Economic History of South Africa*. Cambridge: Cambridge University Press.

Feinstein, Charles, Temin, Peter, and Toniolo, Gianni (1995). "International Economic Organization: Banking, Finance and Trade in Europe between the Wars," in Charles Feinstein (ed.), *Banking, Currency, and Finance in Europe between the Wars*. Oxford: Oxford University Press, 97–106.

Feinstein, Charles, and Watson, Katherine (1995). "Private International Capital Flows in the Inter-war Period," in Charles Feinstein (ed.), *Banking, Currency, and Finance in Europe between the Wars*. Oxford: Oxford University Press, 941–1030.

Feis, Herbert (1966). *1933: Characters in Crisis*. Boston: Little, Brown and Co.

Feldman, Gerald D., Holtferich, Carl-Ludwig, Ritter, Gerhard A., and Witt, Peter-Christian (1982). *The German Inflation Reconsidered: A Preliminary Balance*. Berlin: de Gruyter.

Feldman, Gerald D. (1993). *The Great Disorder: Politics, Economics and Society in the German Inflation, 1914–1924*. Oxford: Oxford University Press.

Felix, David (1971). "Reparations Reconsidered with a Vengeance." *Central European History*, 4, 171–79.

Ferguson, Niall (1995). *Paper and Iron: Hamburg Business and German Politics in the Era of Inflation, 1897–1927*. Cambridge: Cambridge University Press.

Ferguson, Thomas, and Temin, Peter (2003). "Made in Germany: The German Currency Crisis of 1931." *Research in Economic History*, 21, 1–53.

Field, Alexander J. (2003). "The Most Technologically Progressive Decade of the Century." *American Economic Review*, 93, 1399–1413.

Flath, David (2000). *The Japanese Economy*. Oxford: Oxford University Press.

Foreman-Peck, James (1995). *A History of the World Economy: International Economic Relations since 1850*. 2nd ed. London: Harvester-Wheatsheaf.

Fleisig, Heywood (1972). "The United States and the Non-European Periphery during the Early Years of the Great Depression," in Herman van der Wee (ed.), *The Great Depression Revisited*. The Hague: Martinus Nijhoff, 145–81.

Floud, Roderick, and McCloskey, Donald (1994). *The Economic History of Britain since 1700*. 2nd ed. Cambridge: Cambridge University Press.

Freeman, Richard (1998). "Spurts in Union Growth: Defining Moments and Social Processes," in Michael D. Bordo, Claudia Goldin, and Eugene N. White (eds.), *The Defining Moment: The Great Depression and the American Economy in the Twentieth Century*. Chicago: University of Chicago Press, 265–95.

Friedman, Milton, and Schwartz, Anna J. (1963). *A Monetary History of the United States*. Princeton, N.J.: Princeton University Press.

Galbraith, John Kenneth (1955). *The Great Crash, 1929*. London: Hamish Hamilton.

Galenson, Walter, and Zellner, Arnold (1957). "International Comparison of Unemployment Rates," in NBER (National Bureau of Economic Research), *The Measurement and Behavior of Unemployment*. Princeton, N.J.: Princeton University Press, 439–580.

Garraty, John A. (1978). *Unemployment in History: Economic Thought and Public Policy*. New York: Harper and Row.

Garside, William R. (1990). *British Unemployment, 1919–1939: A Study in Public Policy*. Cambridge: Cambridge University Press.

Garside, William R. (ed.) (1993). *Capital in Crisis: International Responses to the Great Depression*. London: Pinter.

Good, David F. (1994). 'The Economic Lag of Central and Eastern Europe: Income Estimates for the Habsburg Successor States,' *Journal of Economic History*, 54, 869–91.

Gordon, Robert J. (2000). "Interpreting the 'One Big Wave' in U.S. Long-Term Productivity Growth," in Bart van Ark, Kuipers Simon, and Kuper Gerard (eds.), *Productivity, Technology and Economic Growth*. Boston: Kluwer, 19–65.

Graham, Frank D. (1930). *Exchange, Prices and Production in Hyperinflation in Germany, 1920–1923*. Princeton, N.J.: Princeton University Press.

Griffiths, Richard T. (ed.) (1988). *The Netherlands and the Gold Standard, 1931–1936*. Amsterdam: NEHA.

Grossman, R. (1994). "The Shoe That Didn't Drop: Explaining Banking Stability during the Great Depression." *Journal of Economic History*, 54, 654–82.

Guillebaud, Claude W. (1939). *The Economic Recovery of Germany*. Cambridge: Cambridge University Press.

Haavisto, Taarmo, and Jonung, Lars (1995). "Off Gold and Back Again: Finnish and Swedish Monetary Policies, 1914–1925," in Charles Feinstein (ed.), *Banking, Currency, and Finance in Europe between the Wars*. Oxford: Oxford University Press, 237–66.

Hamilton, Richard (1982). *Who Voted for Hitler?* Princeton, N.J.: Princeton University Press.

Hannah, Leslie (1979). *Electricity before Nationalisation*, London: Macmillan

Hardach, Gerd (1977). *The First World War 1914–1918*. London: Allen Lane.

Hardach, Karl (1980). *The Political Economy of Germany in the Twentieth Century*. Berkeley: University of California Press.

Harrison, Joseph (1985). *The Economic History of Spain in the Twentieth Century*. Manchester: Manchester University Press.

Harrison, Mark (1988). "Resource Mobilization for World War II: The U.S., U.K., U.S.S.R., and Germany, 1938–1945." *Economic History Review*, 41, 171–92.

Hatton, Timothy J. (1987). "The Outlines of a Keynesian Solution," in Alan Booth and Sean Glynn (eds.), *The Road to Full Employment*. London: Allen and Unwin, 82–94.

Hawley, Ellis (1966). *The New Deal and the Problem of Monopolies: A Study in Economic Ambivalence*. Princeton, N.J.: Princeton University Press.

Hawtrey, Ralph G. (1925). "Public Expenditure and the Demand for Labour." *Economica*, 5, 38–48.

Hawtrey, Ralph G. (1939). *The Gold Standard in Theory and Practice*, 4th ed. London: Longman.

Hayes, Peter (1987). *Industry and Ideology: IG Farben in the Nazi Era*. Cambridge: Cambridge University Press.

Heim, Carol (1998). "Uneven Impacts of the Great Depression: Industries, Regions, and Nations," in Mark Wheeler (ed.), *The Economics of the Great Depression*. Kalamazoo, Mich.: W. E. Upjohn Institute for Employment Research, 29–61.

Hjerppe, Rita (1989). *The Finnish Economy, 1860–1985: Growth and Structural Change*, Helsinki: Bank of Finland.

Hodne, Fritz (1983). *The Norwegian Economy in the Twentieth Century*. London: Routledge.

Hodson, H. V. (1938). *Slump and Recovery, 1929–1937*. Oxford: Oxford University Press.

Holtfrerich, Carl-Ludwig (1986). *The German Inflation, 1914–1923: Causes and Effects in International Perspective*. Berlin: Walter de Gruyter.

Homburg, H. (1987). "From Unemployment Insurance to Compulsory Labour," in R. Evand and D. Grary (eds.). *The German Unemployed*, St. Martin's Press, New York, pp.73–107.

Howson, Susan (1975). *Domestic Monetary Management in Britain, 1919–1938*. Cambridge: Cambridge University Press.

Irwin, Douglas A., and Kroszner, Randall S. (1999). "Interests, Institutions, and Ideology in Securing Policy Change: The Republican Conversion to Trade Liberalization after Smoot-Hawley." *Journal of Law and Economics, 42*, 643–73.

Ito, Takatoshi (1992). *The Japanese Economy*. Cambridge, Mass.: MIT Press.

Jack, D. T. (1927). *The Restoration of European Currencies*. London: King.

Jackson, Julian (1985). *The Politics of Depression in France, 1932–1936*. Cambridge: Cambridge University Press.

Jackson, Julian (1988). *The Popular Front in France: Defending Democracy, 1934–1938*. Cambridge: Cambridge University Press.

Jahoda, Marie, Lazarsfeld, Paul F., and Zeisel, Hans (1971). *Marienthal: The Sociography of an Unemployed Community*. New York: Aldine Atherton.

James, Harold (1985). *The Reichsbank and Public Finance in Germany, 1924–1933*. Frankfurt am Main: Fritz Knapp Verlag.

James, Harold (1986). *The German Slump: Politics and Economics, 1924–1933*. Oxford: Clarendon Press.

James, Harold, Lindgren, Hakan, and Teichova, Alice (eds.) (1991). *The Role of Banks in the Inter-war Economy*. Cambridge: Cambridge University Press.

Johansen, H. (1987). *The Danish Economy in the Twentieth Century*. London: Routledge.

Johnson, Simon, and Temin, Peter (1993). "The Macroeconomics of NEP." *Economic History Review, 46*, 750–67.

Jonung, Lars (1981). "The Depression in Sweden and the U.S.: A Comparison of Causes and Policies," in Karl Brunner (ed.), *The Great Depression Revisited*. The Hague: Martin Nijhoff.

Jonung, Lars, and Ohlsson, Rolf (eds.) (1997). *The Economic Development of Modern Sweden since 1870*. Aldershot: Edward Elgar.

Journal of European Economic History (1984). Special supplement, 13.

Kaiser, D. E. (1980). *Economic Diplomacy and the Origins of the Second World War: Germany, Britain and Eastern Europe, 1930–39*. Princeton, N.J.: Princeton University Press.

Kahn, Alfred E. (1946). *Great Britain in the World Economy*. London: Pitman.

Kaser, Michael C., and Radice, E. A. (eds.) (1985). *The Economic History of Eastern Europe, 1919–1975*, vol. 1, *Economic Structure and Performance between the Two Wars*. Oxford: Oxford University Press.

Kaser, Michael C., and Radice, E. A. (eds.) (1986). *The Economic History of Eastern Europe, 1919–1975*, vol. 2, *Interwar Policy, the War and Reconstruction*. Oxford: Oxford University Press.

Kemp, Tom (1972). *The French Economy, 1913–1939: The History of a Decline*. London: Longman.

Keynes, John Maynard (1919). *The Economic Consequences of the Peace*. London: Macmillan.

Keynes, John Maynard (1931). "An Economic Analysis of Unemployment," in Quincy Wright (ed.), *Unemployment as a World Problem*. Chicago: University of Chicago Press, 34–42.

Keynes, John Maynard (1972). *Collected Works*. Donald E. Moggridge, ed. Vol. 9. London: Macmillan.

Kindleberger, Charles P. (1973). *The World in Depression, 1919–1939*. London: Allen Lane.

Kindleberger, Charles P. (1986). *The World in Depression, 1919–1939*. Rev. Ed. Berkeley: University of California Press.

Kindleberger, Charles P. (1989). "Commercial Policy between the Wars," in Peter Mathias and Sidney Pollard (eds.), *The Cambridge Economic History of Europe*, vol. 8, *The Industrial Economies: The Development of Economic and Social Policies*. Cambridge: Cambridge University Press, 161–96.

Kitson, Michael, and Solomou, Solomos (1990). *Protection and Revival: The British Inter-War Economy*. Cambridge: Cambridge University Press.

Kitson, Michael (1992). "The Move to Autarky: The Political Economy of Nazi Trade Policy." Department of Applied Economics, University of Cambridge, Working Paper No. 9201.

Klein, B. H. (1959). *Germany's Economic Preparations for War*. Cambridge, Mass.: Harvard University Press.

Kuznets, Simon (1966). *Modern Economic Growth: Rate, Structure, and Spread*. New Haven, Conn.: Yale University Press.

Lampe, John R., and Jackson, Martin R. (1982). *Balkan Economic History, 1550–1950: From Imperial Borderlands to Developed Nations*. Bloomington: Indiana University Press.

Landau, Zbigniew, and Tomaszewski, Jerzy (1988). *The Polish Economy in the Twentieth Century*. London: Routledge.

Landes, David (1969). *The Unbound Prometheus: Technological Change and Industrial Development in Western Europe from 1750 to the Present*. Cambridge: Cambridge University Press.

Lary, Hal B. (1943). *The United States in the World Economy*. Washington, D.C.: U.S. Department of Commerce.

Laursen, Karsten, and Pedersen, Jorgen (1964). *The German Inflation, 1918–1923*. Amsterdam: North Holland.

League of Nations (1927). *Report and Proceedings of the World Economic Conference, Held at Geneva 4–23 May 1927*. Vol. 1. Geneva: League of Nations.

League of Nations (1931). *The Agricultural Crisis*. Geneva: League of Nations.

League of Nations (1933). *World Economic Survey 1932/33*. Geneva: League of Nations.

League of Nations (1937). *Monthly Bulletin of Statistics, 18*. Geneva: League of Nations.

League of Nations (1939a). *Review of World Trade, 1938*. Geneva: League of Nations.

League of Nations (1939b). *International Trade Statistics, 1938*. Geneva: League of Nations.

League of Nations (1941). *Europe's Trade*. Geneva: League of Nations.

League of Nations (1945). *Industrialisation and Foreign Trade*. Geneva: League of Nations.

Lee, Bradford A. (1982). "The New Deal Reconsidered." *Wilson Quarterly*, 6, 62–76.

Lester, Richard A. (1939). *Monetary Experiments, Early American and Recent Scandinavian*. Princeton, N.J.: Princeton University Press.

Lewchuk, Wayne (1987). *American Technology and the British Vehicle Industry*. Cambridge: Cambridge University Press.

Lewis, W. Arthur (1949). *Economic Survey, 1919–1939*. London: Allen and Unwin.

Lewis, W. Arthur (1952). "World Production, Prices and Trade, 1870–1960." *Manchester School of Economic and Social Studies*, 20, 105–38.

Lindert, Peter H. (1994). "The Rise of Social Spending." *Explorations in Economic History*, 31, 1–37.

Lindert, Peter H. (2005). *Growing Public*. Cambridge: Cambridge University Press.

Maddison, Angus (1982). *Phases of Capitalist Development*. Oxford: Oxford University Press.

Maddison, Angus (1991). *Dynamic Forces in Capitalist Development: A Long-Run Comparative View*. Oxford: Oxford University Press.

Maddison, Angus (1995). *Monitoring the World Economy, 1820–1992*. Paris: OECD.

Maddison, Angus (2001). *The World Economy: A Millennial Perspective*. Paris: OECD.

Maier, Charles S. (1975). *Recasting Bourgeois Europe: Stabilization in France, Germany and Italy in the Decade after World War I*. Princeton, N.J.: Princeton University Press.

Maizels, Alfred (1965). *Industrial Growth and World Trade*. Cambridge: Cambridge University Press.

Malenbaum, Wilfrid (1953). *The World Wheat Economy, 1885–1939*. Cambridge, Mass.: Harvard University Press.

Mantoux, Étienne (1946). *The Carthaginian Peace—or the Economic Consequences of Mr. Keynes*. Oxford: Oxford University Press.

Margo, Robert (1988). "Interwar Unemployment in the United States: Evidence from the 1940 Census Sample," in B. Eichengreen and T. Hatton (eds.), *Interwar Unemployment in International Perspective*. London: Kluwer Academic Press, 325–52.

Marks, Sally (1978). "The Myths of Reparations." *Central European History*, 3, 231–55.

Martín-Aceña, Pablo (1995). "Spanish Banking in the Interwar Period," in Charles Feinstein (ed.), *Banking, Currency, and Finance in Europe between the Wars*. Oxford: Oxford University Press, 5025–27.

Martin-Aceña, Pablo, and Simpson, James (eds.) (1996). *The Economic Development of Modern Spain since 1870*. Aldershot: Edward Elgar.

Matis, Herbert (ed.) (1994). *The Economic Development of Modern Austria since 1870*. Aldershot: Edward Elgar.

Matthews, Robert C. O., Feinstein, Charles H., and Odling-Smee, John C. (1982). *British Economic Growth, 1856–1973*. Oxford: Oxford University Press.

Mazower, Mark (1991). *Greece and the Inter-War Economic Crisis*. Oxford: Oxford University Press.

McNeil, William C. (1986). *American Money and the Weimar Republic*. New York: Columbia University Press.

Metzler, Mark (2006) *Lever of Empire: The International Gold Standard and the Crisis of Liberalism in Prewar Japan*. Berkeley: University of California Press,

Middleton, Roger (1985). *Towards the Managed Economy: Keynes, the Treasury and the Fiscal Policy Debate of the 1930s*. London: Methuen.

Milward, Alan S. (1965). *The German Economy at War*. London: Athlone.

Milward, Alan S. (1977). *War, Economy and Society, 1939–1945*. London: Allen Lane.

Milward, Alan S. (1984). *The Reconstruction of Western Europe, 1945–51*. London: Methuen.

Milward, Alan S. (1992). *The European Rescue of the Nation State*. Berkeley: University of California Press.

Mindell, David A. (2002). *Between Human and Machine: Feedback, Control, and Computing before Cybernetics*. Baltimore, Md.: Johns Hopkins University Press.

Mitchell, Brian R. (1962). *British Historical Statistics*. Cambridge: Cambridge University Press.

Mitchell, Brian R. (1978). *European Historical Statistics, 1750–1975*. 2nd ed. London: Macmillan.

Mitchell, Brian R. (2003). *International Historical Statistics, 1750–2000*. New York: Palgrave Macmillan.

Moggridge, Donald E. (1972). *British Monetary Policy, 1924–1931: The Norman Conquest of $4.86*. Cambridge: Cambridge University Press.

Moggridge, Donald E. (1989). "The Gold Standard and National Financial Policies, 1913–1939," in Peter Mathias and Sidney Pollard (eds.), *The Cambridge Economic History of Europe*, vol. 8, *The Industrial Economies: The Development of Economic and Social Policies*. Cambridge: Cambridge University Press, 250–314.

Montgomery, Arthur (1938). *How Sweden Overcame the Depression, 1930–1933*. Stockholm: Alb. Bonniers Boktryckeri.

Morgan, E. Victor (1952). *Studies in British Financial Policy, 1914–1925.* London: Macmillan.

Mouré, Kenneth (1991). *Managing the Franc Poincaré: Economic Understanding and Political Constraint in French Monetary Policy, 1928–1936.* Cambridge: Cambridge University Press.

Mowat, Charles Loch (1955). *Britain Between the Wars, 1918–1940.* London: Methuen.

Muhkerji, Saugata (2005). "Evolution of the Non-Agrarian Formal Sector of the Indian Economy through the Nineteenth and Twentieth Century," in Binay Bhushan Chaudhuri (ed.), *The Economic History of India from the Eighteenth to the Twentieth Century.* New Delhi: Centre for Studies in Civilization, 3554–636.

Munting, Roger, and Holderness, B. A. (1991). *Crisis, Recovery, and War: An Economic History of Continental Europe, 1918–1945.* London: Philip Allan.

Neal, Larry (1979). "The Economics and Finance of Bilateral Clearing Agreements in Germany, 1934–8." *Economic History Review,* 32, 391–404.

Nevin, Edward (1955). *The Mechanism of Cheap Money.* Cardiff: University of Wales Press.

Nixon, Edgar B. (ed.) (1969). *Franklin D. Roosevelt and Foreign Affairs, January 1933–February 1934.* Vol. 1. Cambridge, Mass.: Harvard University Press.

Nötel, Rudolf (1986). "International Credit and Finance," in Michael C. Kaser and E. A. Radice (eds.), *The Economic History of Eastern Europe, 1919–1975.* Vol. 2. Oxford: Oxford University Press, 170–295.

Nurkse, Ragnar (1944). *International Currency Experience: Lessons of the Interwar Period.* Geneva: League of Nations.

Obstfeld, Maurice, and Taylor, Alan M. (2004). *Global Capital Markets: Integration, Crisis, and Growth.* Cambridge: Cambridge University Press.

Offer, Avner (1998). "The American Automobile Frenzy of the 1950s," in K. Bruland and P. K. O'Brien (eds.), *From Family Firms to Corporate Capitalism: Essays in Business and Industrial History in Honour of Peter Mathias.* Oxford: Oxford University Press, 315–53.

Ó Gráda, Cormac (ed.) (1994). *The Economic Development of Modern Ireland since 1870.* Aldershot: Edward Elgar.

Ohkawa, Kazushi, and Shinohara, Miyohei (1979). *Patterns of Japanese Economic Development.* Berkeley: University of California Press.

Ohlin, Bertil (1931). *The Course and Phases of the World Economic Depression.* Geneva: League of Nations.

Olney, Martha L. (1991). *Buy Now, Pay Later: Advertising, Credit, and Consumer Durables in the 1920s.* Chapel Hill: University of North Carolina Press.

Orwell, George (1937). *The Road to Wigan Pier.* London: Gollancz.

Overy, Richard James (1994). *War and Economy in the Third Reich.* Oxford: Oxford University Press.

Overy, Richard James (1996). *The Nazi Economic Recovery,* 2nd ed. Cambridge: Cambridge University Press.

Pamuk, Sevket (2005). "The Ottoman Economy in World War I," in Stephen Broadberry and Mark Harrison (eds.), *The Economics of World War I.* Cambridge: Cambridge University Press, 112–36.

Peden, George C. (1988). *Keynes, the Treasury and British Economic Policy*. Houndsmills: Macmillan Education.

Persson, Gunnar (ed.) (1993). *The Economic Development of Modern Denmark since 1870*. Aldershot: Edward Elgar.

Pollard, Sidney (ed.) (1970). *The Gold Standard and Employment Policy between the Wars*. London: Methuen.

Pollard, Sidney (1992). *The Development of the British Economy, 1914–1990*. London: Arnold.

Prados de la Escosura, Leandro (1995) "Growth and Macroeconomic Performance in Spain, 1939–43." CEPR (Centre for Economic Policy Research) Discussion Papers 1104, London: CEPR.

Pryor, Frederic L., Pryor, Zora P., Stadnik, Milos, and Staller, George (1971). "Czechoslovak Aggregate Production in the Inter-war Period." *Review of Income and Wealth*, 17, 35–59.

Radice, E. A. (1985). "General Characteristics of the Region between the Wars," in Michael C. Kaser and E. A. Radice (eds.), *The Economic History of Eastern Europe, 1919–1975*. Vol. 1. Oxford: Oxford University Press, 236–45.

Raff, Daniel M. G., and Summers, Lawrence (1987). "Did Henry Ford Pay Efficiency Wages?" *Journal of Labor Economics*, 5, S57–86.

Rhode, Paul, and Toniolo, Gianni (eds.) (2006). *The Global Economy in the 1990s: A Long-Run Perspective*. Cambridge: Cambridge University Press.

Richardson, Harry W. (1967). *Economic Recovery in Britain, 1932–39*. London: Weidenfeld and Nicolson.

Robbins, Lionel (1934). *The Great Depression*. London: Macmillan.

Romer, Cristina D. (1992). "What Ended the Great Depression?" *Journal of Economic History*, 52, 757–84.

Rossi, N., and Toniolo, Gianni (1993). "Un secolo di sviluppo economico italiano: Permanenze e discontinuità." *Rivista di Storia Economica*, New Series, 10, 145–75.

Rothermund, Dietmar (1996). *The Global Impact of the Great Depression, 1929–1939*. New York: Routledge.

Royal Institute of International Affairs (1932). *World Agriculture: An International Survey*. London: Humphrey Milford.

Royal Institute of International Affairs (1935). *Unemployment, an International Problem: A Report by a Study Group of Members of the Royal Institute of International Affairs*. Oxford: Oxford University Press.

Royal Institute of International Affairs (1937). *The Problem of International Investment*. London: Oxford University Press.

Sanchez-Albornoz, Nicolas (1987). *The Economic Modernization of Spain, 1836–1930*. New York: New York University Press.

Sargent, Thomas J. (1983). "The Ends of Four Big Inflations," in Thomas Sargent (ed.), *Rational Expectations and Inflation*. New York: Harper and Row, 40–109.

Sayers, Richard S. (1976). *The Bank of England, 1891–1944*. Cambridge: Cambridge University Press.

Schnabel, Isabel (2004). "The Twin German Crisis of 1931." *Journal of Economic History*, 64, 822–71.

Schneider, M. (1986). "The Development of State Work-Creation Policy in Germany, 1930–1933," in P. Stachura and F. R. Hirst (eds.), *Unemployment and the Great Depression in Weimar Germany*. New York: St. Martin's Press, 1631–86.

Schubert, Aurel (1991). *The Credit-Anstalt Crisis of 1931*. Cambridge: Cambridge University Press.

Schuker, Stephen A. (1976). *The End of French Predominance in Europe: The Financial Crisis of 1924 and the Adoption of the Dawes Plan*. Chapel Hill: University of North Carolina Press.

Schuker, Stephen A. (1988). *American "Reparations" to Germany, 1919–33: Implications for the Third World Debt Crisis*. Princeton Studies in International Finance, No. 61. Princeton, N.J.

Silverman, D. P. (1982). *Reconstructing Europe after the Great War*. Cambridge, Mass.: Harvard University Press.

Sloan, Alfred P., Jr. (1963). *My Years with General Motors*. Garden City, N.Y.: Doubleday.

Sommariva, Andrea, and Tullio, Giuseppe (1987). *German Macroeconomic History, 1880–1979*. London: Macmillan.

Stachura, Peter D. (ed.) (1986). *Unemployment and the Great Depression in Weimar Germany*. New York: St. Martin's Press.

Svennilson, I. (1954). *Growth and Stagnation in the European Economy*. Geneva: United Nations Economic Commission for Europe.

Stolper, Gustav, Hauser, Karl, and Borchardt, Knut (1967). *The German Economy, 1870 to the Present*. 2nd ed. London: Weidenfeld and Nicolson.

Teichova, Alice (1985). *An Economic Background to Munich: International Business and Czechoslovakia, 1918–38*. Cambridge: Cambridge University Press.

Teichova, Alice (1988). *The Czechoslovak Economy, 1918–1980*. London: Routledge.

Teichova, Alice (1989). "East-central and South-east Europe 1913–1939," in Peter Mathias and Sidney Pollard (eds.), *The Cambridge Economic History of Europe*, vol. 8, *The Industrial Economies: The Development of Economic and Social Policies*. Cambridge: Cambridge University Press, 887–983.

Temin, Peter (1971). "The Beginning of the Depression in Germany." *Economic History Review*, 24, 240–48.

Temin, Peter (1989). *Lessons from the Great Depression*. Cambridge, Mass.: MIT Press.

Temin, Peter (1990). "Socialism and Wages in the Recovery from the Great Depression in the United States and Germany." *Journal of Economic History*, 50, 297–307.

Temin, Peter (1991). "Soviet and Nazi Economic Planning in the 1930s." *Economic History Review*, 44, 573–93.

Temin, Peter (2006). "The 1990s as a Postwar Decade," in Paul Rhode and Gianni Toniolo (eds.), *The Global Economy in the 1990s: A Long-Run Perspective*. Cambridge: Cambridge University Press, 2182–233.

Temin, Peter, and Wigmore, Barrie A. (1990). "The End of One Big Deflation." *Explorations in Economic History*, 27, 483–502.

Thomas, Mark (1988). "Labour Market Structure and the Nature of Unemployment in Interwar Britain," in Barry Eichengreen and Timothy J. Hatton (eds.), *Interwar Unemployment in International Perspective*. Dordrecht: Kluwer Academic Publishers, 971–1048.

Thomas, Terry (1981). "Aggregate Demand in the United Kingdom, 1918–1945," in Roderick Floud and Donald McCloskey (eds.), *The Economic History of Britain since 1700*. Vol. 2. Cambridge: Cambridge University Press, 332–406.

Thomson, David (1966). *Europe since Napoleon*. Harmondsworth: Penguin.

Thorpe, Rosemary (1998). *Progress, Poverty and Exclusion: An Economic History of Latin America in the 20th Century*. Washington, D.C.: Inter American Development Bank.

Timoshenko, Vladimir P. (1953). *World Agriculture and the Depression*. Ann Arbor: University of Michigan Press.

Tipton, F. B., and Aldric, R. (1989). *The Economic and Social History of Europe, 1890–1939*. Baltimore, Md.: Johns Hopkins University Press.

Tomlinson, Jim (1990). *Public Policy and the Economy since 1900*. Oxford: Oxford University Press.

Toniolo, Gianni (1980). *L'economia dell'Italia Fascista*. Rome: Bari Laterza.

Toniolo, Gianni (2005). *Central Bank Cooperation at the Bank for International Settlements*. New York: Cambridge University Press.

Toniolo, Gianni, and Piva, F. (1988). "Unemployment in the 1930s: The Case of Italy," in Barry Eichengreen and Timothy J. Hatton (eds.), *Interwar Unemployment in International Perspective*. Dordrecht: Kluwer Academic Publishers, 221–45.

Tooze, A. (2006). *The Wages of Destruction: The Making and Breaking of the Nazi Economy*. London: Allen Lane.

Trachtenberg, M. (1980). *Reparations in World Politics: France and European Economic Diplomacy, 1916–1923*. New York: Columbia University Press.

Tracy, Michael (1964). *Agriculture in Western Europe: Crisis and Adaptation since 1880*. London: Jonathan Cape.

United Nations (1949). *International Capital Movements during the Interwar Period*. Lake Success, N.Y.: United Nations.

U.S. Department of Commerce (1975). *Historical Statistics of the United States, Colonial Times to 1970*. Washington, D.C.: Government Printing Office.

Van der Wee, Herman, and Blomme, Jan (eds.) (1996). *The Economic Development of Modern Belgium since 1870*. Aldershot: Edward Elgar.

Van Zanden, Jan Luiten (ed.) (1994). *The Economic Development of Modern Netherlands since 1870*. Aldershot: Edward Elgar.

Von Kruedener, Jurgen Baron (ed.) (1990). *Economic Crisis and Political Collapse: The Weimar Republic, 1924–1933*. New York: Berg.

Von Tunzelman, G. Nicholas (1982). "Structural Change and Leading Sectors in British Manufacturing, 1907–68," in C. P. Kindleberger and G. di Tella (eds.), *Economics in the Long View*. Vol. 3. London: Macmillan.

Voth, Hans-Joachim (1995). "Did High Wages or High Interest Rates Bring Down the Weimar Republic? A Cointegration Model of Adjustment in Germany, 1925–1930." *Journal of Economic History, 55*, 8018–21.

Waight, L. (1939). *The History and Mechanism of the Exchange Equalisation Account*. Cambridge: Cambridge University Press.

Walré de Bordes, J. (1924). *The Austrian Crown*. London: King.

Webb, Steven B. (1989). *Hyperinflation and Stabilization in Weimar Germany: Policies, Politics and Market Reactions*. Oxford: Oxford University Press.

Wheeler-Bennett, John W. (1933). *The Wreck of Reparations*. London: Allen and Unwin.

Welk, William (1939). *Fascist Economic Policy*. Cambridge, Mass.: Harvard University Press.

Wicker, Elmus (1996). *The Banking Panics of the Great Depression*. Cambridge: Cambridge University Press.

Williams, John H. (1922) "German Foreign Trade and Reparations Payments." *Quarterly Journal of Economics,* 36, 482–503.

Wolfe, Martin (1957). *The French Franc between the Wars, 1919–1939*. New York: Columbia University Press.

Woytinsky, W. S., and Woytinsky, E. S. (1955). *World Commerce and Government*. New York: Twentieth Century Fund.

Wright, J. F. (1981). "British Interwar Experience," in W. A. Eltis and P. J. N. Sinclair (eds.), *The Money Supply and the Exchange Rate*. Oxford: Oxford University Press, 282–305.

Zamagni, Vera (1993). *The Economic History of Italy, 1860–1990*. Oxford: Oxford University Press.

Index

217